W. W. NORTON & COMPANY

NEW YORK · LONDON

PHOTOGRAPHY *by* **CHRIS TERRY**

FUCHSIA DUNLOP

EVERY GRAIN of RICE

Simple CHINESE HOME COOKING

鋤禾日當午
汗滴和下土
誰知盤中飯
粒粒皆辛苦

The farmer hoes his rice plants in the noonday sun
His sweat dripping on to the earth
Who among us knows that every grain of rice in our bowls
Is filled with the bitterness of his labor.

李紳 Li Shen

INTRODUCTION

The Chinese know, perhaps better than anyone else, how to eat. I'm not talking here about their exquisite haute cuisine, or their ancient tradition of gastronomy. I'm talking about the ability of ordinary Chinese home cooks to transform humble and largely vegetarian ingredients into wonderful delicacies, and to eat in a way that not only delights the senses, but also makes sense in terms of health, economy and the environment.

Not long ago I was invited to lunch in a farmhouse near Hangzhou, in eastern China. In the dining room, the grandmother of the household, Mao Cailian, had laid out a selection of dishes on a tall, square table. There were whole salted duck eggs, hard-boiled and served in their shells, fresh green soy beans stir-fried with preserved mustard greens, chunks of winter melon braised in soy sauce, potato slivers with spring onion, slices of cured pig's ear, tiny fried fish, the freshest little greens with shiitake mushrooms, stir-fried eggs with spring onions, purple amaranth with garlic, green bell pepper with strips of tofu, and steamed eggs with a little ground pork, all served with plain steamed rice. Most of the vegetables on the table were home-grown and the hen's eggs came from birds that pecked around in the yard.

I'll never forget that meal, not only because it was one of the most memorably delicious that I have had in China, but also because it was typical of a kind of Chinese cooking that has always impressed me. The ingredients were ordinary, inexpensive and simply cooked and there was very little meat or fish among the vegetables, and yet the flavors were so bright and beautiful. Everything tasted fresh and of itself. Mrs. Mao had laid on more dishes than usual, because she was entertaining guests, but in other respects our lunch was typical of the meals shared by families across southern China.

European visitors to China since the time of Marco Polo have been struck by the wealth of produce on sale in the country's markets: fresh fish and pork, chickens and other birds, exquisite hams and an abundance of vegetables. The rich variety of ingredients, especially vegetables, in the Chinese diet is still striking. I remember researching an article about school dinners in China in the wake of Jamie Oliver's campaign to improve them in Britain. I came across a group of children at a Chengdu state school lunching, as they did every day, on a selection of dishes made from five or six different vegetables, rice and a little meat, all freshly cooked and extremely appetizing.

More recently, walking around the streets of Beijing, I couldn't help noticing the extraordinarily healthy lunches being eaten by a team of builders outside a construction site. They were choosing from about a dozen freshly cooked dishes made from a stunning assortment of colorful vegetables, flavored, in some cases, with small amounts of meat, and eating them with bowls of steamed rice.

Across the country, a vast range of plant foods are used in cooking. There are native vegetables such as taro and bamboo shoots; imports that came in along the old silk routes from Central Asia such as cucumber and sesame seeds; chillies, corn, potatoes and other New World crops that began to arrive in the late sixteenth century; and more recent arrivals such as asparagus that have become popular in China only in the last few decades. And aside from the major food crops, there are countless local and seasonal varieties that are little-known abroad, such as the Malabar spinach of Sichuan, a slippery leaf vegetable used in soups; the spring rape shoots of Hunan which make a heavenly stir-fry; and the Indian aster leaves that are blanched, chopped, then eaten with a small amount of tofu as an appetizer in Shanghai and the east of China.

Of course, food customs are changing as fast as everything else in China. In the cities, people are eating more meat and fish, dining out more frequently and falling for the lure of Western fast food. Rates of obesity, diabetes and cancer are rising fast. Younger people are forgetting how to cook and I wonder how some of them will manage when their parents are no longer around to provide meals for the family.

The older generation and those living in the countryside, however, still know how to cook as their parents did. They use meat to lend flavor to other ingredients rather than making it the center of the feast; serve fish on special occasions rather than every day; and make vegetables taste so marvellous that you crave them at every meal. It is interesting to see how modern dietary advice often echoes the age-old precepts of the Chinese table: eat plenty of grains and vegetables and not much meat, reduce consumption of animal fats and eat very little sugar. In our current times of straitened economies, overeating and anxiety about future food supplies, traditional Chinese culinary practices could be an example for everyone.

In the past, of course, it was economic necessity that limited the role of meat in the Chinese diet, but, coupled with the eternal Chinese preoccupation with eating well, this habit of frugality has encouraged Chinese cooks to become adept at creating magnificent flavors with largely vegetarian ingredients. In Chinese home cooking,

a small quantity of meat is usually cut up into tiny pieces, adding its savoriness to a whole wokful of vegetables; while dried and fermented foods such as soy sauce, black beans and salt-preserved or pickled vegetables—seasonings I've come to think of as magic ingredients—bring an almost meaty intensity of flavor to vegetarian dishes.

One of the richest aspects of Chinese culture, arguably, is the way so many people know how to eat for health and happiness, varying their diets according to the weather and the seasons, adjusting them in the light of any symptoms of imbalance or sickness and making the most nutritious foods taste so desirable; and yet in China, people generally see this wealth of knowledge as unremarkable. I've lost count of the number of times that Chinese chefs and domestic cooks have told me of their admiration for the "scientific" approach of Western nutrition, without seeming to notice how confused most Westerners are about what to eat, or to consider how much the time-tested Chinese dietary system might have to offer the world.

Chinese cooking has something of a reputation in the West for being complicated and intimidating. It's true that banquet cooking can be complex and time-consuming, but home cooking is generally straightforward, as I hope this book will show. Keep a few basic Chinese seasonings in your larder and you can rustle up a delicious meal from what appear just to be odds and ends. Not long ago, I invited a

friend back for supper on the spur of the moment and had to conjure a meal out of what felt like nothing. I stir-fried half a cabbage with dried shrimps, and leftover spinach with fermented tofu; made a quick twice-cooked pork with a few slices of meat I had in the freezer; and steamed some rice. The friend in question is still talking about the meal. Cooking a few bits and pieces separately, with different seasonings, made a small amount of food seem exciting and plentiful.

The recipes in this book are a tribute to China's rich tradition of frugal, healthy and delicious home cooking. They include meat, poultry and fish dishes, but this is primarily a book about how to make vegetables taste divine with very little expense or effort, and how to make a little meat go a long way. Vegetables play the leading role in most of the recipes: out of nearly 150 main recipes, more than two-thirds are either completely vegetarian or can be adapted to be so, if you choose. Some of the recipes call for more unusual Chinese vegetables that may require a trip to a Chinese or Asian supermarket, but many others demand only fresh ingredients widely available in the West. I have avoided complicated recipes that are more suited to restaurants than home cooking, as well as deep-frying, with a few delicious exceptions.

A large number of recipes come from the places I know best: Sichuan, Hunan and the southern Yangtze region. (Cooks from Sichuan, my first love in terms of Chinese food, are particularly skilled at creating cheap, simple dishes that are extravagantly savory.)

Other recipes are from Hong Kong, Guangdong, Fujian and other regions that I've visited. There is a definite southern bias in the selection, partly because I've spent most time in southern China and partly because southerners, with the diversity of fresh produce available to them all year round, have the most varied and exciting ways with vegetables. I've included some simplified versions of classic recipes from my previous books, and a few unmissable favorites in their original forms.

Chinese home cooking is not about a rigid set of recipes, but an approach to cooking and eating that can be adapted to almost any place or circumstance, so I hope that this book will serve as a collection of inspiring suggestions as much as a manual. Many of the cooking methods and flavoring techniques can be applied to a wide range of ingredients. I've made suggestions for alternatives in many recipes, but feel free to use your imagination and improvise with whatever you can find in your fridge or cupboard. And although I've tested all the recipes with precise amounts of ingredients and seasonings, many are so simple that quantities are not critical: you can add a little more or less of this and that as you please, once you have become familiar with the basic techniques. And, of course, please do use the best, freshest ingredients you can find.

With all the fuss over the Mediterranean diet, people in the West tend to forget that the Chinese have a system of eating that is equally healthy, balanced, sustainable and pleasing. Perhaps it's the dominance of Chinese restaurant food—with its emphasis on meat, seafood and deep-frying as a cooking method—that has made us overlook the fact that typical Chinese home cooking is centered on grains and vegetables.

Culinary ideas from other parts of the world, such as Middle Eastern hummus and halloumi, Thai curry pastes, Italian pasta sauces and North African couscous have already entered the mainstream in many parts of the West. I'd like to see Chinese culinary techniques and ingredients inspiring people in the same way to make the most of local ingredients wherever they are. I regularly use Chinese methods to cook produce I've bought in my local shops and farmers' markets. I have given purple-sprouting broccoli the Cantonese sizzling oil treatment, slow-cooked English rare breed pork in the Hangzhou manner with soy sauce, sugar and Shaoxing wine, steamed Jerusalem artichokes with Hunanese fermented black beans and chilli and prepared mackerel I caught on holiday in Scotland with soy sauce and ginger; all to splendid effect. Sesame oil, soy sauce and ginger may already be on your shopping list and mainstream supermarkets are now stocking Chinese brown rice vinegar and cooking wine; just add Sichuanese chilli bean paste and fermented black beans and you will open up whole new dimensions of taste.

The flavors of some of the simplest recipes in this book will amaze you, I hope, as they still amaze me. Just try Blanched Choy Sum with Sizzling Oil, a dish that takes only 15 minutes to make but is beautiful enough to launch ships, or the Sichuanese sauces for cold chicken, which will transform the way you view leftovers from your Sunday roast or Christmas turkey. Spinach cooked with garlic, chilli and fermented tofu tastes exquisite and is so much more than the sum of its parts. Often, when I cook these dishes, I wonder at the alchemy of it, how such basic techniques can provoke such mesmerizing sensations of flavor.

This book, then, is a collection of recipes and basic Chinese kitchen techniques that I have found to be an inspiration in my own home cooking. I hope you'll find them inspiring too.

BASICS

You don't need many ingredients to get started with Chinese cooking. The following is a list of the seasonings that are the staples of the Chinese larder. (For more information on each seasoning and for a full glossary of Chinese ingredients used in the recipes, with their Chinese pronunciation and Chinese characters, see page 326.) You will also need cooking oil with a high smoke point, such as peanut or rapeseed (see page 344 for detailed advice). And it's really useful to have some stock on hand, either bagged-up homemade stock in the freezer, cans of chicken stock or vegetable stock granules.

Soy sauce (light soy sauce or tamari, and dark soy sauce)
One of the essential seasonings of the Chinese kitchen. Light soy sauce is generally used to add flavor and saltiness to food, dark soy sauce for a caramel color. A good tamari—darker than light soy sauce but richly flavored—can be used instead of light soy sauce.

Chinkiang or Chinese brown rice vinegar
A speciality of the town of Zhenjiang (or Chinkiang) in eastern China, the best is made from fermented glutinous rice with charred rice used to give a deep brown color. It has a mellow, complex flavor and a relatively light acidity.

Chinkiang vinegar can be found in Chinese groceries, while a generic brown rice vinegar is available in some supermarkets.

Toasted sesame oil
With its dark, nutty color and intense aroma, this is never used as a cooking oil, but to add fragrance to dishes. Use it in tiny quantities, and add it to hot dishes right at the end of cooking, as heating it for too long will destroy its fragrance.

Chilli oil
This adds a gorgeous heat and luster to cold dishes and dips. See page 320 for a recipe for making your own.

Dried chillies
An essential of Sichuanese cooking. Use larger, milder red chillies, ideally those known as "facing-heaven" (see photo opposite), rather than smaller, hotter varieties.

Whole Sichuan pepper
Good Sichuan pepper has a fresh, citrussy aroma and the addictive quality of making your lips dance and tingle. It can be used whole, or roasted and ground (see page 322).

A few spices (start with cassia bark and star anise)
These are generally used in combination to give aroma and flavor to broths and stews.

Shaoxing wine
This rice wine is a mild, amber-colored liquor that is often used in marinades to refine the flavors of meat, fish and poultry. Cheap Shaoxing wines for cooking can be found in Chinese supermarkets; they are not recommended for drinking. Many Chinese shops sell some more expensive Shaoxing wines that can be drunk on their own or used in cooking.

Potato flour or cornstarch
The Chinese use a variety of plain starches to thicken sauces and to give a silky mouthfeel to wok-cooked meat, fish and poultry. If you can, use potato flour, which can be found in any Chinese supermarket. Cornstarch is a reasonable substitute.

Fresh ginger, garlic and spring onions
Used separately or in combination, these three vegetables are what the food-writer Yan-kit So called the Chinese "kitchen trinity."

MAGIC INGREDIENTS

One of the reasons simple Chinese cooking is so exciting is the use of what I think of as magic ingredients: richly flavored seasonings that transform common foods into delicacies fit for an emperor. Just as the Italians might use a sprinkle of Parmesan to awaken the tastes of an entire plateful of pasta, or shave white truffle over a simple poached egg to turn it into something ambrosial, Chinese cooks use small amounts of dried shiitake mushrooms, soy sauce, preserved vegetables, dried shrimp and other seasonings to enhance the flavors of fresh produce. Getting to know these magic ingredients is the key to making largely vegetarian ingredients taste so delicious that you won't miss meat at all.

A NOTE ON UMAMI

The word "umami" has come to refer to the rich, savory tastes of some ingredients. It was first used in this way in 1908 by a Japanese scientist who discovered that the irresistible savory taste of kombu seaweed came from its natural glutamates; "umami" was the name he gave to their taste.

Many of the foods that cooks have used for centuries to create intense savory flavors— such as cured hams, Parmesan and dried fish—are now known to be rich in umami

compounds. Umami, it turns out, is just a new word for something good cooks have known about for a very long time. I find umami an invaluable concept in thinking about food, so I use it freely in this book.

Black fermented soy beans
These dry, wizened beans have a rich, complex flavor similar to soy sauce. They are the main ingredient in black bean sauce and can also be used whole in stir-fries and braises. They have been used in Chinese cooking for more than 2,000 years.

Fermented tofu
A soft, cheese-like relish sold as cubes packed in jars of brine, this has an intense flavor a little reminiscent of Roquefort. Eat as a relish to liven up steamed rice or congee, or use in sauces for an enticing flavor and delightful creaminess.

Sichuanese chilli bean paste
Made from salt-fermented chillies and fava beans, this gives a gorgeous savory intensity and deep red color to all kinds of dishes. It is an indispensable seasoning of Sichuanese cooking.

Sweet fermented sauce
A dark, rich, glossy paste used both to boost the savoriness of cooked dishes and as the base of dips for delicacies such as roast pork and crispy duck.

Preserved vegetables
A wide variety of salt-preserved and brine-pickled vegetables are used across China for their salt-sour, umami flavors. They add a delicious savory richness to all kinds of dishes, and are particularly exciting with fresh peas and beans. If you've ever eaten Sichuanese dry-fried beans and wondered about those utterly delicious dark crinkly bits that cling to the beans, they are one of these preserves, Sichuanese *ya cai*. (See page 335 for photos of the most important preserved vegetables.)

Dried shiitake mushrooms
In the same way as Italian porcini, these lend a profound umami richness to other foods and, after soaking, have a pleasingly juicy texture. Their soaking water is delicious in soups, stews and stocks.

Cured ham
As in Spanish and Italian cooking, dark cured hams are used to add rich, savory umami flavors. They are particularly important in the cooking of the Southern Yangtze region and Yunnan.

Dried shimps
These add an intense savory edge. The smallest, which are paper-thin, can be added directly to dishes; larger shrimp are soaked in hot water first.

KITCHEN EQUIPMENT

THE WOK

A good wok is almost essential. I say almost because it's certainly possible to rustle up a Chinese meal without one (as I have done many times, in friends' homes or holiday cottages), but it's not ideal, because stir-frying just isn't the same in a frying pan. The high sides of a wok make it possible to turn and toss ingredients vigorously, and they conduct heat swiftly and evenly. The narrow base (particularly of the round-bottomed kind) also demands much less oil than a frying pan.

A wok is primarily associated with stir-frying, but can also be used to boil, steam, deep-fry, and to roast spices such as Sichuan pepper. If you plan to stir-fry and deep-fry or steam dishes for the same meal, it's useful to own a couple of woks, one to hold oil for deep-frying or water for steaming, the other for stir-frying.

There are several kinds of wok, varying in the materials from which they are made, their bases (flat or curved), their sizes and the arrangement of their handles. In general, I recommend a 12–14 inch wok for home use. Larger Chinese supermarkets sell a variety of sizes; they tend to be cheaper than brand-name woks sold in other shops and just as good.

Carbon steel, round-bottomed

This type of wok, the most typical of a Chinese kitchen, has a curved base and is made from thin carbon steel. If you have a gas stove with a wok stand, this is the best kind to use (it is not suitable for a flat electric stovetop). The carbon steel conducts heat efficiently through the sides, while the curved shape helps you to keep scooping up the ingredients and tossing them with the oil and seasonings that pool in the base. A new carbon steel wok must be scrubbed and seasoned (see page 16).

Over time, the surface of the wok will blacken and acquire a seasoned patina. If you strip this off by using the wok for boiling, re-season the surface afterwards to prevent rusting. This kind of wok is usually sold in various sizes, in Chinese groceries, at very modest prices. Cast-iron woks, which require similar seasoning, may also be found in Chinese shops.

Carbon steel, flat-bottomed

The only difference between this and the one above is its flat base, which makes it suitable for electric stovetops. It must also be seasoned, and re-seasoned if you strip off its protective patina.

Non-stick, flat-bottomed

A fairly recent innovation, this tends to be sold in mainstream shops rather than Chinese stores. Aside from its non-stick qualities, it has the advantage that it won't rust and doesn't need seasoning, but it doesn't produce food that is as sizzly and delicious as that made in a traditional wok. There is also concern that heating empty non-stick pans over high heat may release chemicals that could be damaging to human health and, since heating a wok before you add ingredients is one of the pre-requisites of stir-frying, I'm not convinced that using a non-stick wok for this purpose is a good idea, so I don't recommend it.

Induction wok (flat- or round-bottomed)

An induction stove has rapid heat control and can achieve far higher temperatures than most domestic stovetops. It's also easy to clean (simply wipe the smooth surface). The disadvantages are that you cannot toss the wok, as it only retains heat when its base is touching the burner, and that induction stoves are very expensive.

A note on wok handles

Left to right: wok lid; flat-bottomed wok with one long handle and one "ear" handle; round-bottomed carbon steel wok with two metal "ears"; bamboo wok brush; round-bottomed carbon steel wok with one long handle; wok stand (in top right-hand corner).

Some woks have two "ear" handles on opposite sides, which makes them very stable and so particularly suitable for deep-frying or steaming, when they are filled with large quantities of hot liquid. They can also be used for stir-frying. Other woks have one long handle, which makes the wok easy to hold and move around, but it also makes it less stable, so this kind of wok is less suitable for steaming and deep-frying. If you are only going to have one wok, a good compromise is the kind with a long handle on one side and a small "ear" handle on the other.

Preparing a new wok

With a new carbon steel wok, begin by scrubbing the interior surface with steel wool. Then wash it thoroughly with soapy water, rinse and dry. Heat over a high flame and, when it is really hot, pour in a little cooking oil and carefully smear it over the surface with a good wad of paper towels (protect your hands). Let it cool slightly, then repeat this process twice with fresh towels and oil. Your wok is now ready to use.

Maintaining your wok

After use, a quick scrub under the tap is normally enough to clean a wok. If you do scour the surface, you will need to re-season the wok, heating and oiling it as described above, to prevent rusting. You will also need to re-season your wok after using it for boiling or steaming, because the water will strip off most of its protective patina. There is no need to be precious about traditional woks: they are built to be virtually indestructible. Even if the surface has rusted,

all you need do is scrub away the rust with steel wool and re-season the surface and it will be fit for cooking once more. It is not usually necessary to clean the underside of a wok.

My own woks

In my kitchen, I have one 12 inch, round-bottomed, long-handled, carbon steel wok which I use mainly for stir-frying. I also have a 13 inch, round-bottomed, carbon steel wok with two metal "ears" which I always use for steaming, boiling and deep-frying and, infrequently, for stir-frying. I keep a large (15 inch), round-bottomed, carbon steel wok with two metal "ears" in a cupboard and bring it out on occasions when I want to cook a couple of fish at the same time, say, or something else that demands a little more space.

Apart from these, I have a 13 inch, round-bottomed, long-handled, carbon steel wok I bought from an elderly woksmith in Zhenjiang, eastern China. This man was the third generation of his family in the business, and heated the metal for his woks in a furnace before hammering out the red-hot metal by hand. It is rare to come across a traditional woksmith, and I couldn't resist buying one of his wares.

WOK ACCESSORIES

Wok scoop

Most home cooks in China use a wok scoop to lift and turn the ingredients in a stir-fry, as well as to transfer food on to a serving dish. A spatula or a long-handled spoon are good substitutes.

Chinese ladle

Professional Chinese chefs favor ladles over wok scoops, using them not only to move food around in the wok, but also to scoop up oil, stock or water to add to a dish, to mix up seasonings and to stir the starch-and-water pastes used to thicken sauces. Chinese cooking ladles have a different shape from Western serving ladles; their bowls are more flush to their handles. Western ladles are not suitable for wok cooking because of the sharper angle between their handles and bowls. Chinese ladles can be bought cheaply in good Chinese supermarkets.

Perforated ladle

Used in most professional Chinese kitchens for removing ingredients from cooking oil or water, this can be bought in Chinese stores. A slotted spoon can be used instead.

Bamboo-handled strainer

Available in good Chinese supermarkets, this is ideal for removing ingredients from deep-frying oil.

Bamboo or wooden chopsticks

Used for moving ingredients around in oil or water—to make sure they don't stick to one another—and for tasting. Long-handled cooking chopsticks or regular wooden or bamboo chopsticks can be used.

Clockwise from top left: Bamboo-handled strainer and long chopsticks used for deep-frying; steaming in a wok with a wok rack, a dish to hold food and a wok lid; wok scoop and ladle, both used for stir-frying; using a bamboo steamer in a wok.

Wok brush

A bamboo brush is useful for scrubbing out a hot wok between dishes. If you don't have one, use a scrubbing brush with natural bristles (synthetic bristles might easily melt on the hot wok surface).

Wok lid

This is useful for boiling and simmering and essential to cover the dish if you intend to use your wok as a steamer (see the picture on page 17).

Wok rack

A rack quickly transforms your wok into a steamer. It can also be used to hold food that will be smoked in the wok, over smouldering tea leaves. However, there are other ways to make your own stands from cans or chopsticks (see page 24), so a rack is not essential.

Wok stand

Needed to keep a round-bottomed wok stable when boiling, steaming or deep-frying. Portable stands can be bought in Chinese supermarkets. They are also handy for holding a wok on a countertop when not in use.

Bamboo steamer

Layered bamboo steamers that fit into your wok can be bought cheaply in Chinese supermarkets. Metal steamers can also be used. Take care not to put a cold metal wok lid over a plateful of uncovered food in a steamer, or condensation will drip back on to the food, diluting its natural juices (simply allow the lid to heat in the steam before you place a dish in the steamer). I normally use a steamer that is 11 inches in diameter, sufficient for most

purposes, including steaming a medium-sized fish; I also have a 14 inch steamer for larger fish.

Oil (or sugar) thermometer

Invaluable for deep-frying, to ensure the oil has reached a sufficiently high temperature.

OTHER EQUIPMENT

Chinese cleaver

You can use any kitchen knives for Chinese cooking but a cleaver, once you have grown used to it, is invaluable. A Chinese cleaver is much lighter than a butcher's chopper and surprisingly dexterous. It is suitable not only for cutting up large pieces of food, but also for slicing ginger and garlic. The flat side of its blade can be used to smack ginger to release its fragrance, as well as to scoop up cut ingredients. In fact, a cleaver is usually the only knife in a Chinese home kitchen. Cleavers must be kept very sharp, so they are normally sold alongside whetstones. A typical cleaver blade is 8–9 inches long and 3–4 inches wide, and made from stainless steel. Carbon steel blades are easier to sharpen, but need oiling to prevent rust. The blade of a regular kitchen cleaver may be damaged if you use it to chop bones. For this, ask your butcher to help, or buy a second, heavier cleaver.

Whetstone

Sold with cleavers. They normally have coarse- and fine-grained sides (see page 22).

Measuring spoons

Extremely useful for measuring seasonings accurately.

Rolling pin

You will need this to make your own dumpling wrappers. Chinese rolling pins, which can be found in Chinese shops, are thin and have tapered ends.

Electric rice cooker

If you intend to cook Chinese food on a regular basis, an electric rice cooker is a wise investment. With a rice cooker, you simply measure your rice and water, press a button and relax in the knowledge that your rice will be cooked perfectly and kept hot until you serve it. This means you can devote all your attention to the accompanying dishes. Most rice cookers come with a perforated plastic shelf that can be placed above the rice, so you can steam a little dishful of other food at the same time. Some have a second setting for making perfect congee.

Little bowls and saucers

It is extremely useful to have a few little saucers and bowls around to hold measured ingredients that are ready for the wok. Finely chopped garlic and ginger can be laid out on a little dish and sauces mixed up in bowls. Little saucers can also be used to serve dips for dumplings and other foods.

Serving dishes

You don't need special serving dishes for Chinese food, but it helps to have a selection of different sizes, including a deep bowl for soups and a large oval platter for a whole fish.

Clockwise from top left: A Chinese cleaver; sharpening a cleaver on a whetstone; using a cleaver for horizontal cutting (see page 20); using a cleaver for vertical cutting (see page 20).

CUTTING

Cutting is the first basic skill of the Chinese kitchen. Almost all ingredients are cut into small pieces, partly because of the use of chopsticks, and partly because of the widespread use of stir-frying. Stir-frying demands fine, regular cutting, so ingredients cook quickly and evenly. There's also an aesthetic aspect, as any dish looks far more beautiful if the ingredients are evenly cut.

Any kind of sharp knife can be used, but a cleaver is ideal. Grasp the handle firmly in your right hand (if you are right-handed), and use your index finger to steady the blade. Use your other hand to hold the ingredients. For safety, curl your fingers so the knuckles rest against the blade and your fingertips are tucked away. Always position your thumb behind your fingers and away from the knife.

If you are making a meal that includes last-minute stir-fries, have your ingredients ready to go before you begin: main ingredients neatly cut and marinated, sauces mixed, and bottles of seasonings at the ready. If you are chopping garlic, ginger or spring onions for three different dishes, prepare them all at the same time. Have serving dishes on hand, so you don't have to scramble around the kitchen when each dish is ready.

Enjoy your preparation. I find the cutting for a Chinese meal has a gentle, meditative quality, and calms me after a busy day. It's pleasing, too, to have ingredients cut and laid out on boards when guests arrive.

Basic cutting techniques

Vertical cutting (*qie*): Hold the knife perpendicular to the board; cut in an up-and-down motion (see page 19).

Horizontal cutting (*pian*): Hold the knife parallel to the board and ease it into your ingredient (see page 19).

Basic cutting shapes

A vast vocabulary describes the shapes into which food can be cut. These are some of the most important:

1 | Thumbnail slices (*zhi jia pian*). Just one of many types of slices. Others include thick "domino slices" and broad, thin "ox-tongue" slices.

2 | Slivers or "silken threads" (*si*). Cut spring onions into short sections, then into slivers. Cut other ingredients, such as ginger, into slices, then lay them in a row, overlapping each other, and cut into slivers.

3 | "Horse ears" (*ma'er duo*). Hold your knife at an angle to long ingredients such as spring onions, and cut into thin slices that resemble horses' ears.

4 | Spring onion "flowers," or finely sliced spring onions (*cong hua*). Cut the greens across into very thin slices.

5 | Finely chopped garlic and ginger, or "rice grains" (*mo or mi li*). For ginger, cut into slices, then into slivers, and finally into fine grains. For garlic, slice, then chop into tiny pieces.

6 | Smacked ginger. Smack unpeeled ginger with the flat of a blade to release its juices.

7 | Roll-cut chunks (*gun dao kuai*). A fantastic way of cutting vegetables into chunks with the greatest possible surface area. Hold your knife at an angle to your vegetable, and cut a thick slice. Then roll the vegetable a quarter turn away, and cut another thick slice. Continue.

8 | Strips (*tiao*). Cut into thick slices, and then into strips.

9 | Small cubes (*ding*). Cut your ingredient into thick slices, then strips, and finally small cubes.

Freezing

Freezing meat or poultry for a couple of hours makes cutting thin slices or slivers much easier.

Mandolin

Cheap to buy in Japanese shops, and used to cut crisp vegetables, such as carrot, into thin slices and slivers.

BASIC PREPARATION

SOAKING

Some Chinese ingredients, such as dried mushrooms, dried tofu skin and dried shrimp, must be soaked in hot water from the kettle for 30 minutes or more before cooking.

SALTING

Vegetable ingredients that contain a lot of water, such as cucumber and kohlrabi, are often mixed with a little salt and set aside for 15–30 minutes to draw out some of the liquid, especially when they are to be used in cold dishes. They need to be drained well before use.

MARINATING

There are two main purposes to Chinese marinades. The first is to purify the flavors of meat, fish and poultry by using ingredients such as salt, Shaoxing wine, ginger and spring onion to dispel what the Chinese call "off tastes" (*yi wei*), or "fishy tastes" (*xing wei*). The second purpose is to enhance the flavor of ingredients before cooking: this kind of marinade usually includes salt or soy sauce, Shaoxing wine and a little starch-and-water if a silky texture is required. When the ingredients are cut into small pieces for stir-frying, this kind of marinade is usually added shortly before cooking. A small amount of oil is sometimes mixed into the marinade so the pieces of food won't stick together.

BLANCHING

Vegetables may be blanched in boiling water before stir-frying to "break their rawness" (*duan sheng*). With leafy vegetables, this wilts them and reduces their volume, which makes stir-frying much easier. With crisp-fleshed vegetables, blanching speeds up the stir-frying and makes them easier to handle in the wok. Some vegetables, such as Asian white radish, may be blanched to dispel bitter or peppery tastes. Take care not to over-blanch vegetables so they retain their crispness.

Meat and poultry are sometimes blanched before cooking, for clearer stocks or stews. For stews and cold, cooked meats, you may save time by just rinsing them under the hot tap, or omitting the blanching altogether and simply skimming the liquid very carefully after you have added your meat to the pot and brought it to a boil. For a clear stock or soup and a really professional finish, it's essential to blanch your meats: bring them to a boil in a pot of water and boil for a few minutes to allow impurities to rise to the surface. Throw away the blanching water, rinse the meat carefully under the tap, then cover with fresh water to cook.

USING A WHETSTONE

It is vital to keep your knives extremely sharp. To use a whetstone, wet it and rub with a drop of detergent. Lay it on a damp cloth, at right angles to the edge of a work surface. Lay the knife on its side, diagonally across the whetstone. Raise the top of the blade about a finger's width from the surface. Draw the blade from the bottom right corner of the stone to the top left, so its entire cutting edge, from one end to the other, is drawn across the stone (see photo, page 19). Repeat 10 times. Turn the knife over, raise the top by a finger's width again, and draw the blade from the top left corner of the stone to the bottom right, allowing the entire edge to be drawn across the surface. Repeat 10 times. If your knife is fairly blunt at the beginning, begin by using the coarser side of the stone, then repeat with the finer side.

For best results, sharpen knives little and often. Rinse the blade, and dry well. If you are using a carbon steel, use paper towels to rub it with oil after washing or sharpening, to prevent rust.

BASIC COOKING TECHNIQUES

STIR-FRYING

Stir-frying is the mainstay of Chinese home cooking. Quick and efficient, it preserves the crispness and nutritional richness of vegetables, as well as the tender succulence of meat and poultry.

The basic process

1 | Prepare all your ingredients before you begin.
The main ingredient should be cut and marinated; ingredients chopped; sauces mixed; and any other seasonings you need laid out close to the wok. Make sure you have a serving dish on hand.

2 | Season your wok.
Add a little oil to your wok, swirl around, heat until smoking, then pour off into a heatproof container. This essential step seals the cooking surface so ingredients do not stick and leave a sediment that will burn before the dish is ready.

3 | Add your cooking oil and swirl it around, then immediately add aromatic seasonings such as chillies, ginger and garlic.
Stir-fry these until fragrant, which will take seconds. Trust your nose to tell you when they are ready. Do take care not to let the oil overheat before you add your seasonings, or they may burn.

4 | Add your main ingredient and stir-fry briskly.
If the main ingredient is meat or poultry, separate the pieces.

5 | Add any other ingredients.
Add a sauce if there is one. If you are adding spring onion greens or vinegar, which only require a moment's cooking, add them at the end when the other ingredients are ready. Off the heat, stir in a tiny amount of sesame oil, if using, and turn the food on to a serving dish.

With some stir-fries, one or more ingredients may first be blanched or separately stir-fried before the main dish is cooked. For example, if you are cooking fine slivers of meat with a robust, crunchy vegetable that takes longer to cook than the meat, the vegetable may be blanched or stir-fried separately to "break its rawness," then returned to the wok after the meat slivers have been separated in the hot oil. This way, the meat will not be overcooked by the time the vegetable is ready.

With other stir-fries, all the ingredients are just added in sequence to the wok: this is known in Sichuan as a "small stir-fry" (*xiao chao*), which means a simple, basic stir-fry.

Do not overload your wok, or you won't have enough heat to cook the ingredients properly.

STEAMING

Steaming has been used in Chinese cooking since the Stone Age and remains one of the most important cooking methods. It is a wonderful way to preserve the gentle succulence of fish, poultry and seafood, and the essential taste of any ingredient.

A bamboo steamer is the perfect piece of equipment, but it is not essential: you can also use a stainless steel or aluminium steamer-saucepan of the kind used in Western cooking, or you can steam food in your wok without a bamboo steamer (see page 24).

Make sure your wok is stable before you use it for steaming: a wok stand is essential when using a round-bottomed wok.

Using a bamboo steamer
Choose one that will fit in your wok, with the appropriate lid. To hold your ingredients, select a heatproof dish that will sit nicely inside the steamer, with ⅜ in (1cm) or more around the edge to allow steam to circulate. Make sure it's deep enough to hold the juices that will emerge.

Place the steamer in the wok, then put in your dish of ingredients. Fill the wok with boiling water to just above the base of the steamer and bring to a boil over high heat.

Cover the steamer with its lid and steam. Make sure the wok does not boil dry: top up with hot water from the kettle if necessary.

Re-season the surface of a carbon steel wok after steaming, to prevent rusting.

Using a wok without a bamboo steamer

Lay a metal trivet in the base of your wok. Make sure it is stable. Add boiling water from the kettle, filling to within ⅜ in (1cm) of the trivet. Cover with a wok lid and bring to a boil over a high flame. Lay your dishful of ingredients on the trivet, cover with the hot wok lid and steam.

If you don't have a trivet, you can improvise: one of my Hong Kong friends recommends using an empty tuna can, with top and base removed, instead! Another suggests using three wooden or bamboo chopsticks, their ends meeting in the base of a wok, as a stand for the dish.

In Hunan, where steaming is widely used, they often steam a small stack of bowls in a tall pressure cooker, with a trivet at the bottom and chopsticks separating the bowls.

Using a steel or aluminum steamer-saucepan

Fill the base of the pan with water, cover and bring to a boil. When the lid is hot, raise it, lay your dishful of food in the steamer layer, cover and steam.

Steaming without a steamer or wok

Any broad saucepan with a lid can be used. Place a trivet in the base, add water, lay on a dish of food, cover and steam.

DEEP-FRYING

Deep-frying is not an everyday method in Chinese home cooking and very few recipes in this book demand it. It is, however, ideal for some foods, including eggplant.

To use a wok for deep-frying, make sure it is completely stable (use a wok stand with a round-bottomed wok). A two-handled wok is more stable than a one-handled wok.

Ideally, use an oil or sugar thermometer: if you don't have one, it's useful to know that a stale cube of bread will brown in 60 seconds at 350°F, ideal for deep-frying.

You need less oil to deep-fry in a round-bottomed wok than in a saucepan. If you cook in small batches, you can use as little as 1–1½ cups (300–400ml) oil.

Long-handled cooking chopsticks are handy for moving ingredients around in the oil. Remove food from the oil with a bamboo strainer or perforated spoon.

OIL-SIZZLING

I wanted to make separate mention of this method (*you lin*), used very widely in Cantonese cooking, because it is so simple and quick and produces such devastatingly delicious results. It works like this: you blanch or steam your main ingredients (perhaps a whole fish or some leafy green vegetables), and lay them out neatly on a serving plate. You scatter them with slivered spring onions and ginger.

You heat a little oil until it emits a thin smoke, then pour it over the onions and ginger, which sizzle and smell wonderful. You then pour over soy sauce, usually diluted with hot water.

This sounds ridiculously easy—which it is—but it's one of the finest Chinese cooking methods. It adds a sublime edge of flavor to good-quality ingredients, while allowing their natural flavors to shine through. Blanched Choy Sum with Sizzling Oil, and Steamed Sea Bass with Ginger and Spring Onion, are two classic examples in this book.

SLOW-COOKING

There are many different ways of slow-cooking in the Chinese kitchen: one that features prominently in this book is "red-braising" (*hong shao*), in which ingredients are slow-cooked with soy sauce and/or other deeply colored flavorings.

Traditionally, Chinese kitchens lacked ovens, so all cooking was done over a stove (people went to specialist food shops to buy roasted or baked goods). For this reason, most Chinese stews and soups are cooked on the stovetop, on a very low flame. A slow oven achieves much the same result with greater convenience and, since most Western kitchens have ovens, I've given instructions for using them where appropriate.

PLANNING A CHINESE MEAL

A Chinese meal consists at its simplest of rice, noodles, bread or other grain foods (known as *fan* or, literally, "cooked rice"), served with shared accompanying dishes (known as *cai*, which literally means "vegetables" or "greens"). At their simplest, these other dishes might be pickled vegetables or fermented tofu; at their most extravagant they might include dozens of concoctions made with rare and expensive ingredients. A typical home-cooked meal for most people, however, consists of a few simple dishes made mainly with vegetables, with relatively small amounts of fish, meat or poultry.

Cold dishes are normally laid on the table at the start of the meal, and hot dishes added as they emerge from the stove. A soup may be served alongside other dishes, or at the end of the meal; at home, it will normally be drunk from the same rice bowl used for the other food. Dessert is absent as a concept in Chinese culinary culture. Some sweet dishes may be served alongside savory dishes at main meals, particularly in places like Suzhou in the east, while sweet snacks are eaten from time to time across China and sugar is used here and there as a seasoning in savory dishes. Most meals end with fruit rather than sweetmeats.

When I'm cooking Chinese food for friends at home, I never make a dessert, but serve fresh fruit and Chinese tea after the meal, with dishes of chocolates or Middle Eastern sweetmeats on the table for those who crave something sweet.

Some of the dishes in the rice, noodle and dumpling chapters can serve as entire meals on their own, with perhaps just a salady cold dish as an accompaniment. Otherwise, the dishes in this book are intended to be served with bowls of rice or noodles, as part of a fuller Chinese meal.

When deciding what to cook, try to ensure that you have a variety of colors, flavors and textures on the table, because much of the pleasure of a Chinese meal lies in dipping back and forth between contrasting dishes. A spicy stir-fry can be balanced by a gentle soup; a ruddy, full-flavored Sichuanese braise with a fresh green vegetable; a dry dish with something sauced. If you have several lightly flavored dishes on offer, try to include one that is either salty or spicy or soy-rich (strongly flavored dishes go particularly well with plain steamed rice).

Do try to avoid constructing a meal consisting entirely of stir-fries that you will have to cook at the very last minute, which can be exhausting. When feeding a party of six, for example, try to include a slow-cooked dish that you can prepare well in advance and warm up slowly on a backburner, as well as one or two delectable cold dishes to serve as appetizers, so there is less for you to do at the last minute. Chinese people also like to serve a soup with every meal, which may be as simple as some good-quality stock with a few vegetable leaves and a little tofu, but Westerners don't regard it as essential, so only include it if you want to.

A great advantage of the Chinese meal is that different dietary requirements can easily be accommodated with grace and ease. I often find myself cooking for diverse groups of people in which, for example, one person is vegetarian, one doesn't eat any pork and so on, and it's simple to keep everyone happy, because individuals just help themselves to those dishes that agree with them and avoid those that don't. And, of course, dairy products are entirely absent from the vast majority of Chinese dishes. If you use tamari soy sauce, most dishes won't contain any wheat either, so catering for friends who have these common food avoidances is no problem at all.

One other useful tip is that some Chinese dishes mix more than happily with dishes from other culinary traditions. I sometimes serve Sichuanese red-braised beef with mashed potatoes. A Chinese soup can be enjoyed at the start of a non-Chinese meal, and there's no reason why you can't serve the leftovers of a Western stew, or a salad, as one dish of a Chinese meal. (I've even, on occasion, eaten cubes of Roquefort instead of fermented tofu with my breakfast congee!) The essence of the Chinese way of eating lies in the overall structure of a meal, with its grains and shared dishes, rather than in any particular dish or ingredient.

I've included a few suggested menus (see pages 30–31), which may be useful as guides.

SERVING QUANTITIES

Because Chinese dishes are normally shared by everyone at the table, serving quantities are worked out differently from the way they are in Western cuisines. Basically, you need to make sure there's at least enough rice for everyone to eat their fill, and then the quantities of the other dishes are flexible. A single dish of meat or tofu and vegetables may suffice for a very casual meal for two (though adding another simple vegetable dish won't take long and makes more of a spread). On the other hand, if I'm making a quick lunch when I'm at home on my own and using up leftovers, I may end up eating three or four small dishes with my rice: yesterday's soy bean salad, perhaps, one egg stir-fried

with a single tomato, a little spinach stir-fried with chopped garlic, and so on.

In planning a meal, I suggest you think in terms of serving rice or noodles with one accompanying dish per person and perhaps one extra. So, if you are cooking lunch for one, a bowl of noodles with one or two dishes will do; for four people, five dishes is perfect. For a special occasion, increase the number of dishes, especially cold appetizers that can be made in advance. And if you suddenly have an extra, unexpected guest, it doesn't matter: just add another rice bowl and pair of chopsticks to the table and the dishes will go further.

AT THE CHINESE TABLE

For simple home-cooked meals, a table setting will consist of just rice bowls and chopsticks. The rice bowl is used to hold rice and other dishes, as well as soup, which may be drunk directly from the bowl.

For more formal settings, a small plate is laid underneath each rice bowl. The plate can be used to hold pieces of food taken from the common dishes in the center of the table. It may also be used to hold bones, shells, whole spices and other unwanted bits and pieces.

Chopsticks may, in a more formal setting, be laid on chopstick stands. Spoons are offered for drinking soup and for eating soft ingredients such as silken tofu. China spoons are most traditional and their shape makes them very suitable for

using with rice bowls, but metal spoons may also be used.

At home, people normally help themselves with their own chopsticks to the shared dishes in the center of the table; in more formal settings, shared "public chopsticks" or serving spoons may be offered alongside each dish. It's a good idea to provide serving spoons if your guests are not confident chopstick-users.

It's perfectly polite, in a Chinese context, to raise your rice bowl to your lips so you can push rice into your mouth or drink your soup. It is also polite to spit bones on to your saucer, gently and quietly, and to place choice morsels of food into other people's rice bowls. It is not polite, in a Chinese context, to rummage around in a shared dish, or to touch food with your chopsticks that you don't intend to eat.

The photograph opposite shows a meal for four. The menu includes Sichuanese Spiced Cucumber Salad, Spinach in Ginger Sauce, Fish-fragrant Eggplant, Cold Chicken with a Spicy Sichuanese Sauce, Steamed Sea Bass with Ginger and Spring Onion, and Stir-fried Garlic Stems with Mushrooms, served with plain white rice.

AFTER THE MEAL

Rather than dessert, the Chinese usually serve fresh fruit at the end of a meal. In a smart restaurant, you might be offered iced platters of beautifully cut watermelons, pineapples, oranges and apples; at home, whole fruit may be served with little paring knives for peeling.

My favorite place for after-dinner fruit is the Dragon Well Manor restaurant in Hangzhou, where they always serve the best of the season, often gathered earlier the same day from the farms that supply their kitchens. There might be small, crisp peaches, pale green and just blushed with pink; orange loquats, their juicy flesh a little tart and arresting, their flavor reminiscent of passion fruit; or fresh jujubes, mottled and crunchy as apples. Once they gave me a full, ripe peach that had been stewed with crystal sugar, served in its sweet broth in a china pot.

At home in London, I also like to serve my guests fruit after dinner. I love offering some of the more unusual Chinese fruits they may not know, such as longans or "dragon eyes," whose dull brown shells encase delicately sweet, jade-white flesh; loquats from my local Turkish supermarket; or ripe persimmons that can be sliced open and eaten with a spoon, like soft-boiled eggs. There are also the better-known Chinese fruits, such as lychees, with their dragon-like pink and scaly skins and shiny secret pits. The luxuriant sweetness of this fruit is associated with the decadence of the northern Tang Dynasty court, because of the legend that the Emperor Xuanzong ordered relays of horsemen to carry lychees all the way from southern China to please his beloved concubine Yang Guifei. Peaches are the favored fruit of the mythical Immortals (steamed buns in the shape of peaches, their white dough dusted with pink coloring, are served at birthdays in parts of China, as symbol of longevity). The golden skins of mandarins make them an auspicious fruit for the Chinese New Year.

With fruit and sweetmeats, Chinese tea makes a beautiful postscript to dinner. Sometimes I'll serve Dragon Well green tea, with its spear-like leaves and nutty fragrance; sometimes a honeyed oolong, brewed in a small clay pot and served in tiny porcelain bowls. Or perhaps soothing pu'er, made in a pot and poured into rough earthenware bowls, which is the perfect digestif. And if people prefer something herbal before sleeping, I might give them chrysanthemum tea, made from tight knots of dried yellow flowers that "bloom" in the hot water and have a delicate, almost artichoke-like scent. This tea looks lovely when brewed in tall glasses, with a few gouqi berries to add a splash of color.

A NOTE ON DRINKS

Tea The classic accompaniment to the Cantonese dim sum breakfast, Chinese teas or herbal infusions (such as chrysanthemum tea) may also be served alongside other kinds of meals.

Beer Light bottled beers are popular accompaniments for more casual meals.

Grape wines Red wine is now fashionable in Chinese cities, but whites tend to be a better match for Chinese food. Rieslings, Grüner Veltliners and Pinot Gris can go well with spicy dishes; Champagne is often delicious with gentler flavors; oaky whites are best avoided. If you prefer to drink red, pick lighter, fruitier wines, not those with heavy tannins (Pinot Noirs are a good bet).

Chinese wines and spirits Shaoxing wine is served with food in eastern China, while fiery grain vodkas are more common elsewhere. Grain alcohols are always served with dishes, never with rice or noodles.

MENU IDEAS

Except for those that include noodles, all menus are intended to be served with plain white or, if you prefer, brown rice. Most Chinese people like to serve a simple soup with any rice-based meal.

As in the rest of this book, work on the premise of one dish per person, with perhaps one extra.

Please remember that these are simply suggestions; there are infinite possibilities.

FOR TWO PEOPLE

Menu 1
Cold chicken with a spicy Sichuanese sauce	48
Hangzhou fava beans with ham	158
Spinach with chilli and fermented tofu	170

Menu 2
Smacked cucumber with sesame and preserved mustard greens	34
Twice-cooked pork	96
Bok choy with fresh shiitake	180

Menu 3
Tiger salad	66
Red-braised beef with tofu "bamboo"	108
Stir-fried greens with dried shrimp	172

Menu 4
Classic dan dan noodles	280
Spinach in ginger sauce	64

Vegetarian menu 1
Smacked cucumber in garlicky sauce	34
Pock-marked old woman's tofu	76
Stir-fried beansprouts with Chinese chives	164

Vegetarian menu 2
Silken tofu with avocado	42
Sichuanese dry-fried green beans	150
Stir-fried choy sum with ginger and garlic	177

Vegetarian menu 3
Smoked tofu with celery and peanuts	44
Stir-fried eggs with tomatoes	128
Stir-fried broccoli with chilli and Sichuan pepper	174

Vegetarian menu 4
Ho fun rice noodles with mushrooms	272
Sichuanese green soy bean salad	38

FOR FOUR PEOPLE

Menu 1
Spinach in ginger sauce   64
Steamed chicken with Chinese sausage
and shiitake mushrooms   114
Fish-fragrant eggplant   210
Stir-fried green soy beans
with snow vegetable   162
Soup with vegetables and meatballs   248

Menu 2
Sichuanese spiced cucumber salad   36
Spinach with sesame sauce   67
Steamed sea bass with ginger
and spring onion   136
Bear's paw tofu   80
Stir-fried garlic stems with mushrooms   206

Menu 3
Smacked cucumber in garlicky sauce   34
Sichuanese green soy bean salad   38
Gong bao chicken with peanuts   118
Stir-fried celery with lily bulb
and macadamia nuts   196
Blanched choy sum with sizzling oil   168

Menu 4
Cold chicken with a spicy Sichuanese sauce   48
Kohlrabi salad with sesame oil   62
Red-braised pork   94
Green or romano beans with
black bean and chilli   154
Stir-fried choy sum with ginger and garlic   177

Vegetarian menu 1
Silken tofu with avocado   42
Sichuanese spiced cucumber salad   36
Twice-cooked Swiss chard   186
Stir-fried oyster and shiitake mushrooms
with garlic   232
Sichuanese dry-fried green beans   150

Vegetarian menu 2
Pock-marked old woman's tofu   76
Golden Chinese chive omelette   204
Blanched choy sum with sizzling oil   168
Stir-fried cucumber with wood ear   216
Fava bean and snow vegetable soup   244

Vegetarian menu 3
Smoked tofu with celery and peanuts   44
Spinach in ginger sauce   64
Fish-fragrant eggplant   210
Stir-fried peas with chilli and
Sichuan pepper   152
Stir-fried garlic stems with mushrooms   206

FOR SIX PEOPLE

Menu 1
Cold chicken with a spicy Sichuanese sauce   48
Delectable lotus root salad   70
Braised trout in chilli bean sauce   140
Red-braised pork   94
Hangzhou eggplant   212
Stir-fried choy sum with ginger and garlic   177
Taro and arugula soup   250

Menu 2
Kohlrabi salad with sesame oil   62
Smoky eggplant with garlic   63
Red-braised beef with tofu "bamboo"   108
Steamed sea bass with ginger
and spring onion   136
Black bean chicken   116
Stir-fried oyster and shiitake
mushrooms with garlic   232
Blanched choy sum with sizzling oil   168

Menu 3
Smacked cucumber with sweet
and sour sauce   34
Smoky eggplant with garlic   63
Pipa tofu   78
Steamed sea bass with ginger
and spring onion   136
Green or romano beans with black bean
and chilli   154
Bok choy with fresh shiitake   180

Vegetarian menu
Tofu "bamboo" with spring
onion-flavored oil   46
Smacked cucumber with sesame
and preserved mustard greens   34
Pock-marked old woman's tofu   76
Fish-fragrant eggplant   210
Sichuanese dry-fried green beans   150
Spinach with chilli and fermented tofu   170

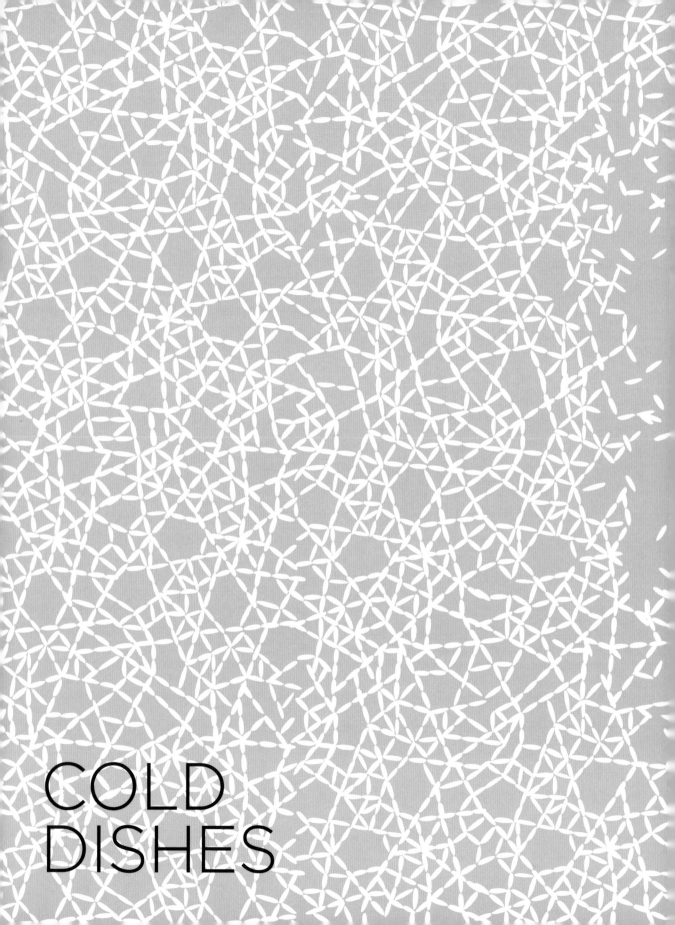

COLD
DISHES

My honorary Sichuanese aunt, Li Shurong, is a famously good cook. Whenever I'm in the Sichuanese capital, Chengdu, she feeds me with her magnificent fish in pickled chilli sauce, her unforgettable red-braised pork, and other homemade dishes. If she notices I am tired or sad, she is even more attentive in her culinary ministrations. And every so often, she includes me in a weekend feast with her extended family.

Like many Chinese home cooks, Li Shurong has a few cold dishes at the ready when her guests arrive, to whet their appetites and occupy them while she stir-fries the vegetables and finishes off her soups and stews. She might have rustled up a quick, spicy fava bean salad, cut some preserved duck eggs into rainbow segments, or steamed and sliced up some of her homemade winter sausages and laid them on a plate with a dip of ground chillies.

Cold appetizers, rather than the deep-fried titbits typical of Chinese restaurants in the West, open the meal in many parts of China, including Beijing, Shanghai and Sichuan Province. They might be as simple as some fried peanuts and a cucumber salad with a spicy dressing, or as elaborate,

in a glamorous restaurant, as a checkerboard of 16 different delicacies, made with ingredients beautifully cut and arranged in each dish like the petals of a flower. Modest or extravagant, they make a delightful start to the meal, both for the eater and for the cook, who can make them in advance and concentrate, at the last minute, on the hot dishes that must be served fresh from the wok.

Some of the vegetable dishes in this chapter make refreshing accompaniments to a simple lunch of noodles or dumplings, as well as appetizers. And don't feel obliged to eat them only in a Chinese context, because many of them work splendidly as Western-style starters, or as part of a mixed buffet lunch. I've often served a Sichuanese cold-dressed chicken dish for a summer lunch party alongside, perhaps, an Arabian carrot salad, a green salad, a potato salad and bread. And my Boxing Day lunches invariably include cold meats with Sichuanese seasonings: turkey treated like chicken in a spicy sauce; beef sliced and tossed with chilli oil, roasted nuts and celery or cilantro. Similarly, there's no reason why you can't serve a dish of charcuterie or a salad as appetizers at the start of an otherwise Chinese meal.

Most of the dishes that follow are extremely easy to make; some, like the Smacked Cucumber in Garlicky Sauce, take about 10 minutes from start to finish; others can be cooked in advance and swiftly assembled when you want to eat. A few dishes found in other chapters can also be included in a spread of appetizers, such as Spicy Buckwheat Noodles or Mrs. Yu's Sweet and Spicy Cold Noodles. You can also serve leftover cold meats, sliced and laid out on a plate with little piles of ground chillies and ground roasted Sichuan pepper; smoked or spiced tofu (sliced, laid out prettily on a plate and drizzled with chilli oil); or edamame soy beans, served in the pod. As in the rest of the book, allow one dish for each guest, perhaps with one extra.

SMACKED CUCUMBER IN GARLICKY SAUCE
SUAN NI PAI HUANG GUA 蒜泥拍黄瓜

This exceptionally quick and easy dish was a favorite of mine at the now demolished and much-missed Bamboo Bar, a small restaurant just outside the Sichuan University campus. The serving girls there, who lodged like sardines in the attic at the top of the old wooden building, used to mix up the seasonings behind the counter, taking spoonfuls of garnet-red chilli oil and dark soy sauce from the bowls in the glass cabinet beside them and tossing the cucumber in the piquant sauce. The combination of seasonings, known as "garlic paste flavor" (*suan ni wei*), is a Sichuanese classic, with its garlicky pungency and undercurrent of sweetness: the same sauce may be used to dress fresh fava beans, thinly sliced cooked pork (perhaps mixed with fine slivers of carrot and Asian radish), boiled pork dumplings or wontons, and many other ingredients. You may use sweet, aromatic soy sauce instead of light soy sauce if you have it in stock (see page 322).

The cucumber is smacked before cutting to loosen its flesh and help it absorb the flavors of the sauce. Try not to smash it into smithereens!

1 cucumber (about 11 oz/300g)
½ tsp salt
1 tbsp finely chopped garlic
½ tsp sugar
2 tsp light soy sauce
½ tsp Chinkiang vinegar
2 tbsp chilli oil
A pinch or two of ground roasted Sichuan pepper, (optional)

Lay the cucumber on a chopping board and smack it hard a few times with the flat blade of a Chinese cleaver or with a rolling pin. Then cut it, lengthways, into four pieces. Hold your knife at an angle to the chopping board and cut the cucumber on the diagonal into ⅛–⅜ in (½–1cm) slices. Place in a bowl with the salt, mix well and set aside for about 10 minutes.

Combine all the other ingredients in a small bowl.

Drain the cucumber, pour over the sauce, stir well and serve immediately.

VARIATIONS

A sweet-and-sour sauce for smacked cucumber
A lovely variation. Smack, cut and salt the cucumber as in the main recipe, but dress it with the following seasonings: ½ tsp salt, 1 tbsp finely chopped garlic, 2 tsp sugar, 2 tsp Chinkiang vinegar, 1 tsp light soy sauce and, if you fancy a bit of heat, 2 tbsp chilli oil.

Smacked cucumber with sesame and preserved mustard greens
For a nutty, savory flavor, smack, cut and salt the cucumber as in the main recipe, but dress it with the following seasonings: 2 tbsp Sichuan preserved mustard greens (*ya cai*), 1 tsp finely chopped garlic, 1 tbsp runny sesame paste, 1½ tsp clear rice vinegar, 1 tsp sesame oil and salt to taste.

SICHUANESE SPICED CUCUMBER SALAD
QIANG HUANG GUA 熗黃瓜

This swiftly stir-fried cucumber, infused with the smoky aromas of chillies and Sichuan pepper and the subtle fragrance of sesame oil, is normally served at room temperature and can be made a few hours in advance of your meal. It uses the Sichuanese *qiang* cooking method, in which a brief blast of heat in the wok drives the flavors of the spices into the main ingredient. It is usually served as an appetizer, or as a side dish with a selection of Sichuanese "small eats," such as the slippery dragon wontons, "glassy" steamed dumplings and Lai glutinous rice balls for which the regional capital Chengdu is famed.

1 cucumber (about 11 oz/300g)
½ tsp salt
2 tbsp cooking oil

4–5 dried chillies, snipped in half, seeds discarded as far as possible
½–1 tsp whole Sichuan pepper
1 tsp sesame oil

Cut the cucumber in half lengthways and scoop out the pulp and seeds with a teaspoon (I usually eat them as I go along). Then cut each half into about three sections and slice each section into thin strips. Place the pieces in a bowl, sprinkle with the salt, mix well and set aside for at least 30 minutes.

Drain the cucumber and shake dry.

Heat a wok over a high flame. Pour in the cooking oil, swirl it quickly around, then add the chillies and Sichuan pepper. Stir-fry the spices until the chillies are darkening but not burned, then add the cucumber. Stir-fry very briefly to heat the surface of the cucumber and drive in the flavors of the oil. Off the heat, stir in the sesame oil and turn on to a serving dish.

VARIATION

Spiced potato sliver salad

If you've never tasted a dish like this, prepare to be surprised. It's a simple concoction of potato slivers enlivened by scorched chillies and Sichuan pepper, but the potatoes are deliberately cooked so fleetingly that they retain some of their raw crunchiness. Peel 11 oz (300g) potatoes (larger ones will be easier to cut). Cut them evenly into the thinnest possible slices, then into slivers; you may use a mandolin for this, if you have one. Place the slivers in a bowl of lightly salted cold water as you work, so they don't discolor.

Bring a panful of water to a boil and blanch the potato slivers for about two minutes; they should remain crisp. Turn them into a sieve, refresh under the cold tap and shake dry. Place in a bowl and add 1½ tbsp clear rice vinegar and salt to taste. Now make the spicy oil: snip eight dried chillies in half and discard their seeds as far as possible. Heat 3 tbsp cooking oil in a wok over a medium flame. Add the chillies and 1 tsp whole Sichuan pepper and sizzle gently until the chillies are darkening but not burned. Add the oil and spices to the potato with 2 tsp sesame oil, mix well, then serve.

SICHUANESE GREEN SOY BEAN SALAD
XIANG YOU QING DOU 香油青豆

Young soy beans, which can be bought fresh in places where they are cultivated and are otherwise available cooked and frozen, are a strikingly beautiful green and delicately savory in flavor. In the West, they are most often encountered in their pods, with the Japanese name edamame. Although the Chinese eat them this way too (see page 72), they also like to serve the shelled beans as an appetizer, sometimes just with a little red pickled chilli for color, sometimes mixed with preserved mustard greens and other ingredients as in this recipe. Leave out the preserved vegetable if you don't have it to hand.

Salt
7 oz (200g) fresh or defrosted frozen green soy beans (shelled weight)
2 oz (50g) Sichuan preserved vegetable (*zha cai*)

½ oz (25g) carrot
A small piece of red bell pepper or fresh red chilli
1–2 tsp sesame oil

Bring a panful of water to a boil, add salt, then the soy beans. Return to a boil. If you are using fresh soy beans, cook for about five minutes, until tender, then drain and refresh immediately under the cold tap; if you are using defrosted frozen beans, simply blanch them for a few seconds, drain and refresh.

Cut the preserved vegetable, carrot and red pepper into small squares of a similar size to the beans. Bring a little water to a boil, then blanch the carrot and pepper, separately, for a minute or two, until tender but still crunchy. Drain and refresh these, too.

Mix the beans and other vegetables together with salt and sesame oil to taste.

SICHUANESE FAVA BEAN SALAD
LIANG BAN HU DOU 涼拌胡豆

The Sichuanese name for fava beans is *hu dou*, or "barbarian" beans, because they are thought to have entered China along the old silk routes from Central Asia. Dried and spiced, the beans are a favored snack all over China; fermented, they are one of the essential ingredients of the fabulous Sichuanese chilli bean paste. They are also eaten fresh, in season.

One of my favorite uses for the fresh beans is a Sichuanese salad in which they are tossed with slivers of lettuce stem and the leaves and juicy stalks of *ze'er gen*, a local vegetable with a refreshing, sour fruitiness to its taste that is sometimes called "Chinese watercress" or "fish grass." *Ze'er gen* is hard to find outside China, so this recipe offers a version of the dish made with other lettuces and cucumber. The same sauce may be used to dress fava beans alone. If you can find tiny, very young beans, simply blanch them: there is no need to pop them out of their skins.

Salt
7 oz (200g) shelled fava beans
4 oz (100g) cucumber
Generous handful of baby spinach or lettuce of your choice, washed and dried

For the dressing
2 tsp light soy sauce
½ tsp sugar
¼ tsp Chinkiang vinegar
1–2 tbsp chilli oil with ½ tsp of its sediment
1 garlic clove, crushed (optional)
A few good pinches of ground, roasted Sichuan pepper (optional)

Bring a panful of water to a boil. Lightly salt, add the beans and boil for about four minutes, until tender. Drain and rinse under the cold tap, then pop the beans out of their skins. Cut the cucumber section in half lengthways, scoop out and discard the pulp, then cut the flesh lengthways into thin slivers.

Combine the dressing ingredients in a small bowl.

When you are ready to serve, combine the salad ingredients in a bowl, pour over the dressing and mix well.

SILKEN TOFU WITH SOY SAUCE
XIAO CONG BAN DOU FU 小蔥拌豆腐

Many years ago I spent a surreal week in the northern city of Lanzhou, hanging out with some artist friends and a bunch of local gangsters. One of my friends had a complicated business connection with the gangsters, which meant that we were obliged to spend endless hours humoring them in the private rooms of local restaurants while they chain-smoked, showed off, knocked back cupfuls of eye-watering liquor and bossed around their sycophantic minions.

It was a ghastly experience, but at least one good thing did come out of it: this marvellous recipe. I first tasted it in a restaurant next to the hotel where I was staying that week—which listed it as a Taiwanese delicacy—and it was love at first bite. The silken tofu, as tender as crème caramel, is livened up with spring onions, soy sauce and a sizzling of oil, and this dish takes minutes to make.

7 oz (200g) silken tofu
2 spring onions, green parts only
1½ tbsp cooking oil

2 tbsp light or tamari soy sauce diluted with 1 tbsp water
1 tsp sesame oil

Turn the block of silken tofu out on to a serving dish. Cut the block into ⅛ in (½cm) slices, then push down gently so the slices lean towards one end of the dish (see photo on page 43). Thinly slice the spring onion greens and scatter them over the tofu.

Heat the oil in a wok or small pan until it is hot enough to produce a dramatic sizzle when you drip it on to the spring onions (test a few drops to make sure). Then pour the rest of the hot oil all over the spring onions, which will begin to smell delicious as they sizzle. Pour over the diluted soy sauce and the sesame oil and serve.

VARIATION

Silken tofu with preserved duck eggs
Slice the tofu and place it on a serving dish, as in the main recipe. Pour over 2 tbsp light or tamari soy sauce diluted with 1 tbsp water and 1 tsp sesame oil. Coarse-chop one or two peeled preserved duck eggs and scatter them over the tofu. Garnish with 2 tbsp finely sliced spring onion greens or chopped cilantro.

SILKEN TOFU WITH AVOCADO
E'LI DOU FU 鱷梨豆腐

One warm autumn night in Taipei, a few years ago, I left the lights of the city behind and drove out to a restaurant in the southern hills. I left my shoes at the door and padded across tatami mats to a candlelit dining room, where the owner, dressed like a Buddhist monk, joined me for tea as the frogs and cicadas sang outside. He told me about his travels abroad, his interest in Chinese medicinal theory and the old literati culture, and how all these influenced his cooking. "The food here expresses my own philosophy," he told me. "My dishes are my life."

The meal that followed was a kind of miracle that I've never forgotten. It drew on ancient Chinese traditions, the flavors of Taiwanese street food, Taiwan's legacy as a Japanese colony and even the owner's travels in Europe, blending a miscellany of ingredients with uncommon artistry. One of the dishes I ate that night was a freshly made silken tofu topped with raw sea urchin, a hint of wasabi, soy sauce and a wedge of avocado. What took me by surprise was the delicate sympathy between the tender tofu and the ripe, buttery avocado: a simply wonderful combination. The following dish is inspired by Mr. Li's creation. If you happen to have any, top with a little raw sea urchin. Don't even think of using an unripe avocado!

7 oz (200g) silken tofu
2 tbsp light or tamari soy sauce diluted with 1 tbsp water
A hint of wasabi paste (optional)
½ tsp sesame oil
½ perfectly ripe avocado, sliced

Turn the block of silken tofu out on to a serving dish. Cut the block into ⅛–⅜ in (½–1cm) slices, then push down gently so the slices lean towards one end of the dish.

Pour over the diluted soy sauce (with the wasabi stirred in, if you wish) and sesame oil. Top with the avocado and serve immediately.

SMOKED TOFU WITH CELERY AND PEANUTS
LIANG BAN DOU FU GAN 涼拌豆腐乾

When I was a student at Sichuan University, there was a street market just outside the campus that overflowed with seasonal produce. Farmers would crouch behind stalls with their produce, perhaps just a single ingredient, piled up on bamboo trays. One old woman sat behind an array of spices that included blood-red chillies and dusky pink Sichuan pepper, while the butchers hung their pink-and-white slabs of meat on blackened iron frames. And then there was a man with a glass cabinet of spicy hors d'oeuvres and relishes on the back of his bicycle cart: piquant concoctions of pickled tubers and dried radish, tofu skin and other vegetarian tidbits. The following mixture was always one of my favorites. It takes about 10 minutes to prepare and makes a wonderful appetizer. You can use either fried or roasted peanuts: both are delicious, differing mainly in the mouthfeel of the moist or crunchy nuts.

3½ oz (100g) smoked or spiced firm tofu
3 celery sticks (about 4 oz/125g)
1 oz (30g) Fried or Roasted Peanuts (see page 325)

1½ tbsp chilli oil with ½ tbsp of its sediment, to taste
Good pinch of sugar
Salt, to taste

Cut the tofu into ⅜ in (1cm) cubes. De-string the celery sticks, cut them lengthways into ⅜ in (1cm) strips, then into small pieces to match the tofu. Bring some water to a boil in a saucepan, add the celery and blanch for 30–60 seconds; it should remain a little crunchy. Remove to a colander and cool immediately under the cold tap, then shake dry.

Combine all the ingredients in a bowl and mix well. Serve.

VARIATION

Simple firm tofu salad

This satisfying appetizer can be can be rustled up in minutes if you have the tofu, sesame seeds and a spring onion or two in the fridge. Toast 1 tsp sesame seeds in a dry wok or frying pan until fragrant and starting to turn golden, then put in a small bowl to stop the cooking. Cut 4 oz (125g) spiced firm tofu into thin slices or slivers and combine with 2 tbsp finely sliced spring onion greens, ½ tsp sugar, 2 tbsp chilli oil, with or without its sediment, ½ tsp sesame oil and salt to taste. Scatter with the sesame seeds and serve.

There are many types of spiced, firm tofu: I use lightly spiced squares for this recipe, pale brown on the outside, about ⅜ in (1cm) thick and the texture of Edam cheese, found in my local Chinatown, but you might find some that is a dark caramel color. The same seasonings can be used to dress tofu "bamboo" (soaked to reconstitute, see page 46), or very thin sheets of firm tofu, cut into tagliatelle-like ribbons. Some people add crushed garlic to the sauce, others chopped cilantro or ground roasted Sichuan pepper. And if you want to keep the flavors even simpler, just toss the tofu in a little soy sauce and sesame oil, with the spring onion greens and sesame seeds as a garnish.

TOFU "BAMBOO" WITH SPRING ONION-FLAVORED OIL
CONG YOU FU ZHU 蔥油腐竹

Dried tofu sticks, known in Chinese as tofu "bamboo," are made from the protein-rich skins that are lifted from the surface of simmering soy milk, crumpled and rolled into sticks before drying. After a good soak, the dried "bamboos" absorb flavors beautifully and have a satisfying, slightly elastic texture. In this dish, which looks plain but tastes delicious, they are encouraged to drink in the savory tastes of stock and fried spring onions. Any leftovers can be cut into smaller pieces, tossed with boiled green soy beans and chopped "snow vegetable" (*xue cai*), then seasoned with salt and sesame oil, for another wonderful salad.

4 sticks of dried tofu "bamboo" (about 2 oz/60g)
4 spring onions, white parts only
1½ x 2 in (3 x 5cm) strips of Sichuanese pickled chilli, fresh red bell pepper, or chilli

1½ tbsp cooking oil
2 slices of peeled ginger
2 garlic cloves, sliced
½ cup (100ml) chicken or vegetable stock
½ tsp salt (optional)
½ tsp sesame oil

Soak the "bamboos" in hot water from the kettle for an hour or so, until they have softened. Then drain well, squeeze out any excess water and cut into 2 in (5cm) lengths, discarding any remaining hard bits.

Cut the spring onion whites into 2 in (5cm) sections and smack gently but firmly with the side of a cleaver or a rolling pin to loosen (don't smash them to pieces). If using Sichuanese pickled chilli, discard the seeds as far as possible.

Heat the oil in a wok over a medium flame. Add the spring onions, ginger and garlic and stir-fry gently for a couple of minutes until the onions are golden and the oil smells delicious. Pour in the stock with the tofu and salt and bring to a boil (if you are using storebought stock that is already salty, you may not need this extra salt). Boil, stirring intermittently, until the liquid has almost completely evaporated. Towards the end of the cooking time, add the red pepper or chilli strips. Turn off the heat, stir in the sesame oil and allow to cool.

Lay the sections of "bamboo" neatly on a plate to serve, with the chilli or pepper for a splash of color.

COLD CHICKEN WITH A SPICY SICHUANESE SAUCE
LIANG BAN JI 涼拌雞

This is one of the most marvellous of all Sichuanese culinary ideas. The cold chicken is dressed with seasonings that generally include soy sauce and chilli oil, with sugar, sesame oil, vinegar, crushed garlic and ground, roasted Sichuan pepper added according to taste or mood. It's very easy to make and stunningly delicious, as I hope you'll agree. Ever since I first lived in Sichuan, this kind of dish has been part of my everyday kitchen repertoire. I've often served a spicy chicken salad alongside other dishes that are more ambitious or complicated to make, and yet this tends to be the one that everyone raves about the most.

I don't actually use a recipe for this, any more than I would use a recipe to mix up a vinaigrette, so it's different every time I make it. The following version and its variation, which I've measured, are lip-smackingly wonderful, but do please think of them as templates rather than immutable instructions, and improvise as you will. You might want to add more chilli oil in winter, or more refreshing vinegar when the weather is hot and sultry, while a spritz of crushed garlic can be quite enlivening. You can also serve the dressed chicken on a bed of sliced cucumber, or toss some salad greens, perhaps arugula or watercress, into the mix.

In China, they normally poach a whole chicken (see page 50), then chop it up bones and all, but you can equally well use boneless meat. And don't forget that this is also a marvellous way of using up leftover roast chicken or turkey: the meat won't be quite as moist and fresh-tasting as that of a poached bird, but it's still delicious (and you can add extra chicken stock to the sauce to moisten, if necessary).

About ³⁄₄ lb (300–350g) cold, cooked chicken, without bones (see page 50 for poaching instructions)
3 spring onions
¼ tsp salt
1 tbsp sesame seeds (optional)

For the sauce
2 tbsp light soy sauce
1½ tsp Chinkiang vinegar
1½ tsp sugar
1 tbsp chicken stock
3–4 tbsp chilli oil with ½ tbsp of its sediment (or more, if you wish)
¼–½ tsp ground, roasted Sichuan pepper, to taste
1 tsp sesame oil

Cut or tear the chicken as evenly as possible into bite-sized strips or slivers and place them in a deep bowl. Cut the spring onions at a steep angle into thin slices. Mix them and the salt with the chicken. If using sesame seeds, toast them gently in a dry wok or frying pan for a few minutes, until they are fragrant and starting to turn golden, then tip out into a small dish.

Combine all the sauce ingredients in a small bowl.

When you are ready to eat, pour the sauce over the chicken, and mix well with chopsticks or salad servers. Arrange on a serving dish and sprinkle with sesame seeds, if desired.

VARIATION

Another sauce for cold chicken
2 tbsp light soy sauce
2 tsp finely chopped or crushed garlic
2 tbsp chicken stock
3 tbsp chilli oil (with or without its sediment)
½ tsp ground, roasted Sichuan pepper
½ tsp sesame oil

COLD CHICKEN WITH GINGER AND SPRING ONION
YOU LIN JI 油淋雞

This is my recreation of a dish I ate in a Hong Kong restaurant with my friend Susan and some of her friends. We were actually there for the green bell pepper crab, an electrifying potful of fresh crustacean with whole strands of fresh green peppercorns, but I couldn't help being distracted by this delicious starter. It uses the classic Cantonese method in which sizzling hot oil is used to awaken the heady fragrances of a ginger and onion garnish. On that warm Hong Kong night, I think we had half a chicken, chopped up on the bone, but this recipe uses boneless thigh meat for convenience. A couple of generously sized thighs give enough for four to six people as a starter, with other dishes. It's best to use poached chicken, which will be beautifully moist. I've given a method for poaching the meat here.

You can use a similar method to finish hot, freshly steamed chicken if you like: equally fabulous. Just chop the raw chicken, on or off the bone, lay it in a shallow bowl with a little Shaoxing wine, steam it through, then season with the chopped ginger, spring onion, oil and soy sauce as in this recipe.

2 cold, cooked boneless chicken thighs (about 9 oz/250g in total)
2 tbsp finely chopped ginger
2 spring onions, finely sliced
3½ tbsp cooking oil
3 tbsp light or tamari soy sauce mixed with 1 tbsp water

Cut the chicken evenly into very thin slices and lay them neatly in a serving dish. Scatter with the ginger and spring onions.

Heat the oil over a high flame until hot enough to create a dramatic sizzle when you spoon it over the ginger and onions (try first with a drop to make sure). Then pour the oil evenly over the ginger and spring onions, drizzle with the diluted soy sauce and serve.

To poach a chicken for Chinese cold dishes

You may use any cold, cooked chicken for the recipes in this book, but poached chicken is particularly silken and succulent. The classic Chinese method is to place a whole bird in a measured amount of boiling stock, return it to a boil, then leave it to cool in the liquid. If the measuring is accurate, the chicken will be just cooked by the time the stock is cool, but still a little pink around the bones. This produces chicken flesh that is moist but still a little taut, exactly the way Chinese gourmets like it. It's a little dicey for home cooks, because of the health risks if the chicken is not sufficiently heated, so in general I recommend using the following method.

Allow the chicken to come to room temperature before you start. Bring to a boil enough water to immerse your bird, without too much room to spare in the pan. Place the chicken in the water, return it quickly to a boil, then skim. Add a piece of ginger, unpeeled and slightly crushed, with a couple of spring onions (white parts only), also crushed. Partially cover the pan with a lid, reduce the heat so the liquid just murmurs gently and poach for about 30 minutes, depending on the size of the chicken. Pierce the thigh joint deeply with a skewer to see if the bird is done: the juices that emerge should run clear, not pink and bloody (you may find it easiest to remove the bird from the pan to do this). When the chicken is just cooked, remove it from the pan and rinse it in cold running water. Set aside to cool.

If you are using smaller amounts of chicken, such as a boned thigh or two, poach them similarly but in less water and for a shorter time. And if you are using a spectacularly good free-range capon or another fine bird, consider poaching it whole, chopping it up on the bone, and serving it at room temperature with nothing but a dip of tamari soy sauce.

VEGETARIAN CLAY BOWL "CHICKEN"
BO BO FU ZHU 鉢鉢腐竹

The Chinese are masters at devising vegetarian versions of meat, fish and poultry dishes that fool not only the eye, but also the palate. In Buddhist temple restaurants, tofu, sweet potato and mushrooms may be cunningly fashioned into convincing replicas of crab meat and shrimp, abalone and shark's fin, not to mention more humble foods such as meatballs and fish. To imitate cold chicken, the chefs often roll up sheets of fresh "tofu leather" (*dou fu pi*), bind them tightly in muslin and steam them into a semblance of flesh.

This simpler version of "chicken" uses only the dried rolls of tofu "bamboo" (*fu zhu*), that can be found in most Chinese groceries: all you need do is soak them in hot water for an hour or so before use. For a more intense flavor, begin by simmering the tofu using the method for Tofu "Bamboo" with Spring Onion-flavored Oil (see page 46).

5 sticks of dried tofu "bamboo" (about 3 oz/75g)
½ tbsp sesame seeds
1½ oz (40g) Fried or Roasted Peanuts (see page 325)
3 tbsp finely sliced spring onion greens
Small handful of fresh cilantro, chopped

For the sauce
1 tbsp light soy sauce
½ tsp sugar
2 tsp sesame paste
¼–½ tsp ground roasted Sichuan pepper, to taste
4–5 tbsp chilli oil, with its sediment
½ tsp sesame oil
Salt, to taste

Soak the "bamboos" in hot water from the kettle for about an hour, until they are supple. Shake and squeeze the rolls dry. Holding the knife at an angle, cut them diagonally into bite-sized pieces, discarding any sections that remain hard. Place the pieces in a serving bowl.

Toast the sesame seeds gently in a dry wok or frying pan for a few minutes, until they are fragrant and starting to turn golden, then remove to a dish. Combine all the sauce ingredients in a small bowl.

Pour the sauce over the tofu "bamboo," then scatter over the peanuts, sesame seeds, spring onions and cilantro. Mix everything together before eating.

CLAY BOWL CHICKEN
BO BO JI 鉢鉢雞

In rural Sichuan, earthenware bowls are commonly used both for steaming food and for serving. Steamed dishes such as belly pork with dark mustard greens, and sweet glutinous rice with red bean paste, were once the centerpieces of wedding and funeral feasts. Nowadays, you'll find old-fashioned steaming bowls used to give a rustic touch to restaurant dishes. (The delightful-sounding Chinese name of this dish, for example, is because the *bo*, or *b ozi*, of the *bo bo ji* means a rough earthenware bowl, and *ji* is chicken.) Like other Sichuanese cold chicken dishes, this is easy to make but extravagantly delicious. The crunch of the peanuts and the fresh, urgent pungency of the cilantro are a pleasing contrast to the silky chicken.

For the sauce
1 tbsp light soy sauce
½ tsp sugar
2 tsp sesame paste
1 tbsp chicken stock or water
¼–½ tsp ground roasted Sichuan pepper, to taste
4–5 tbsp chilli oil, with its sediment
½ tsp sesame oil
Salt, to taste

½ tbsp sesame seeds
4 oz (100g) beansprouts (optional)
7 oz (200g) cold, cooked chicken
1 oz (25g) Fried or Roasted Peanuts (see page 325)
3 tbsp finely sliced spring onion greens
Small handful of fresh cilantro, chopped

Toast the sesame seeds gently in a dry wok or frying pan for a few minutes, until they are fragrant and starting to turn golden, then put in a dish. Blanch the beansprouts (if using) briefly in boiling water to wilt them, refresh under the cold tap, then shake and squeeze dry. Mix the sauce ingredients together in a small bowl.

Pile the beansprouts in the center of a serving bowl (an earthenware one, if you like). Cut or tear the chicken evenly into bite-sized strips and lay it over the beansprouts. Pour over the sauce, then scatter over the peanuts, sesame seeds, spring onions and cilantro. Mix everything together before eating.

PRESERVED DUCK EGGS
LIANG BAN PI DAN 涼拌皮蛋

The first time I encountered these dark, mysterious-looking eggs, with their gelatinous brown "whites" and creamy grey yolks, I was terrified. But their appearance is misleading, because they actually taste quite like eggs, but more intense and delicious (when I've blindfolded friends before giving them their first taste, they've enjoyed them without any hesitation). They are made by coating raw duck eggs with a thick, alkaline paste that "cooks" the eggs by transforming their chemical structure. No one's quite sure who invented this method, but there are some colorful legends about its origins. Some say an elderly tea house owner found some eggs that his ducks had laid in a pile of wood ash and tea leaves and discovered their shiny dark flesh to be marvellously tasty. Others tell of a farmer who stumbled across some eggs his ducks had laid in a lime pit behind his house. Whoever it was who first decided to try tasting a black and smelly old egg, one has to admire their courage. The names "1,000-year-old eggs" and "century eggs," by the way, are Western inventions: in Chinese they are simply called "skin eggs," *pi dan*.

The Cantonese like to serve the eggs with a little vinegar and slivered ginger, but I prefer to use Sichuanese seasonings, as in this recipe.

3 preserved duck eggs
½ green bell pepper, thin-skinned and slightly hot if possible
A tiny amount of red bell pepper for color (optional)
1 tbsp light or tamari soy sauce
½ tsp Chinkiang vinegar
1 tbsp chilli oil, with its sediment if desired

Peel the preserved eggs and rinse them under the cold tap if necessary, to wash away any fragments of shell. Cut them into segments and arrange these in a circle around a serving plate, like the petals of a flower. Finely chop the pepper(s) and pile up in the center of the plate. Mix the soy sauce and vinegar together.

Just before serving, trickle the soy sauce mixture and the chilli oil over the eggs and peppers.

VARIATION

Sour-and-hot preserved duck eggs
Add 2–3 tsp Chinkiang vinegar to the sauce and garnish with a little finely chopped pickled green or red chilli instead of the fresh green bell pepper.

SICHUANESE NUMBING-AND-HOT BEEF
MA LA NIU ROU 麻辣牛肉

At a food conference in Chengdu a few years ago, I met the daughter of the couple who are immortalized in the name of the dish "man-and-wife lung slices" (*fu qi fei pian*). In the 1930s her parents, a pair of street vendors, charmed the citizens of Chengdu not only with their fiery, lip-numbing snack of beef offal (including head, skin, tongue, heart and tripe) laced with roasted nuts and fragrant oils, but with their happy and harmonious marriage, which is why the dish ended up with its "man-and-wife" name. Preparing the classic dish at home, which involves cleaning and cooking tripe as well as the other bits and pieces, can be a palaver, but this version, made with beef shin instead, uses the same scintillating spices, and it has had a rapturous reception whenever I've served it. The beef can be prepared a couple of days in advance and kept in the refrigerator; just slice and dress it when you're ready. It's not essential to use all the serving flourishes, but try to have at least something nutty and something green.

If you wish to make this in large quantities for a party, prick your chunks of shin all over with a skewer, rub in salt, a generous slosh of Shaoxing wine and plenty of crushed ginger and spring onions and marinate overnight before cooking.

¾ lb (325g) stewing beef or beef shin, boneless and in one piece
2 oz (50g) ginger, unpeeled, cut into thick slices
2 spring onions, crushed slightly
2 star anise
1 piece of cassia bark, or ⅓ of a cinnamon stick
½ tsp whole Sichuan pepper
2 cloves
1 tbsp Shaoxing wine
2 tsp salt

For the sauce
⅛ tsp ground roasted Sichuan pepper
1 garlic clove, very finely chopped
1 tsp light soy sauce
3–5 tbsp chilli oil, with its sediment, to taste
¼ tsp sesame oil

To serve
1 tsp sesame seeds (optional)
Handful of fresh cilantro, coarsely chopped
2 tbsp finely sliced spring onion greens
1 celery stick, de-stringed and finely chopped
Good handful of Fried Peanuts (see page 325), roughly chopped or crushed with a mortar and pestle

Rinse the beef very thoroughly in cold and then hot water to remove any bloodiness (under the tap will do). Then place in a saucepan, cover with water and bring to a boil. Skim the liquid. Then add the ginger, spring onions, spices, Shaoxing wine and salt, and return to a boil. Cover and cook over a very low flame for about two hours. When the beef is cooked, set it aside to cool, reserving ⅓ cup (75ml) of the cooking liquid. (The beef and liquid can be kept in the fridge for a few days. The leftover liquid can be frozen and re-used on another occasion to give a spiced flavor to firm tofu, hard-boiled eggs, peanuts, chicken wings, beef or offal of your choice.)

Gently toast the sesame seeds, if using, in a dry wok or frying pan for a few minutes, until they are fragrant and starting to turn golden, then tip into a dish.

When you wish to serve the beef, cut it into fairly thin slices and place in a serving dish. If the reserved beef cooking liquor has become jellied, let it stand at room temperature or gently warm it through until it is liquid once more, then allow to cool a little. Combine all the sauce ingredients with the beef cooking liquor in a small bowl, mix well and pour over the beef. Scatter over the other ingredients and serve. Give everything a good mix and invite your guests to help themselves.

SWEET-AND-SOUR SPARE RIBS
TANG CU PAI GU 糖醋排骨

Sweet-and-sour ribs are not difficult to make, but they do take a little time because the recipe has several stages. However, they can be prepared a day or two in advance and refrigerated (just return them to room temperature before serving). In my experience they are always incredibly popular, with their sticky sauce and chewily tender flesh. They are served as an appetizer in many parts of China: this particular recipe is from my *Revolutionary Chinese Cookbook*.

Ask your butcher to cut the spare ribs into bite-sized sections. You can do this at home but it's quite a job, for which you need a heavy cleaver. And, as suggested in the recipe, you can omit the deep-frying, but the ribs won't be quite as compellingly fragrant if you do. The following recipe yields a good bowlful of ribs, but given their popularity and the slightly time-consuming cooking method, it's a good idea to make double, saving some for another meal.

1¼ lb (500g) meaty spare ribs, cut into bite-sized sections
2 x 1 oz (30g) pieces of ginger, crushed
4 spring onions, white parts only, crushed
1 tbsp Shaoxing wine
Salt

Cooking oil, for deep-frying (optional), plus 3 tbsp more
2 tsp dark soy sauce
¼ cup (60g) sugar
1 tbsp Chinkiang vinegar
1 tsp sesame oil
1 tsp sesame seeds (optional)

Place the ribs in a panful of water and bring to a boil over a high flame. Skim the water, then add one of the pieces of ginger, two spring onion whites, the Shaoxing wine and about 1 tsp salt. Boil for 15 minutes until the meat is cooked and tender. Drain thoroughly and set aside, reserving ¾ cup (200ml) of the cooking liquid.

If you are going to deep-fry the ribs, heat the deep-frying oil to 350–400°F (180–200°C). Add the ribs and fry until golden. Drain and set aside.

Pour the 3 tbsp oil into a seasoned wok over a high flame. Add the rest of the ginger and spring onions and fry until fragrant. Add the ribs and toss for a couple of minutes in the fragrant oil. Pour in the reserved cooking liquid and add the soy sauce and the sugar. Boil over a high flame, spooning the liquid over the ribs, until the sauce has reduced to a heavy, syrupy consistency. Season with with salt to taste if you need it (remember the liquid will be reduced to a glaze, so take care not to over-salt). Add the vinegar and cook for another minute or two until the flavors have fused. Off the heat, stir in the sesame oil and leave to cool. (The ribs are normally served at room temperature.)

If you are using the sesame seeds, toast them very gently in a dry wok or frying pan until they are fragrant and starting to turn golden. Scatter them over the ribs just before serving.

SLIPPERY WOOD EAR SALAD WITH CILANTRO
XIANG CAI MU ER 香菜木耳

Wood or cloud ear mushrooms, also known as Chinese black fungus, derive their name from the way they grow in rows of "ears" on damp wood. When you buy them, the hard, crinkled pieces are as light as paper; soaked in hot water, they expand into sleek, rippling waves. The mushrooms retain their slippery crispness even after cooking and are appreciated for this delectable mouthfeel rather than any inherent flavor. In this brisk, refreshing salad, the wood ears are complemented by the arresting tastes of cilantro, chilli and vinegar. It's a good dish for rousing the palate for anyone feeling sluggish before a meal.

Handful of dried wood ear mushrooms (about ⅓ oz/10g dry, 4 oz/100g after soaking)
1 tsp finely chopped garlic
1 tbsp roughly chopped cilantro leaves

1–2 tsp chopped salted, pickled or fresh red chillies, to taste
½ tsp clear rice vinegar
Salt, to taste
1 tsp sesame oil

Soak the mushrooms in hot water from the kettle for at least 30 minutes. Then pinch or cut out and discard any hard, knobbly bits and tear or cut the rest into bite-sized pieces. Rinse, then shake dry.

Combine all the ingredients in a bowl and serve.

KOHLRABI SALAD WITH SESAME OIL
XIANG YOU PIE LAN 香油苤藍

Kohlrabi is known in some parts of China, rather poetically, as a "jade turnip," on account of its luminous green flesh. It is an underrated vegetable that sparkles in this simple Sichuanese appetizer. I like to serve it alongside richer dishes at the start of a meal, or as a fresh, zesty complement to a bowlful of noodles if I'm rustling up a quick lunch for one or two. The recipe and its variations were taught to me by Chef Zhang Xia ozhong of Barshu restaurant.

1 kohlrabi (about 14 oz/400g)
1¼ tsp salt
2 tbsp finely sliced spring onion greens

For the sauce
1 tsp light soy sauce
1 tsp finely chopped garlic
1 tsp Chinkiang vinegar
¼ tsp sugar
1 tsp sesame oil

Peel the kohlrabi and cut it into very thin slices. Cut the slices into very thin slivers. Place in a bowl, add the salt and mix well, scrunching with your hand to squeeze the salt into the kohlrabi shreds. Set aside for at least 10 minutes.

Drain off the water that will have emerged from the kohlrabi and squeeze the slivers as dry as possible. Add all the sauce ingredients, mix well, then serve with the spring onion greens scattered on top.

VARIATIONS

Kohlrabi salad with sour-and-hot dressing
Add 2 tsp more Chinkiang vinegar than the recipe above, as well as 1½ tbsp chilli oil with ½ tbsp chilli sediment, to the sauce. You can add a few good pinches of ground roasted Sichuan pepper or a dash of Sichuan pepper oil if you wish.

Asian white radish with sesame oil (or sour-and-hot dressing)
Cut Asian radish into fine slivers and salt it in the same way as the kohlrabi. Serve it with either of the two sauces above.

SMOKY EGGPLANT WITH GARLIC
HUO SHAO QIE ZI 火燒茄子

The smoky flavor of charred eggplant is the soul of the Middle Eastern dish *baba ghanoush* and it's also used in this Sichuanese appetizer. The recipe is based on one I tasted at a restaurant in rural Sichuan that specialized in old-fashioned cooking methods and insect cooking. The fridge there was full of extraordinary grubs and six-legged creatures, while the kitchen had a wood-burning wok range. A young chef crouched behind the range, tending the food he was cooking in the glowing embers. There was a whole duck caked in mud, as well as paddy eels, eggplant and green bell peppers strung up on bamboo skewers. The duck was slow-cooked for three or four hours, while the eels and vegetables were quickly burned, peeled and dressed with local seasonings. I adored this Sichuanese variation on the charred eggplant theme.

2 eggplant (about 1¼ lb/600g)
2 tsp light soy sauce
2 tsp Chinkiang vinegar
2 tbsp chilli oil with its sediment

1–2 tsp finely chopped garlic, to taste
½ tsp sesame seeds
2 tbsp finely sliced spring onion greens

Prick each eggplant a couple of times with a fork, then lay them on a very low gas flame and allow them to soften and char, turning from time to time for even cooking (this can take up to an hour, so it's best done when you have other chores in or near the kitchen).

When the skins have blackened and the flesh is soft and pulpy within, remove them from the stove and allow to cool.

Strip away the burned skin and tear the eggplant into strips, discarding the seeds as far as possible. Pile on a serving dish and pour or scatter over the other ingredients. Mix well before eating.

SPINACH IN GINGER SAUCE
JIANG ZHI BO CAI 薑汁菠菜

This is a most refreshing appetizer, with juicy leaves in a delicate dressing of ginger, mellow vinegar and sesame oil. The combination of seasonings is known as "ginger-juice flavor," and comes from the canon of classic Sichuanese flavor combinations. It can be used to dress many other vegetables, such as green beans, which should also be blanched and then refreshed under the cold tap before dressing. I've also had asparagus, a relatively recent import to China, served in this way.

Do use fresh bunched spinach for its wonderfully juicy texture (baby spinach leaves tend to melt away when you blanch them).

11 oz (300g) fresh bunched
  spinach
1 tbsp cooking oil
1 tbsp very finely chopped
  ginger
2 tsp Chinkiang vinegar
1 tsp light soy sauce
1½ tbsp chicken stock or water
Salt
½ tsp sesame oil

Bring a large panful of water to a boil (4–6 cups/1–1½ liters will do).

Wash and trim the spinach. When the water has boiled, add the oil, then the spinach and blanch for about 30 seconds. Drain the spinach and refresh in cold water, then shake dry in a colander. Gently squeeze it to remove as much water as possible.

Combine the ginger, vinegar, soy sauce and stock or water in a small bowl, with salt to taste. Add the sesame oil.

Lay the spinach leaves out on a chopping board and cut them across into about four sections. Pile these sections neatly on a serving plate. Give the sauce a stir and pour it over the spinach.

TIGER SALAD
LAO HU CAI 老虎菜

The tiger is a symbol of strength and valor in China and also, along with the wolf, of ferocity and danger. This dish, with its lacing of fresh green chilli, can be as fierce as a tiger, hence the name. It's generally held to be a northern invention, though it's now popular across China and there are many different versions.

Green chillies and cilantro seem to be the essential ingredients: some cooks mix them with cucumber or tomato, while others use sliced onions (salted for a while to draw out some of their pungency). The final salad tends to have a refreshing, sour-hot taste. It's particularly good for stimulating the appetite, as an accompaniment to alcohol, or to cut richer dishes. This version is inspired by one served at Yiwanju, a restaurant specializing in old Beijing dishes: the chef there, Xi Guyang, told me how to make it. There is no need to be particular about quantities: just assemble it as you would a simple salad and add as much or as little chilli as you please.

½ cucumber
Salt
Good handful of fresh
   cilantro
1–2 mild green chillies, to taste

¼ tsp sugar
2 tsp Chinkiang vinegar
½ tsp sesame oil
Ground white pepper

Cut the cucumber in half lengthways, then cut each half into three sections. Cut each section lengthways into thin slices and put the slices into a bowl. Sprinkle with ½ tsp salt, mix well and set aside for 30 minutes or so.

Wash the cilantro, trim off the ends of the leafy stems and cut into lengths to match the cucumber slices. (If you are using cilantro that is sold as leaves only, rather than on the stem, simply chop it roughly.) Thinly slice the chilli(es), discarding stem and seeds.

Combine the sugar, vinegar and sesame oil in a small bowl, with salt and pepper to taste (you may prefer not to add salt, because the cucumber will already be a little salty).

When you are ready to serve, drain the cucumber and squeeze gently to get rid of excess water. Combine with the cilantro and chilli, pour over the dressing and mix well.

SPINACH WITH SESAME SAUCE
MA JIANG BO CAI 麻醬菠菜

In southern China, it is still possible to find small backstreet workshops producing artisanal sesame oil and paste. The paste, richer and darker than Middle Eastern tahini, with a wonderful roasty aroma, is an essential ingredient in many appetizers and noodle dishes. It may be offered as a dip for batons of fresh cucumber, or mixed into a sauce for various vegetables, including the juicy spinach in this recipe.

The Sichuanese like to use the same sauce to dress *you mai cai*, a kind of crisp lettuce with no head and long, spear-like leaves. Trimmed and cut lengthways into quarters, it resembles the tails of the mythical phoenix, which is why this dish is known as "phoenix tail lettuce" in sesame sauce. (This particular variety of lettuce can be hard to find outside China, but the sauce is also lovely poured over a couple of hearts of romaine or little butter lettuces: this dish appears in the background to the photograph of Twice-cooked Pork on page 96.)

11 oz (300g) fresh bunched spinach
1 tbsp cooking oil, plus more if needed

For the sauce
1 tsp sesame seeds
4 tbsp oil-topped sesame paste
1 tsp sesame oil
2–3 pinches of sugar
Salt

Bring some water to a boil in a large saucepan (4–6 cups/1–1½ liters will do).

Wash and trim the spinach. When the water has boiled, add the 1 tbsp cooking oil, then the spinach and blanch briefly to wilt the leaves. Drain the spinach, refresh in cold water, then shake dry in a colander. Gently squeeze it to remove as much water as possible, then cut into chopstickable sections.

Toast the sesame seeds gently in a dry frying pan until they are starting to turn golden, then tip into a dish and set aside to cool.

Blend the sesame paste and sesame oil in a bowl, adding some oil from the top of the sesame paste jar if necessary to achieve a thick pouring consistency, like heavy cream. If there isn't enough oil in the jar, use cooking oil instead. Add the sugar and salt to taste.

Arrange the spinach neatly on a plate. Pour the sauce over it, sprinkle with the sesame seeds and serve.

VARIATION

Sour-and-hot spinach
Prepare the spinach as in the recipe above, but dress it with a sauce made from the following seasonings: 2 tsp Chinkiang vinegar, 2 pinches of sugar, salt to taste and 1½ tbsp chilli oil. The same sauce is also good with purslane, similarly blanched.

RADISHES IN CHILLI OIL SAUCE
QIANG LUO BO 熗蘿蔔

This is a beautiful and stunningly simple dish to rouse the appetite at the start of a meal. Small red radishes are not a traditional Chinese vegetable, but a recent import. This recipe is based on one from a book of simple recipes for home cooking, *Ji ben jia chang cai (shu cai pian)*, or *Basic Domestic Dishes*.

2 bunches of small red radishes
³/₄ tsp salt
1 tsp sugar
2 tbsp light soy sauce

2 tbsp chilli oil with its sediment
½ tsp sesame oil

Trim the radishes. Smack them lightly with the side of a cleaver or a rolling pin; the idea is to crack them open, not smash them to bits.

Add the salt and mix well. Set aside for 30 minutes.

Combine the sugar and soy sauce in a small bowl. Add the chilli and sesame oils.

When you are ready to eat, drain the radishes—which will have released a fair amount of water—and shake them dry. Pour the prepared sauce over them, mix well and serve.

DELECTABLE LOTUS ROOT SALAD
MEI WEI OU PIAN 美味藕片

The so-called "root" of the lotus is actually the underwater stem of the waterlily. Other parts of the plant can also be eaten: the seeds, a traditional symbol of fertility, are made into soups and sweetmeats; the thin flower stems are delicious stir-fried; the broad lily leaves are used to wrap meat or poultry for an aromatic steaming, or a mud-baked "beggar's chicken"; I've even tasted the delicate white waterlilies themselves, in a lyrical soup of assorted water plants. The root, cut into slices, has an ethereal quality, with its crisp, crystalline flesh and snowflake pattern of holes, which this colorful salad shows off beautifully.

1 tbsp dried shrimp (optional)
A couple of small crinkly pieces of dried wood ear mushroom
1 section of fresh young lotus root (about 7 oz/200g)
1 tsp finely chopped ginger
2½ tsp clear rice vinegar

1 tsp sugar
A few small horse-ear (diagonal) slices of red chilli or bell pepper, for color
1 spring onion, green part only, sliced diagonally
1 tsp sesame oil
Salt, to taste

Soak the dried shrimp (if using) and the wood ears, separately, in hot water from the kettle for at least 30 minutes.

Bring a panful of water to a boil. Break the lotus root into segments and use a potato peeler to peel them. Trim off the ends of each segment and slice thinly and evenly: each slice will have a beautiful pattern of holes.

Blanch the lotus root slices in the boiling water for a minute or two; they will remain crisp. (Make sure you blanch them soon after cutting, or the slices will begin to discolor.) Refresh in cold water and drain well.

Drain the wood ears and the shrimp (if using). Tear the wood ears into small pieces.

Combine all the ingredients together in a bowl and mix well.

GREEN SOY BEANS, SERVED IN THE POD
MAO DOU 毛豆

Young green soy beans, served in the pod, have become popular in Japanese restaurants in the West, which is why they are often known by their Japanese name, edamame. They are also a favorite snack in Sichuan, where they might be offered with beer, alongside salted duck eggs, peanuts and aromatic cold meats. In Chinese, they are known as *mao dou*, "hairy beans," because of the furry skins of their pods.

Salt
One ½ oz (20g) piece of ginger, unpeeled

A few pinches of whole Sichuan pepper
About 11 oz (300g) frozen soy beans in their pods

Bring a panful of water to a boil and add salt. Crush the ginger slightly with the flat of a cleaver blade or a rolling pin and add to the pan with the Sichuan pepper and the beans.

Return to a boil, then reduce the heat and simmer for about five minutes. Drain well and serve at room temperature.

Invite your guests to squeeze the beans from the pods and eat them. The furry pods should be discarded.

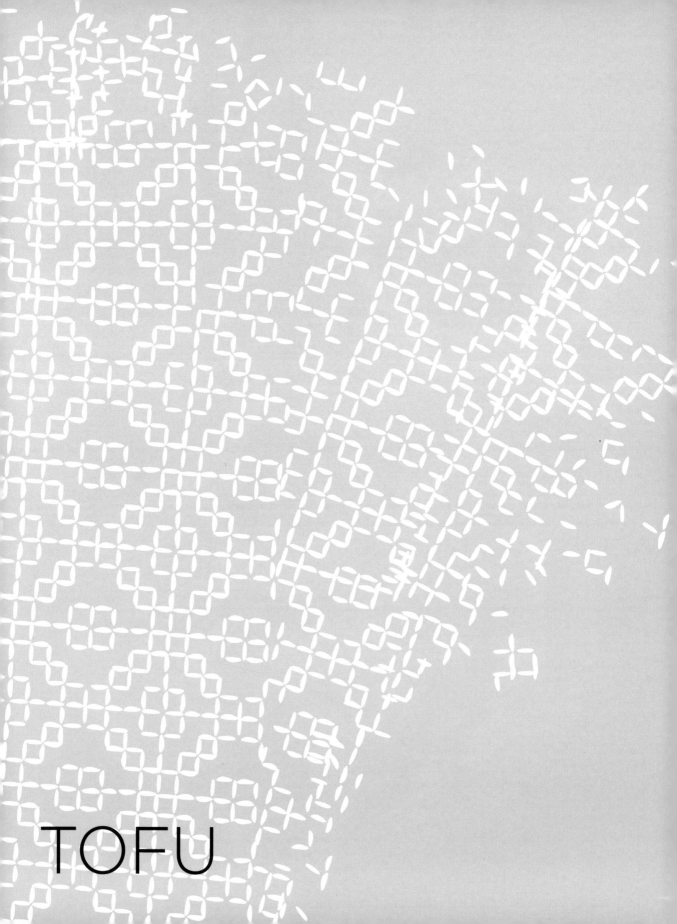

TOFU

The Chinese have, throughout history, shown a remarkable preference for selecting and cultivating the most nutritious food plants available to them. The soy bean, which has been grown in China for more than three millennia, is richer in protein than any other plant food. It contains all the amino acids essential for human health, in the right proportions. Along with rice and leafy greens, it is one of the cornerstones of the largely vegetarian traditional diet. Young green soy beans are eaten fresh, as a vegetable, but far more important are the dried beans, which are transformed through ancient technologies into fermented seasonings and tofu.

Tofu is formed by soaking dried soy beans in water, grinding them with fresh water to give soy milk, straining out the solid residue of the beans, then heating the milk and adding a coagulant to set the curds. The set curds may be eaten as they are, or pressed to rid them of excess water and make them firmer. Tofu-making is a process that has been known in China since at least the tenth century AD, although legend traces its invention back further, to the second century king, Liu An.

Some Westerners still seem to think of tofu as some sackcloth-and-ashes sustenance for vegans, and a sad substitute for meat. In China, however, it is one of the most ubiquitous foodstuffs and wonderful when you acquire a taste for it. In its most basic form it may be plain, but then so is ricotta cheese; tofu is so gentle and innocent, so richly nutritious, so kind to earth and conscience. And of course,

as a vehicle for flavor, it's amazing. No one could accuse a Sichuanese Pock-marked Old Woman's Tofu of being insipid; in my experience even avid meat-eaters enjoy it. And who could resist the juicy charms of a Cantonese Pipa Tofu? (You'll find both recipes in this chapter.)

Plain tofu is only one of the myriad forms of this shape-shifting food. The unpressed curd, known as "silken" tofu or bean "flower," has the delightful, slippy texture of pannacotta. Eaten with a spoon, it is perfect comfort food. Just thinking about Sichuanese Sour-and-hot Silken Tofu—with its zesty dressing of pickles, soy sauce, chilli and crunchy nuts—makes my mouth water.

Plain white tofu can be deep-fried into golden puffs, or pressed into blocks or sheets as thin as leather. After pressing, this "firm" tofu can be simmered in a spiced broth or smoked over wood embers to give it a wonderful flavor. Stir-fry it with a fresh vegetable such as celery or chives, serve it with rice and you have a very satisfying supper. And for high cheesy tastes, look no further than fermented tofu, a magical cooking ingredient and a stupendous relish that is utterly addictive. Add some to a wokful of stir-fried spinach and you'll see what I mean.

Some 300 years ago, the Qing Dynasty poet and gourmet Yuan Mei lampooned those who were impressed by ostentatious delicacies, writing that a well-cooked dish of tofu, humble though it might be, was far superior in taste to a bowlful of expensive

bird's nest. I hope, when you try some of these recipes, that you'll agree.

Some tips on using tofu

– Blanch plain white tofu in hot salted water before use, to freshen up its flavor and warm it before you combine it with other ingredients.

– When adding seasonings to simmering white tofu in a broth or sauce, to avoid breaking up the pieces of tofu, simply push them gently with the back of your wok scoop or ladle to allow the ingredients to mingle, rather than stirring.

– Don't let tofu boil vigorously for too long unless you want it to become porous and slightly spongey in texture.

– Freezing tofu changes its texture completely: the formation of water crystals creates a honeycomb of holes, so the thawed tofu has a chewy, spongey texture. Northern cooks do this deliberately, because the thawed tofu absorbs the flavors of sauces rather beautifully; but don't try it if you want a tender mouthfeel.

– Cover any leftovers of fresh white tofu in water, store them in the refrigerator, and use within a couple of days.

A note on names

English speakers may refer to tofu as beancurd or bean curd. Tofu is overwhelmingly the most widely known word for this foodstuff, which is why I have chosen to use it in this book.

POCK-MARKED OLD WOMAN'S TOFU (VEGETARIAN VERSION)
MA PO DOU FU 麻婆豆腐

Mapo doufu is one of the best-loved dishes of the Sichuanese capital, Chengdu. It is named after the wife of a Qing Dynasty restaurateur who delighted passing laborers with her hearty braised tofu, cooked up at her restaurant by the Bridge of 10,000 Blessings in the north of the city. The dish is thought to date back to the late nineteenth century. Mrs. Chen's face was marked with smallpox scars, so she was given the affectionate nickname *ma po*, "Pock-marked Old Woman."

The dish is traditionally made with ground beef, although many cooks now use pork. This vegetarian version is equally sumptuous. Vegetarians find it addictive: one friend of mine has been cooking it every week since I first taught her the recipe some 10 years ago. In Sichuan, they use garlic leaves (*suan miao*) rather than baby leeks, but as they are hard to find, tender young leeks make a good substitute, as do spring onion greens. You can also use the green sprouts that emerge from onions or garlic bulbs if you forget about them for a while (as I often do). This dish is best made with the tenderest tofu that will hold its shape when cut into cubes.

1–1¼ lb (500–600g) plain white tofu
Salt
4 baby leeks or spring onions, green parts only
4 tbsp cooking oil
2½ tbsp Sichuan chilli bean paste
1 tbsp fermented black beans, rinsed and drained
2 tsp ground red chillies (optional)
1 tbsp finely chopped ginger
1 tbsp finely chopped garlic
½ cup (100ml) vegetarian stock or water
¼ tsp ground white pepper
2 tsp potato flour mixed with 2 tbsp cold water
¼–½ tsp ground roasted Sichuan pepper

Cut the tofu into ¾ in (2cm) cubes and leave to steep in very hot, lightly salted water while you prepare the other ingredients (do not allow the water to boil or the tofu will become porous and less tender). Slice the baby leeks or spring onion greens at a steep angle into thin "horse ears."

Heat a wok over a high flame. Pour in the cooking oil and swirl it around. Reduce the heat to medium, add the chilli bean paste and stir-fry until the oil is a rich red color and smells delicious. Next add the black beans and ground chillies (if using) and stir-fry for a few seconds more until you can smell them too. Then do the same with the ginger and garlic. Take care not to overheat the seasonings; you want a thick, fragrant sauce and the secret of this is to let them sizzle gently, allowing the oil to coax out their flavors and aromas.

Remove the tofu from the hot water with a perforated spoon, shaking off excess water, and lay it gently in the wok. Push the tofu tenderly with the back of your ladle or wok scoop to mix it into the sauce without breaking up the cubes. Add the stock or water, the white pepper and salt to taste and mix gently, again using the back of your scoop so you don't damage the tofu.

Bring to a boil, then simmer for a few minutes to allow the tofu to absorb the flavors of the seasonings. Add the leek slices (if using) and nudge them into the sauce. When they are just tender, add a little of the flour-and-water mixture and stir gently as the liquid thickens. Repeat once or twice more, until the sauce clings to the seasonings and tofu (don't add more than you need). If you are using spring onions rather than leeks, add them now and nudge them gently into the sauce.

Pour the tofu into a deep bowl. Sprinkle with the ground roasted Sichuan pepper and serve.

PIPA TOFU
PI PA DOU FU 琵琶豆腐

The pear-shaped pipa (pronounced pee-par), or Chinese lute, is one of the best-known Chinese musical instruments. This Cantonese dish derives its name from the resemblance of the tofu puffs, scooped out of spoons like French quenelles, to the instrument. It's a little complicated to make, because the tofu puffs have to be shaped and deep-fried, but it's a richly rewarding dish and one of my favorites. The golden "lutes," their pale flesh speckled with color, are sumptuously juicy in their savory sauce.

Some cooks add a little raw minced shrimp to the tofu mixture to enhance its flavor, and use pork stock and oyster sauce for the gravy, but I prefer to make a completely vegetarian version, because it's one of those dishes that really doesn't need meat. You can, if you wish, fry the tofu puffs a day in advance and keep them in the refrigerator. Another suggestion is to double the mixture for the tofu puffs, serve half of the finished puffs immediately with a spiced salt dip (see variation) and use the rest to make the main recipe the following day.

The puffs may also be served in a fish-fragrant sauce to sumptuous effect. Simply substitute them for the fried eggplant on page 210.

For the tofu puffs
1 dried shiitake mushroom
9 oz (250g) plain white tofu
2 tbsp very finely chopped carrot (about 2 oz/50g)
1 tbsp finely chopped cilantro
1 large egg white
3 tbsp potato flour
Salt
Ground white pepper
At least 1½ cups plus 2 tbsp (400ml) cooking oil, for deep-frying

For the sauce
2 dried shiitake mushrooms
1 spring onion
A few slices of peeled ginger
A few slices of carrot, for color
A few slices of fresh red chilli
1 cup (250ml) vegetarian stock or mushroom soaking water
1 tbsp Shaoxing wine
1 tbsp light or tamari soy sauce
⅛ tsp dark soy sauce
1 tsp potato flour mixed with 1 tbsp cold water
1 tsp sesame oil

Soak all the mushrooms in 1 cup plus 2 tbsp (300ml) hot water for at least 30 minutes. Drain, reserving the water. Discard the stalks. Finely chop one mushroom and thinly slice the other two. Blitz the tofu to a paste in a food processor. Mix in the chopped mushroom, carrot, cilantro, egg white, flour, ¼ tsp salt and some pepper. Slice the spring onion white on the diagonal and cut the green into 1¾ in (4cm) lengths.

Rub a couple of dessertspoons with oil. In a wok, heat the oil to 375°F (190°C). Scoop up spoonfuls of tofu mixture and slide them gently into the oil. (Slide each into a different area of the wok, so they don't stick.) Do not fry more than five spoonfuls at a time. Leave for a couple of minutes until golden, then flip over for another minute or two. Remove from the oil with a slotted spoon and drain on paper towels. Continue until you have fried all the mixture, skimming the oil between batches. Pour off the oil and wipe out the wok. Return it to a high heat with 2 tbsp fresh oil. Add the ginger, spring onion whites, carrot, sliced mushrooms and chilli and stir-fry until they smell wonderful. Pour in the stock or mushroom water, bring to a boil and add the Shaoxing wine, soy sauces and salt and pepper to taste. Add the puffs and simmer for a minute or two. Give the potato flour mixture a stir and add, stirring as the liquid thickens to the consistency of heavy cream. Throw in the spring onion greens, stir, then, off the heat, mix in the sesame oil and serve.

VARIATION

Tofu puffs with salt and Sichuan pepper
Instead of the sauce, serve the puffs immediately after frying with a little dipping dish of three parts salt to one part ground roasted Sichuan pepper, a classic "salt-and-pepper" dip for deep-fried foods.

BEAR'S PAW TOFU
XIONG ZHANG DOU FU 熊掌豆腐

This exotic-sounding dish is actually just a version of the everyday Sichuanese dish "homestyle tofu" (*jia chang dou fu*). It takes its name from the fact that the fried slices of tofu have a puckered appearance like that of bear's paw, a legendary (and now notorious) banquet delicacy. Most Sichuanese cooks would add a little pork to the dish, frying it off in the oil before they add the chilli bean sauce, but it's equally delicious without. You can shallow-fry the tofu slices if you prefer: they'll be equally tasty, but may disintegrate in the sauce. With a dish of leafy greens and plenty of rice, bear's paw tofu makes a very satisfying supper for two.

1 lb (450g) plain white tofu
³/₄ cup (200ml) cooking oil, for deep-frying
2 tbsp Sichuanese chilli bean paste
3 garlic cloves, sliced
An equivalent amount of ginger, also sliced

3 baby leeks or spring onions, sliced diagonally into "horse ears," white and green parts separated
³/₄ cup (200ml) vegetarian stock
½ tsp sugar
½–1 tsp light soy sauce
½ tsp potato flour mixed with 2 tsp cold water

Cut the tofu into 1³/₄–2 in (4–5cm) squares or rectangles, about ³/₈ in (1cm) thick. Heat the oil in a seasoned wok over a high flame to 350–375°F (180–190°C). Fry the tofu slices in a few batches for a few minutes until golden, then set aside.

Pour all but 3 tbsp of the oil into a heatproof container. Reduce the heat to medium, then return the wok to the stove with the chilli bean paste. Stir-fry until the oil is red and richly fragrant. Add the garlic, ginger and leek or spring onion whites and fry until they, too, are fragrant. Then add the stock and the tofu and bring to a boil. Reduce the heat slightly, season with the sugar and soy sauce and simmer for three to four minutes until the liquid is reduced and the tofu has absorbed some of the flavors of the sauce.

Add the leek or spring onion greens and stir briefly until just cooked. Finally, stir the potato flour mixture, scatter it into the center of the wok, and stir until the sauce has thickened. Turn out on to a serving dish.

SPICY FIRM TOFU WITH GARLIC STEMS
SUAN TAI CHAO XIANG GAN 蒜薹炒香乾

In my experience, vegetarians adore this swift stir-fry, which is based on a Sichuanese supper dish that would normally be made with pork (see page 98). It takes just a few minutes to prepare and a few minutes to cook, and is almost a meal in itself with a bowlful of rice. If you'd rather, substitute green or red bell pepper—or a mixture of both—for the garlic stems.

6 oz (175g) garlic stems
4 oz (100g) firm tofu (spiced or smoked)
2 tbsp cooking oil
1 tbsp Sichuan chilli bean paste
½ tbsp fermented black beans, rinsed and drained
¼ tsp sugar

Cut the garlic stems into 1¾ in (4cm) sections. Cut the tofu into strips of similar dimensions.

Heat the oil in a seasoned wok over a medium flame. Add the chilli bean paste and black beans and stir-fry to release their flavors. When the oil is red and fragrant, add the garlic stems and tofu.

Increase the heat to high, then stir-fry for about three minutes until everything is piping hot and the garlic stems have become sweet and tender. Stir in the sugar towards the end of the cooking time. Serve.

SUZHOU BREAKFAST TOFU
SU ZHOU DOU HUA 蘇州豆花

In the old part of Suzhou, where the boatmen sing as they ply the canals and the landscaped gardens offer a refuge from the clamor of city life, a sprawling mansion is home to the Wumen Renjia restaurant, which specializes in traditional Suzhou cuisine. At breakfast time, the restaurant serves a vast array of congees, pickles, sweet pastries and dumplings, and, best of all, this classic street snack: warm, custardy tofu served with a delectable selection of savory garnishes. If you have silken tofu on hand, it takes about 10 minutes to prepare, if that. And if you'd rather not eat it for breakfast, serve it as an appetizer.

The same garnishes can be served with warm soy milk to delicious effect. At the Dragon Well Manor restaurant in Hangzhou, fresh stone-ground soy milk is offered at the start of a feast, like a soup or an aperitif, to calm the spirits and refresh the palate. Many local guests are moved to sweet nostalgia by this old-fashioned treat, which reminds them of the street vendors of their childhoods, who rose early to grind their soaked beans and simmer their milk. To try it, simply warm up unsweetened soy milk and season it to taste with the garnishes listed here.

This is best eaten with a spoon, either on its own or with rice.

Salt
11 oz (300g) silken tofu
1 tbsp finely chopped Sichuan preserved vegetable (*zha cai*)
2 tsp paper-thin dried shrimp
1 tbsp dried laver seaweed, torn into tiny pieces
1½ tbsp finely sliced spring onion greens
2 tsp light or tamari soy sauce
1 tsp sesame oil

Bring enough water to cover the tofu to a boil in a saucepan. Salt it lightly. Use a spoon to scoop up large pieces of the tofu, which will have a texture a little like pannacotta, and transfer them to the water. Simmer very gently for about five minutes to heat through. Meanwhile, prepare your other ingredients.

When the tofu is ready, use a slotted spoon to transfer it to the serving bowl and break up the chunks into smaller pieces. Scatter over all the other ingredients and serve.

FIRM TOFU WITH GREEN BELL PEPPER
QING JIAO DOU FU GAN 青椒豆腐乾

This is one of the easiest and most ubiquitous of Chinese dishes, and one of those served at a perfect lunch I attended in a farmhouse in Zhejiang province. For a more complex flavor, pre-fry the peppers as in the recipe, then sizzle some slices of garlic and ginger in the hot oil before you add the tofu and, later, return the peppers to the wok.

Firm tofu holds its shape when cut and stir-fried. For this recipe you can use plain firm tofu which is white, or spiced tofu which is usually golden. It is also delicious stir-fried with Chinese chives (see page 201).

4¼ oz (125g) plain or spiced firm tofu
1 green bell pepper (about 5 oz/150g)

2 tbsp cooking oil
A little light soy sauce
Salt

Cut the tofu evenly into bite-sized strips. Discard the pepper stem, membranes and seeds and cut into strips to match the tofu.

Heat a wok over a high flame. Add the pepper and dry-fry until nearly cooked. Set aside.

Return the wok to a high flame. Add the oil, swirl it around, then add the tofu. Stir-fry until hot and tinged with gold, then add the peppers. Stir-fry briefly to reheat the peppers, seasoning with soy sauce and salt to taste.

STIR-FRIED TOFU WITH BLACK BEAN AND CHILLI
XIANG LA DOU FU GAN 香辣豆腐乾

This colorful, sizzly stir-fry is the kind of dish you might find served in a "dry wok" (*gan guo*), a miniature wok over a tabletop burner. The main flavoring is Laoganma black bean sauce, a scintillating relish made in Guizhou from fermented black soy beans, chilli oil and other seasonings that has become popular all over China. The rich, oily black beans are much closer to Sichuanese black beans than the dry-salted kind sold in Cantonese supermarkets. Meat-eaters will find a pork variation of the recipe below.

5 oz (150g) firm tofu (spiced or smoked)
2 garlic cloves
An equivalent amount of ginger
5–10 dried chillies, to taste
1/4 red onion
1/4 red bell pepper
1/4 green bell pepper
2/3 celery stick, de-stringed

2 spring onions
3 tbsp cooking oil
3 tbsp Laoganma black bean sauce
1/2 tsp whole Sichuan pepper
1/4 tsp sugar
Ground white pepper
Light soy sauce
1 tsp sesame oil

Cut the tofu into 2 in (5cm) strips, each 3/8 in (1cm) thick. Peel and slice the garlic and ginger. Snip the chillies in half with a pair of scissors and discard their seeds as far as possible. Peel the onion and cut lengthways into strips of a similar thickness to the tofu. Cut the peppers and celery into strips of similar dimensions. Cut the spring onions into 2 in (5cm) lengths, keeping the green and white parts separate.

Heat the oil in a seasoned wok over a medium flame. Add the black bean sauce, chillies and Sichuan pepper and stir-fry until wonderfully fragrant. Then add the ginger and garlic and sizzle for a few moments more. Add the onion, peppers, celery and spring onion whites, increase the heat to high and stir-fry until hot and fragrant.

Season with the sugar, a good pinch of pepper and light soy sauce to taste. Add the tofu and continue to stir-fry until it is hot and everything smells delicious, adding the spring onion greens towards the end of the cooking time. Remove from the heat, stir in the sesame oil and serve.

VARIATION

Twice-cooked pork with black bean and chilli
Cut 1/2 lb (225g) cooked, cooled belly pork (with skin) into thin slices. Heat 1 tbsp cooking oil in a seasoned wok over a medium flame, add the pork, then stir-fry until the slices have curled up and the meat smells delicious. Then follow the recipe above from the second paragraph, sizzling the seasonings in the oil, then adding the vegetables and further seasonings with the addition of 1/2 tbsp Shaoxing wine. Return the pork and finish with the sesame oil as in the main recipe.

SILKEN TOFU WITH PICKLED MUSTARD GREENS
SUAN CAI DOU HUA 酸菜豆花

This is an unassuming but marvellous dish, a gentle marriage of soothing tofu and delicate pickles in a savory broth. Eat it with a spoon as you curl up on the sofa, or ladle it over your rice and let the white grains soak up its juices, enjoying the contrast of the bright green spring onion with the understated jade-and-ivory of pickles and tofu. At its most basic, made with a vegetarian stock or even water, it's the epitome of old-fashioned, rustic cooking, although a good chicken stock makes it more luxurious. You can even add chicken slivers, if you want (see the variation below).

1 oz (30g) pickled mustard greens
1½ tbsp cooking oil
1 cup plus 2 tbsp (300ml) chicken or vegetable stock
Salt
Ground white pepper
11 oz (300g) silken tofu
1½ tsp potato flour mixed with 1½ tbsp cold water
2 tbsp finely sliced spring onion greens

Cut the pickled greens evenly into slivers.

Heat the oil in a seasoned wok, add the slivered greens and stir-fry briefly until fragrant. Add the stock, bring to a boil and season with salt and white pepper, to taste. Use a spoon to scoop large pieces of the tender tofu into the water. Let it warm gently and absorb the flavors of the stock.

When the tofu has heated through, adjust the seasoning if necessary. Then give the potato flour mixture a stir and, in a couple of stages, add enough of it to thicken the stock to a lustrous gravy (mix it in by pushing the tofu gently with the back of a wok scoop or ladle rather than stirring, so you don't break it up completely).

Tip into a serving bowl, scatter with the spring onions and serve.

VARIATION

Silken tofu with chicken slivers and pickled mustard greens

Slice the pickled mustard greens as in the main recipe above. Cut one small chicken breast (5 oz/150g) evenly into fine slivers, add a marinade of ½ tsp salt, 1 tsp Shaoxing wine, 1 tsp potato flour, 2 tsp cold water and 1 tsp cooking oil and mix well.

Follow the instructions above to make the main recipe, but don't scatter the spring onion greens over the dish.

Clean the wok, season and add another 1½ tbsp cooking oil. When hot, add the marinated chicken slivers and stir-fry to separate. When they are just cooked, spoon them on to the prepared tofu dish, add the spring onion greens and serve.

SOUR-AND-HOT SILKEN TOFU
SUAN LA DOU HUA 酸辣豆花

This is one of my favorite Sichuanese dishes, a tender bowlful of slippy tofu dressed in a heart-warming mixture of chilli oil, mellow vinegar and other seasonings, with a crunchy garnish. Chengdu street vendors use similar seasonings to serve their own silken tofu, which they make at home and carry around, still warm from the stove, in a pair of red-and-black wooden barrels suspended from a bamboo shoulder pole. This version of the dish was taught to me by Chef Zhang Xiaozhong of Barshu restaurant. Traditionally, the crisp element of the garnish might be a mixture of deep-fried noodles and deep-fried soy beans, but Bombay mix (a crispy, crunchy Indian snack mix) makes a perfect substitute. This dish is best eaten with a spoon, either on its own or with rice.

Salt
11 oz (300g) silken tofu
1 tbsp Chinkiang vinegar
2 tsp light soy sauce
2 tbsp chicken stock
2 tbsp chilli oil with 1 tbsp of its sediment
1 tsp sesame oil
1 tbsp finely sliced spring onion greens
½ tsp finely chopped garlic
1 tbsp finely chopped Sichuan preserved vegetable (*zha cai*)

To serve
1 tbsp finely chopped Sichuan preserved vegetable (*zha cai*)
1 tbsp finely sliced spring onion greens
Small handful of Bombay mix

Bring to a boil in a saucepan enough water to cover the tofu. Salt it lightly. Use a spoon to scoop large pieces of the tender tofu into the water. Simmer it very gently for about five minutes to heat it through.

While the tofu is warming up, you can prepare your other ingredients. Place them all, except for the garnishes, in the serving bowl with ¼ tsp salt and give the mixture a stir.

When the tofu is ready, use a slotted spoon to transfer it to the serving bowl and break up the chunks into smaller, spoonable pieces. Scatter with the garnishes and serve.

MEAT

Until recently, meat was considered a luxury in China. Most people ate it only rarely, as the longed-for relish that added richness and flavor to a diet based on grains and vegetables. Only at the Chinese New Year—when every rural household slaughtered a pig and feasted on its meat throughout the holiday—was flesh at the center of the Chinese dinner table. I remember one man telling me that in the bitter years of the 1960s and 1970s, when even grain was scarce, he would use a single slice of belly pork to wipe his hot wok and lend his vegetables some of its savor, before putting it away to use another time; others have told me that they had tantalizing dreams about meat.

Even in times of plenty, moderation in diet has traditionally been seen as a sign of good character in China, and images of the *tao tie*, a mythological beast that is thought to represent the vice of gluttony, have served as a warning against self-indulgence. The epitome of the evil ruler in China is the last king of the ancient Shang Dynasty, who not only hosted orgies, but entertained his guests with a "lake of wine and a forest of meat." In contrast, the sage Confucius showed his self-restraint in a fastidious approach to food and drink, refusing to eat food that had not been properly cut or cooked and not allowing himself to eat more meat than rice.

Although in recent decades, with rising living standards and the advent of factory farming, meat has become cheaper and more widely available,

many people, especially in the countryside, still live mainly on rice or noodles, with plenty of vegetables and tofu and small amounts of delicious meat. It's the kind of dietary system recommended more and more by those around the world who are concerned about the environmental consequences of factory farming and the effects on the body of eating too much grain-fed, intensively reared flesh.

The Chinese food system lends itself readily to the frugal use of meat. Most ingredients are cut into small pieces so they can be cooked quickly and eaten with chopsticks. As little as half a chicken breast or a couple of slices of bacon, stir-fried with vegetables, can be shared by a whole family, while a potful of red-braised pork or a whole fish, served alongside a few vegetable dishes, is enough meat for a group. (The idea of serving an entire steak or sea bass for each person is unthinkable in traditional Chinese terms.) Tofu, cooked with mouthwatering seasonings, is a rich source of protein, while the use of preserved vegetables and fermented sauces gives largely vegetarian ingredients the tempting savory tastes associated with meat.

For the ethnic Han majority in China, "meat" means pork unless otherwise stated. Lamb and mutton are sometimes eaten in the north, with its proximity to nomadic pasturelands, and are strongly associated with the Muslim and Mongolian minorities. In the south they are traditionally disdained for their "muttony taste" and generally eaten infrequently. Beef plays a minor

role in traditional Chinese cooking: in the past oxen were primarily regarded as beasts of burden and there were periodic bans on their slaughter for meat. Other kinds of flesh—including goat, rabbit, venison and other game—are eaten in some regions and on some occasions.

Pork, the mainstay of Chinese meat cooking, is eaten fresh, brined, smoked, salt-cured and, in some areas, pickled. And, frankly, I don't know anyone who does pork better than the Chinese, with their marvellous hams and bacons, their sumptuous roasts and slow braises, and their skilful use of just a little meat to bring magic to a whole potful of vegetables.

The recipes that follow, which include some of the most delicious Chinese meat dishes I know, are designed to be eaten with vegetable dishes as part of a Chinese meal. A dish of twice-cooked pork uses a relatively small amount of meat and will feed four or more people when served with other dishes. Red-braised pork or beef will go further if you add vegetables or tofu to the pot. Lamb may be used as a substitute for beef in some recipes, and either lamb, beef or chicken for pork, especially in stir-fries (Muslim restaurants in China usually serve beef or mutton versions of classic pork dishes). But whatever meat you choose, I recommend putting the expense into quality rather than quantity and buying the best you can afford.

RED-BRAISED PORK
HONG SHAO ROU 紅燒肉

Red-braised pork may be one of the most common of all Chinese dishes, but it is also one of the most glorious, a slow stew of belly pork with seasonings that may include sugar, soy sauce, Shaoxing wine and spices. Every region seems to have its own version: this is my favorite, based on recipes I've gathered in eastern China. If my experience is anything to go by, you won't have any leftovers. My guests tend to finish every last morsel and usually end up scraping the pot. If your guests are more restrained, leftover red-braised pork keeps very well for a few days in the refrigerator and a good spoonful makes a wonderful topping for a bowl of noodles (see page 284). I don't recommend freezing it, however, as this ruins the delicate texture of the fat.

This recipe will serve four to six as part of a Chinese meal. To make it go further, add more stock or water and a vegetarian ingredient that will soak up the sauce most deliciously. Puffy, deep-fried tofu is a fine addition to red-braised pork, as are hard-boiled eggs, dried tofu "bamboo" and the little knotted strips of dried tofu skin that can be found in some Chinese supermarkets (the latter two should first be soaked in hot water until supple). In rural households in China, they often add dried vegetables such as string beans and bamboo shoots, which should also be pre-soaked. You can also use root vegetables such as potato, taro or carrot, or peeled water chestnuts: just make sure you cook the vegetables with the pork for long enough to absorb its flavors, and adjust the seasoning as necessary.

To reduce the amount of oil in the final dish, make it in advance and refrigerate overnight. Then scrape off the layer of fat on the surface and keep it in the refrigerator to add to your stir-fried mushrooms or other vegetables. If you prefer a less fatty cut, pork ribs or shoulder are also magnificent red-braised. And you can, if you like, cook the pork slowly in an oven instead of on the burner—not very Chinese, but often more convenient (for this, preheat the oven to 300°F/150°C/gas mark 2).

1¼ lb (500g) boneless pork belly, with skin, or shoulder
2 tbsp cooking oil
4 slices of unpeeled ginger
1 spring onion, white part only, crushed slightly
2 tbsp Shaoxing wine
2 cups plus 2 tbsp (500ml) chicken stock or water, plus more if needed
1 star anise

Small piece of cassia bark or cinnamon stick
Dash of dark soy sauce
2 tbsp sugar
Salt, to taste
A few lengths of spring onion greens, to garnish

Cut the pork into ¾–1 in (2–3cm) chunks.

Pour the oil into a seasoned wok over a high flame, followed by the ginger and spring onion and stir-fry until you can smell their aromas. Add the pork and stir-fry for a couple of minutes more. Splash in the Shaoxing wine. Add the stock, spices, soy sauce, sugar and 1 tsp salt. Mix well, then transfer to a clay pot or a saucepan with a lid.

Bring to a boil, then cover and simmer over a very low flame for at least 1½ hours, preferably two or three. Keep an eye on the pot to make sure it does not boil dry; add a little more stock or hot water if necessary. Adjust the seasoning and add the spring onion greens just before serving.

TWICE-COOKED PORK
HUI GUO ROU 回鍋肉

This simple, hearty supper dish is one of the best-loved and most delicious in Sichuanese cuisine. I remember once interviewing three top Chengdu chefs for a magazine article, and each of them independently told me that of all the culinary riches Sichuan had to offer, this was their favorite dish. There is something about the rich, fragrant meat, cooked in a sizzle of intensely flavored seasonings and set off by the garlicky freshness of the leeks, that is utterly irresistible. It's the perfect accompaniment to a bowl of plain steamed rice.

The name *hui guo rou* literally means "back-in-the-pot" meat, because the pork is first boiled, then stir-fried.

It must be allowed to cool completely before you embark on the final dish: if you try to slice it warm, the layers of fat and lean meat will separate. Recently, I've taken to buying a large piece of belly pork from a really good butcher, boiling it, leaving it to cool and slicing. I then freeze the slices in thin layers, in twice-cooked pork-sized portions. The frozen slices can be cooked, which means that I'm never more than about 15 minutes away from a plateful of twice-cooked pork, a very happy state.

7 oz (200g) boneless pork belly, with skin
6 baby leeks, trimmed (or Chinese leaf garlic)
2 tbsp cooking oil or lard
1 tbsp Sichuan chilli bean paste
1 tsp sweet fermented sauce
2 tsp fermented black beans, rinsed and drained
½ tsp dark soy sauce
½ tsp sugar
Salt, to taste (optional)
A few slices of fresh red chilli or bell pepper for color

Place the pork in a saucepan, cover with water and bring to a boil, then simmer gently until just cooked through (probably about 20 minutes, depending on dimensions): lift it from the water with a slotted spoon and pierce with a skewer to make sure the juices run clear. Let it cool a bit, then refrigerate for several hours or overnight to cool completely.

When the meat is completely cold, slice it thinly. Each slice should have a strip of skin along the top. If your slices are very large, you may wish to cut them into a couple of pieces; each slice should make a good mouthful. Holding your knife at an angle, cut the leeks into diagonal slices.

Add the oil or lard to a seasoned wok over a high flame, add the pork slices, reduce the heat to medium and stir-fry until they have become slightly curved, some of their fat has melted out and they smell delicious. Then push the slices to the side of the wok and tip the chilli bean paste into the space you have created at the bottom. Stir-fry the paste until the oil is red and fragrant, then add the sweet fermented sauce and the black beans. Stir-fry for a few seconds more to release their aromas, then mix everything together, adding the soy sauce, the sugar and salt to taste, if you need it.

Finally, add the leeks or leaf garlic and the red pepper and continue to stir-fry until they are just cooked. Serve.

VARIATIONS

Many kinds of vegetable ingredients can be used instead of the leeks or leaf garlic. In Sichuan, the classic accompaniment to the pork is garlic leaves (*qing suan* or *suan miao*), which can occasionally be found in Chinese supermarkets in the West. You might use another Chinese variety of garlic, *jiao tou*, slicing the whole stems and bulbs on the diagonal; white onions, sliced; red or green bell peppers or a mixture of both (first stir-fry them separately to "break their rawness"); salt-preserved cabbage or mustard greens (first rinse them to get rid of excess salt); even spinach leaves.

SALT-FRIED PORK WITH GARLIC STEMS
YAN JIAN ROU 鹽煎肉

Like twice-cooked pork, this invigorating supper dish relies on chilli bean paste and fermented black beans for what they call its "homestyle flavor." Unlike twice-cooked pork, it requires no advance preparation, so with the right ingredients on hand you can knock out a plateful in less than 30 minutes. And with its fresh, pungent greens and intensely flavored meat, it's really all you need for a quick meal for one or two, with a good bowlful of rice, of course. Feel free to vary the vegetable ingredient as you please: red or green bell peppers, baby leeks or sliced onions would all be magnificent.

4 oz (100g) belly pork, without skin
5 oz (150g) garlic stems
3 tbsp cooking oil or lard
Pinch of salt

1 tbsp Sichuan chilli bean paste
1 tbsp fermented black beans, rinsed and drained
½ tsp sugar

Cut the pork into thin slices, each with a good mixture of fat and lean. Cut the garlic stems into 1¾ in (4cm) sections, discarding any fibrous parts at their bases.

Add the oil or lard to a seasoned wok over a high flame, then add the pork, reduce the heat to medium and stir-fry until the slices are curved and tinged with gold and the oil is clear, adding a good pinch of salt about halfway through the cooking time.

Use a wok scoop or ladle to move the pork to one side of the wok. Add the chilli bean paste and black beans to the oil that pools in the space you have created and stir-fry them briefly until the oil is red and fragrant. Then mix everything together, add the sugar and then the garlic stems.

Increase the heat to high and stir-fry until the garlic stems are cooked (taste one to check: when they are ready, their aggressive raw pungency will have mellowed to a sweet garlickiness). Serve.

BRAISED PORK WITH POTATOES
TU DOU SHAO ROU 土豆燒肉

This heart-warming stew is one of those you find on display outside Sichuanese restaurants specializing in braised dishes, simmering away in a clay pot on a stove alongside, perhaps, beef with bamboo shoots, spare ribs with carrots, pork with soy beans, and other concoctions. The chilli bean paste gives the stew a gorgeous richness. Make the dish with carrots instead of potatoes if you prefer, or a mixture of the two, or indeed with another root vegetable of your choice. Pork ribs may be used instead of shoulder.

This recipe makes a good amount of stew, so you may wish to make it when you are feeding a large group of people, or to serve it over a couple of meals.

1¼ lb (500g) boneless pork shoulder
2 spring onions
3 tbsp cooking oil
2½ tbsp Sichuan chilli bean paste
½ oz (20g) ginger, peeled and sliced
3 cups (750ml) chicken stock or water
1 tbsp Shaoxing wine
11 oz (300g) potatoes

Cut the pork into 1½ in (3cm) chunks. Rinse thoroughly under the hot tap, or blanch in boiling water. Separate the green and white parts of the spring onions. Crush the whites slightly with the side of a cleaver blade or a rolling pin and cut the greens into 1½—1¾ in (3–4cm) sections.

Heat the oil in a seasoned wok over a medium flame. Add the chilli bean paste and stir-fry gently until it smells wonderful and the oil is richly red. Add the ginger and spring onion whites and continue to stir-fry until you can smell them, too. Then add the pork, stock or water and Shaoxing wine and bring to a boil.

Turn the contents of the wok into a saucepan, partially cover and simmer for an hour or so, until the pork is tender.

Peel the potatoes and cut into chunks to match the pork. Add them to the pan, return to a boil, then simmer for another 20 minutes or so until the potatoes are tender. Adjust the seasoning if necessary (though the saltiness of the chilli bean paste means you probably won't need extra salt). Serve in the cooking pot or in a deep bowl, scattered with the spring onion greens.

STIR-FRIED BEEF WITH BLACK BEAN AND CHILLI
JIA CHANG NIU ROU 家常牛肉

The punchy flavors of Laoganma sauce, a spicy relish made from fermented black beans and dried chillies in oil, give an enticing lift to this colorful stir-fry of beef and peppers. Served with plain white rice, it's enough for a quick, hearty supper for two.

11 oz (300g) lean sirloin or another tender steak
¼ red bell pepper
¼ green bell pepper
Small bunch of cilantro (about 1½ oz /40g)
3 tbsp cooking oil
2½ tbsp Laoganma black bean sauce

Salt
1 tsp sesame oil

For the marinade
½ tsp dark soy sauce
1 tsp light soy sauce
1 tsp Shaoxing wine
1½ tsp potato flour

Cut the beef into ⅜ in (1cm) strips, each 2–2½ in (5–6cm) long. Stir the marinade ingredients with 2 tsp water, add to the meat and set aside while you prepare the other ingredients. Cut the peppers into strips to match the beef. Coarsely chop the cilantro.

Heat the oil in a seasoned wok over a high flame. When it is really hot, add the beef and stir-fry until the strips start to separate. Add the peppers and continue to stir-fry until the beef is nearly cooked. Then add the black bean sauce and stir, adding salt to taste. When everything is hot and smells delicious, stir in the cilantro. Finally, remove from the heat, add the sesame oil and serve.

TUZI'S SLOW-COOKED RIBS WITH RED FERMENTED TOFU
NAN RU PAI GU 南乳排骨

There's a wonderful travellers' hostel in the village of Manjuelong, on the outskirts of Hangzhou, where I stay when I'm craving fresh air, greenery and good cheer. The village is famous for its osmanthus blossoms, which are used as an ingredient in sweet dishes and appreciated for their intoxicating fragrance; in the autumn osmanthus season people flock here in the evenings to breathe in the sweet floral air. The hostel itself has a popular restaurant where a female chef known as "Rabbit" (*tu zi*), conjures up a mixture of traditional and fusion dishes from local ingredients supplemented with European, east Asian and south Asian herbs she's been given or has picked up on her travels.

This is my attempt to recreate Rabbit's fabulous pork ribs cooked with red fermented tofu, a typical seasoning of the Lower Yangtze region. The tofu has a vibrant red color which comes from red yeast rice and lends the sauce a rich, almost biscuity fragrance. If you can get it, add a little extra red yeast rice towards the end to give the sauce an intense crimson luster.

Do use chunks of pork shoulder or belly instead of ribs, if you prefer.

1½ lb (750g) meaty pork ribs, shoulder or belly
½ cup (100ml) Shaoxing wine
2 oz (50g) red fermented tofu, mashed into a paste with 3 tbsp juices from the jar
2 tbsp cooking oil

½ oz (25g) ginger, unpeeled, crushed slightly
2 spring onions, white parts only, crushed slightly
1 tbsp sugar
1 tsp ground red yeast rice, *hong qu fen* (optional)

Ask your butcher to chop the ribs into bite-sized pieces. (They'll be equally delicious if you cook them whole, but more difficult to eat with chopsticks.) Add the Shaoxing wine to the fermented tofu and mix well.

If using an oven, preheat it to 300°F (150°C/gas mark 2).

Pour the oil into a seasoned wok over a high flame, add the ribs and fry until lightly browned, stirring from time to time. Then add the ginger and spring onions and stir-fry until you can smell their fragrances. Turn the ribs, ginger and spring onions into a heatproof pot that has a tight-fitting lid. Add the fermented tofu mixture, sugar and ½ cup (100ml) water, stir well and bring to a boil. Cover with the lid and cook over a low flame or in the oven for 30 minutes.

Add the ground red yeast rice, if using, topping up with water from the kettle if necessary to prevent the pot boiling dry. Give it a good stir, then continue to cook for another 30 minutes. Increase the heat to reduce the sauce further, if desired, before serving.

BOWL-STEAMED PORK IN RICE MEAL
FEN ZHENG ROU 粉蒸肉

In the old days in the Sichuan countryside, steamed dishes like this were part of every feast. The fatty pork was a luxury and the cooking method made it possible to serve vast numbers of people: towers of bamboo steamers could be set up over makeshift stoves, each layer bearing a multitude of little bowls. When the guests arrived, the lids of the steamers could be whipped off and the food swiftly distributed to the waiting tables. For this reason, rural feasts were often known as "three steamed dishes and nine bowls" (*san zheng, jiu kou*), or "nine big bowls" (*jiu da wan*). Despite its homely appearance, this dish is glorious: one friend declares it his favorite among all the many dishes of mine he's tasted. It's certainly Sichuanese comfort food at its best: just thinking about it makes me sigh with pleasure. The sumptuously seasoned pork, soft and glutinous in its rice meal coating, melts away into the peas. Eat it with plain rice or, even more perfect, stuffed inside lotus leaf buns (see page 315), which you can serve on the side.

This dish is easy to make but takes two hours to steam and, of course, you have to keep an occasional eye on it to make sure it doesn't boil dry. The only bother is grinding the rice meal, for which you need a blender, but this can be made in quantity and stored in a jar. (You may find it in your local Chinese supermarket, labeled "steam powder"; see Glossary, page 342, for more information.) The whole dish can be made in advance and heated through in a steamer or microwave when you want it. You will need a heatproof bowl about 7 in (18cm) in diameter and 2 in (5cm) deep to make this recipe.

5 oz (150g) peas (about
   1 lb/450g in the pod)
Salt
5 tbsp rice meal (see note
   below)
½ cup (100ml) chicken stock
¾ lb (350g) boneless pork
   belly, with skin
1–2 tbsp finely sliced spring
   onion greens

For the marinade
1½ tbsp chilli bean paste
2 tsp fermented tofu
2 tsp Shaoxing wine
1 tsp finely chopped ginger
⅛ tsp ground white pepper
¼ tsp dark soy sauce

Place the peas in a bowl and add ¼ tsp salt, 1 tbsp of the rice meal and 2 tbsp of the stock. Mix well. Cut the pork into slices like very thick bacon slices, about 4 in (10cm) long and 1¼–1¾ in (3–4cm) thick, and place in a bowl. Add all the marinade ingredients, the remaining rice meal and stock, and ¼ tsp salt, and mix well.

Arrange the pork slices over the sides and base of your bowl in an overlapping pattern, leaving no holes, with the strip of skin on each piece of meat resting on the bowl. Fill with the peas, spread evenly so the top layer is fairly flat. Bring plenty of water to a boil in a wok or steamer, lay the bowl on the rack, cover and steam over medium heat for two hours.

Remove the bowl from the steamer. Cover with a deep plate, then swiftly invert. Remove the bowl, leaving a bowl-shaped mound of meat and peas. If it subsides slightly in its tenderness, don't worry, it'll taste fantastic. Sprinkle with the sliced spring onions and serve.

To make your own rice meal
Place 5 oz (150g) dry Thai fragrant rice, 1 star anise and a couple of pieces of cassia bark in a dry wok. Heat over a medium flame for about 15 minutes, stirring, until the rice grains are brittle, yellowish and aromatic. Remove from the wok and allow to cool. Pluck out and discard the spices. Using a grinder or blender, grind the rice coarsely, until it has the consistency of fine couscous. Store in an airtight jar until needed.

BEEF WITH CUMIN
ZI RAN NIU ROU 孜然牛肉

Cumin is not a typical spice in mainstream Chinese cooking. It carries with it the aroma of the bazaars of Xinjiang in the far northwest of the country, where ethnic Uyghur Muslims sprinkle it over their lamb kebabs and add it to their stews and *polos* (the local version of pilafs). It is, however, found in spice shops all over China, and non-Uyghur cooks use it from time to time. I came across the original version of this sensational recipe in a restaurant in Hunan called Guchengge, and it became one of the most popular in my *Revolutionary Chinese Cookbook*.

The only snag with the Guchengge recipe is that it uses the restaurant technique of pre-frying the beef in a wokful of oil. Here, I've reworked the recipe as a more simple stir-fry. The texture isn't quite as silky as in the original version, but it's much easier to make and still absolutely delicious, as I hope you'll agree.

9 oz (250g) trimmed sirloin or another tender steak
½ red bell pepper
½ green bell pepper
4 tbsp cooking oil
1½ tsp finely chopped ginger
2 tsp finely chopped garlic
1 fresh red chilli, deseeded and finely chopped (optional)
2 tsp ground cumin
2–4 tsp dried chilli flakes, to taste
2 spring onions, green parts only, finely sliced
1 tsp sesame oil

For the marinade
1 tsp Shaoxing wine
¼ tsp salt
½ tsp light soy sauce
¾ tsp dark soy sauce
1½ tsp potato flour

Cut the beef into thin bite-sized slices. Stir the marinade ingredients with 1½ tbsp water and mix well into the meat. Trim the peppers and cut them into strips ⅜–¾ in (1–2cm) wide, then diagonally into diamond-shaped slices.

Add 3 tbsp of the oil to a seasoned wok over a high flame and swirl it around. Add the beef and stir-fry briskly to separate the slices. When the slices have separated but are still a bit pink, remove them from the wok and set aside.

Return the wok to the flame with the remaining oil. Add the ginger and garlic and allow them to sizzle for a few seconds to release their fragrances, then tip in the peppers and fresh chilli, if using, and stir-fry until hot and fragrant. Return the beef slices to the wok, give everything a good stir, then add the cumin and dried chillies. When all is sizzlingly fragrant and delicious, add the spring onions and toss briefly. Remove from the heat, stir in the sesame oil and serve.

RED-BRAISED BEEF WITH TOFU "BAMBOO"
FU ZHU SHAO NIU ROU 腐竹燒牛肉

This gently spicy, slow-cooked stew is the perfect thing for a winter's evening. The tofu soaks up the flavors of the meat and has a delightful texture. If you'd rather, you can use chunks of winter vegetables instead: carrot, potato and turnip all work well. Dried bamboo shoots, soaked to soften then cooked with the beef from the beginning, make another wonderful variation. (You can see a version made with Asian radish in the background of the photograph of the soy bean salad on page 39.) If you have any leftovers, use them as a topping for Buckwheat Noodles with Red-braised Beef (see page 286).

1 lb (450g) stewing beef or boneless beef shin
2 tbsp cooking oil
2½ tbsp Sichuan chilli bean paste
½ oz (25g) piece of ginger, unpeeled, crushed slightly
2 spring onions, white parts only, crushed slightly

1 star anise
1½ tsp sweet fermented sauce
3 cups (750ml) chicken stock, plus a little more, if needed
2 tbsp Shaoxing wine
2 sticks of tofu "bamboo," or dried tofu knots (see Glossary, page 326)

Cut the beef into ¾–1 in (2–3cm) chunks. Bring a panful of water to a boil, add the beef and return to a boil. When a froth has risen to the surface, tip the beef into a colander, drain and rinse.

Heat the oil in a seasoned wok over a medium flame. Add the chilli bean paste and stir-fry until the oil is red and richly fragrant. Add the ginger, spring onions and star anise and continue to stir until you can smell them. Add the sweet fermented sauce and stir-fry for a few moments more before pouring in the stock.

Place the beef and Shaoxing wine in a saucepan or a clay pot and pour over the contents of the wok. Bring to a boil, then partially cover the pan, reduce the heat and simmer for a couple of hours, until the meat is beautifully tender. When the beef has started its slow cooking, set the tofu to soak in hot water from the kettle.

Shortly before you wish to serve the dish, drain the tofu and cut on the diagonal into ¾–1½ in (2–3cm) sections to complement the beef, discarding any pieces that remain hard. Add it to the stew and heat through (you may add a little more stock or hot water from the kettle if you need it), then serve.

SLOW-COOKED BEEF BRISKET WITH BERRIES
QING DUN NIU ROU 清燉枸杞牛肉

One of my favorite Chinese soups is a speciality of Chongqing: a rich, nourishing oxtail broth, cooked for many hours, then served with a beautiful scattering of scarlet gouqi berries and a handful of cilantro. The same method can be used to cook beef and it works perfectly with brisket, one of those nostalgic cuts of meat that I adored as a child. In the original recipe, a whole chicken is used to enrich and elevate the flavor of the beef, but stewing the meat in a rich chicken stock works well.

If you want to be Chinese about it, serve the beef in the soup, either in the cooking pot or in a china bowl; invite your guests to help themselves to pieces of meat with chopsticks or a serving spoon, dip them into the chilli sauce before eating, and then drink a bowl of soup. You may also remove the meat from the soup before serving and serve it on a separate platter, alongside the dip and the soup.

Asian white radish is a classic and most delicious addition. Simply peel the radish, cut into finger-thick strips, boil for a few minutes until tender (and to remove any pepperiness), then add it to the beef and simmer for a few minutes to absorb the flavors of the broth. You can also add other vegetables, such as potatoes, carrots or celery, which don't require blanching.

1½ lb (750g) beef brisket
2 oz (50g) ginger, unpeeled
5¼ cups (1¼ liters) good-quality chicken stock
⅓ cup (75ml) Shaoxing wine
1 tsp Sichuan pepper
2 tbsp gouqi berries, rinsed
Handful of chopped cilantro (optional)

For the dip
1 tbsp cooking oil
4 tbsp Sichuan chilli bean paste
2 tsp finely chopped ginger
1 tsp sesame oil

Bring a panful of water to a boil. Untie the brisket, if necessary, add it to the water, return to a boil, then boil for three to four minutes to allow any impurities to rise to the surface. Pour off the water and rinse the beef thoroughly under the tap. Crush the ginger slightly with the flat of a cleaver or rolling pin.

Place the brisket in a heavy-bottomed saucepan or a casserole pot, cover with the chicken stock and bring to a boil. Skim. Add the Shaoxing wine, ginger and Sichuan pepper and return to a boil. Then cover and simmer over a very low heat or in a gentle oven (preheated to 300°F/150°C/gas mark 2) for at least three hours (some recipes suggest more than five), until the brisket is meltingly tender.

To make the dip, add the oil to a seasoned wok over a medium flame. Swirl it around, add the chilli bean paste and stir-fry until the oil is red and smells delicious. Add the ginger and stir-fry a little longer until you can smell its fragrance. Off the heat, stir in the sesame oil, then transfer the mixture to a small dipping dish.

Ten minutes or so before you are ready to eat, strain out and discard the ginger and Sichuan pepper, using a slotted spoon or tea strainer. Remove the meat from the pot to a chopping board and cut it into finger-thick strips. Return it to the pot with the gouqi berries for 10 minutes more.

Serve in the cooking pot or a deep china bowl, with a scattering of fresh cilantro, if you like. Serve the dip alongside.

CHICKEN
& EGGS

Every Chinese person knows that the best chickens are reared in the countryside, where they peck around the rice fields and vegetable plots, seeking out stray seeds and insects. They are known as *tu ji*—literally "earth chickens"—the Chinese term for birds that Westerners would call free-range, organic or traditionally reared. I've eaten the best, most unforgettable chicken of my life in Chinese farmhouses. One chicken stew, made from a bird reared by the parents of my friend Fan Qun and cooked over a wood fire in rural Hunan for the New Year's feast, was dreamily delicious, the platonic ideal of chickenness.

For the Chinese, as in many other cultures, chicken soup is an important tonic food. (New mothers are often fed chicken soup during their month of confinement, to replenish their energies after the birth.) In the past, chicken was a luxury meat. It was eaten on special occasions, or brewed up with pork ribs and ham to make fine banquet stocks in rich homes and fancy restaurants. Older hens, scrawny but flavorful, were used for soups and stews; young capons for cold chicken dishes and stir-fries. Almost every part of the chicken is still used in the Chinese kitchen: the innards might be stir-fried with something fresh or pungent and the rest of the bird cooked whole; or the breasts and leg meat used for flavorful wok-cooked dishes and the rest added to the stock pot. In restaurants, you'll find the wing tips, stewed in a spiced broth, offered as a special delicacy; the feet (known as "phoenix claws") are another snack to be savored.

There is something very satisfying about buying a whole bird from a farmers' market and using every bit of it at home. Think of cutting away the breasts and using them in Gong Bao Chicken with Peanuts; poaching the thighs and serving them as Cold Chicken with a Spicy Sichuanese Sauce, or using them to whip up a Black Bean Chicken. Stew the heart and liver in a little spiced broth and dip them in salt, ground chillies and ground roasted Sichuan pepper. And then make the rest of the bird into a stock, with a little ginger and spring onion, and use it as the base for the evening's soup, or store it in the freezer for another time.

Perhaps the most wonderful thing about the chicken in Chinese cooking, however, is the way a little bit of its meat or fat can lend rich, savory flavors to vegetable dishes. Half a chicken breast, sliced or slivered and simply marinated, adds an extra dimension of deliciousness to a wokful of mushrooms or vegetables (see Stir-fried Oyster Mushrooms with Chicken). Leftovers from a Western-style roast chicken can be given the Sichuanese treatment: sliced or slivered, bulked out with salad leaves and served with a lavishly spicy dressing; or piled on top of a bowl of cold buckwheat noodles. Chicken stock is a perfect base for all kinds of soups, while the golden fat that solidifies at the top of a panful of cooling stock is often added to mushrooms or greens just before they are served, like a magical elixir of umami flavor.

Chicken is the bird most often cooked at home in China, which is why it's the focus of the recipes that follow. Duck is also enjoyed, but cooked less often at home than in restaurants and in the workshops of specializt food producers, whose ovens, large woks for deep-frying and smokeries are designed to make the most of its luxuriantly fragrant fat. Many Chinese people will buy roasted, smoked or stewed duck and serve it with home-cooked dishes. Leftover duck can be chopped up and used in fried rice, with a little preserved vegetable, or in soupy rice (used in place of salt pork); and the carcass makes a fabulous stock to which you can add Chinese cabbage and tofu for a comforting soup.

Goose is another fowl that is enjoyed in certain parts of China, but rarely cooked in a domestic kitchen. Pheasants and pigeons are rarer treats; game birds such as pheasants may be fried in oil, then slow-cooked, as in the Braised Chicken with Chestnuts, or simply stewed in a clay pot with a little Shaoxing wine, ginger and medicinal herbs for a tonic soup.

Finally, eggs might be stir-fried with tomatoes or made into a Golden Chinese Chive Omelette; they may also be fried on both sides (to make what are known as "pocket eggs") and laid on top of a bowl of noodles. Duck eggs are sometimes eaten in omelettes, but are more often salted or preserved in alkalis to make the striking delicacy known in the West as "1,000-year-old eggs."

STEAMED CHICKEN WITH CHINESE SAUSAGE AND SHIITAKE MUSHROOMS
HE YE ZHENG JI 荷葉蒸雞

This delicate Cantonese dish is no trouble at all to make. All you need to do is cut up chicken thighs, Chinese sausage and mushrooms, mix them with a few seasonings and steam them for 15 minutes. The chicken retains a silky tenderness and the sausage and mushrooms impart a heady hit of umami. The chicken is traditionally wrapped in a lotus leaf, which lends an exquisite fragrance, but it's lovely even without this extra touch. You can buy dried lotus leaves in good Chinese supermarkets.

2 dried shiitake mushrooms
3 boneless chicken thighs (11½ oz/330g)
1¾ oz (45g) Chinese wind-dried sausage, or ¾ oz (30g) Chinese or Spanish ham

For the marinade
⅓ oz (10g) ginger, unpeeled, plus ½ oz (20g) ginger, peeled and sliced
½ tsp salt
¼ tsp sugar
½ tbsp Shaoxing wine
2 tsp potato flour mixed with 2 tsp cold water
2 tsp cooking oil

Soak the dried mushrooms for at least 30 minutes in hot water from the kettle.

Cut the chicken into strips about 1cm wide and put it in a bowl. Crush the whole piece of ginger with the flat of a cleaver or a rolling pin, put in a cup and cover with water (the water will immediately take on its fragrance). Add 1 tbsp of this water to the chicken, along with the salt, sugar, Shaoxing wine, and potato flour mixture, and mix well. Finally, add the sliced ginger and the oil and stir (I find it easiest to use my hand for this mixing).

Cut the wind-dried sausage at an angle into thickish slices (if you are using ham, slice it thinly). Cut the soaked mushroom caps, at an angle, into thin slices, discarding the stalks.

Spread out the chicken strips, as far as possible in a single layer, in a shallow bowl that will fit into your steamer. Lay the mushrooms and sausage slices neatly over the top. Place the bowl in the steamer, cover, then steam over a high heat for about 15 minutes, until the chicken pieces are just cooked through. Serve.

To wrap the chicken in a lotus leaf
Soak the dried lotus leaf in hot water from the kettle for at least 15 minutes. When the leaf is soft and supple, use scissors to cut a piece large enough to wrap the chicken completely (if the leaf is broken, use two layers). Lay the leaf, or leaves, in the steamer. Arrange the chicken, sausage slices and mushrooms on the leaf as described in the main recipe above, then turn in the edges of the leaf to wrap it up into a parcel. Cover the steamer and steam over a high heat for about 15 minutes, until the chicken is cooked through. Gently remove the lotus leaf parcel to a serving dish, or serve in the steamer. Your guests can unwrap it at the table.

BLACK BEAN CHICKEN
DOU CHI JI DING 豆豉雞丁

This is a slightly simplified version of a delicious dish from the Hunanese firework-producing city of Liuyang. In the original, the chicken is deep-fried; here, it is simply stir-fried, so it keeps its succulent mouthfeel. The seasonings remain the same as in the original recipe. You can omit the chillies, or increase them, according to taste. Fermented black beans are among the most distinctive Hunanese seasonings, especially when used in combination with chillies.

Here, as in many Chinese dishes, an apparently small amount of meat goes a long way: serve this with two or three vegetable dishes and rice and it will be enough for four people. You could use chicken breast instead if you prefer.

2 boneless chicken thighs (8 oz/225g)
1 smallish green bell pepper, or ½ each red and green bell pepper
3 tbsp cooking oil
3 garlic cloves, peeled and sliced
An equivalent amount of ginger, peeled and sliced
2 tbsp fermented black beans, rinsed and drained
1–2 tsp ground chillies, to taste
Salt
2 tbsp finely sliced spring onion greens
1 tsp sesame oil

For the marinade
1 tbsp Shaoxing wine
¼ tsp salt
1½ tsp potato flour
1 tsp light soy sauce
1 tsp dark soy sauce

Cut the chicken into ⅜–¾ in (1–2 cm) cubes and put into a bowl. Stir together the marinade ingredients, add to the chicken and mix well.

Cut the pepper(s) into small squares to match the chicken. Heat a wok over a high flame, add 1 tbsp of the oil, then the peppers and stir-fry until hot and slightly cooked, but still crisp. Remove and set aside.

Reheat the wok over a high flame. Add the remainder of the oil, swirl it around, then add the marinated chicken and stir-fry to separate the pieces. When they have separated and are starting to become pale, add the garlic and ginger and stir-fry until they smell delicious. Add the black beans and stir a few times until you can smell them. Then add the ground chillies and return the peppers to the wok. Continue to stir-fry until the chicken is just cooked through and everything is sizzlingly delicious, seasoning with salt to taste. Then stir in the spring onions and, off the heat, the sesame oil. Serve.

GONG BAO CHICKEN WITH PEANUTS
GONG BAO JI DING 宮保雞丁

As far as I'm concerned, this is one of the ultimate chicken dishes: quick and easy to make and thrillingly delicious. The cooking method is *xiao chao*, "small stir-fry," in which all the ingredients are simply added to the wok in succession. With its kick of scorched chilli, tingle of Sichuan pepper and gentle sweet-sour sauce, it's a typically Sichuanese combination of flavors. The crunchy peanuts, juicy spring onions and succulent chicken also give it a delightful mouthfeel.

The dish is named after a late Qing Dynasty governor of Sichuan, Ding Baozhen, who is said to have enjoyed eating it. You'll find versions of this dish, often known in English as Kung Po chicken, on virtually every Chinese restaurant menu, but this is the real Chengdu version. This recipe first appeared in my book *Land of Plenty*.

2 boneless chicken breasts, with or without skin (11–12 oz/300–350g in total)
3 garlic cloves
An equivalent amount of ginger
5 spring onions, white parts only
A handful of dried chillies (about 10)
2 tbsp cooking oil
1 tsp whole Sichuan pepper
3 oz (75g) roasted peanuts (to make your own, see page 325)

For the marinade
½ tsp salt
2 tsp light soy sauce
1 tsp Shaoxing wine
1½ tsp potato flour

For the sauce
1 tbsp sugar
¾ tsp potato flour
1 tsp dark soy sauce
1 tsp light soy sauce
1 tbsp Chinkiang vinegar
1 tsp sesame oil
1 tbsp chicken stock or water

Cut the chicken as evenly as possible into ½ in (1½cm) strips, then cut these into small cubes. Place in a small bowl. Add the marinade ingredients together with 1 tbsp water, mix well and set aside while you prepare the other ingredients.

Peel and thinly slice the garlic and ginger and chop the spring onions into chunks as long as their diameter (to match the chicken cubes). Snip the chillies in half or into sections. Discard their seeds as far as possible. Combine the sauce ingredients in a small bowl.

Heat a seasoned wok over a high flame. Add the oil with the chillies and Sichuan pepper and stir-fry briefly until the chillies are darkening but not burned (remove the wok from the heat if necessary to prevent overheating).

Quickly add the chicken and stir-fry over a high flame, stirring constantly. As soon as the chicken cubes have separated, add the ginger, garlic and spring onions and continue to stir-fry until they are fragrant and the meat just cooked through (test one of the larger pieces to make sure).

Give the sauce a stir and add it to the wok, continuing to stir and toss. As soon as the sauce has become thick and shiny, add the peanuts, stir them in and serve.

EVERYDAY STIR-FRIED CHICKEN
XIAO JIAN JI 小煎雞

This simple but extremely delicious supper dish uses the *xiao chao* ("small stir-fry") method that is typical of the Sichuanese home kitchen, which is to say that all the ingredients are added to the wok in sequence, so the cooking takes a matter of minutes. Serve it with rice and a couple of stir-fried vegetables and you have an easy but satisfying meal for three or four.

Most Chinese people would use thigh meat in this dish because of its superior flavor, but you can use breast if you prefer. And you can also vary the vegetables as you please: sliced mushrooms or peppers, or a small handful of soaked cloud ear mushrooms, would all work very well. Another popular Sichuanese dish, pork slices with black wood ear mushrooms (*mu'er rou pian*), uses the same method: just substitute sliced pork for the chicken and wood ear for the cucumber.

2 boneless chicken thighs, with or without skin (8 oz/225g)
Small section of cucumber (1½–2 in/4–5cm will do)
⅔ celery stick
1 garlic clove
An equivalent amount of ginger
1 spring onion, white part only
1 fresh red chilli, or Sichuan pickled red chilli
3 tbsp cooking oil

For the marinade
¼ tsp salt
1 tsp potato flour
1 tsp Shaoxing wine
1 tsp light soy sauce

For the sauce
¼ tsp sugar
½ tsp potato flour
1 tsp Shaoxing wine
2 tsp light soy sauce
½ tsp Chinkiang vinegar
1 tbsp chicken stock or water

Lay the chicken thighs out on a chopping board. Whack them up and down with the back of your knife to tenderize them, then cut into ⅛ in (½cm) slices along the grain of the meat. Place in a small bowl. Add the marinade ingredients along with 2 tsp water and mix well.

Cut the piece of cucumber in half lengthways and discard the seeds. Then cut lengthways into ⅛ in (½cm) strips. De-string the celery and cut into strips to match the cucumber. Peel and thinly slice the garlic and ginger. Cut the spring onion white and chilli on the diagonal into thin "horse-ear" slices. Combine the sauce ingredients in a small bowl.

Heat the oil in a seasoned wok over a high flame. Add the chicken and stir-fry briskly. When the pieces have separated, add the garlic, ginger, spring onion and chilli and stir-fry until you can smell their fragrance and the chicken is almost cooked but still a little pink. Add the cucumber and celery and stir-fry until they are piping hot.

Give the sauce a stir, pour it into the center of the wok and stir quickly as it thickens and clothes the pieces of chicken. Serve.

BRAISED CHICKEN WITH DRIED SHIITAKE MUSHROOMS
XIANG GU SHAO JI 香菇燒雞

If you are cooking a Chinese supper for several people, it's always helpful to include a slow-cooked dish such as this, that can be prepared in advance and just heated up when you wish to eat it. (Simply follow the recipe until it has been simmered for 30 minutes beforehand, then reheat, reduce and scatter with spring onions and sesame oil when you wish to serve.)

Serve this smokily delicious stew with a cold appetizer or two and a couple of stir-fried vegetables and you'll have a wonderful meal for four people.

8 dried shiitake mushrooms
4 boneless chicken thighs
  (about ¾ lb/350g)
2 spring onions
2 tbsp cooking oil
½ oz (20g) ginger, peeled and
  sliced
2 tbsp Shaoxing wine
About ¾ cup (200ml) chicken
  stock or water
1 tbsp sugar
2 tsp dark soy sauce
Salt
1 tsp sesame oil

Set the dried mushrooms to soak in hot water from the kettle for at least 30 minutes. Cut the soaked mushrooms into quarters, reserving their soaking water. Cut the chicken into pieces of a similar size to the mushrooms. Cut the spring onions into 2 in (5cm) sections and separate the white and green parts. Crush the white parts slightly with the side of a cleaver or a heavy object.

Add the oil to a seasoned wok over a high flame, swirl it around, then add the chicken and stir-fry for a few minutes until the pieces are lightly browned. If you like, pour off any excess oil at this stage (keep it for stir-frying vegetables, to which it will add a lovely umami flavor). When the chicken is nearly done, add the ginger and spring onion whites and allow the hot oil to release their fragrances.

Add the Shaoxing wine, stir a few times, then add the mushrooms, mushroom soaking water and enough stock or water to make up about 1 cup plus 2 tbsp (300ml). Add the sugar, soy sauce, and salt to taste.

Bring to a boil, skim if necessary, then cover the wok, reduce the heat and simmer gently for 30 minutes, stirring from time to time. (I usually transfer the mixture from a wok to a saucepan for the simmering, so that the wok can be freed up for cooking other dishes.)

Remove the lid, increase the heat and reduce the liquid to thicken the sauce. Adjust the seasoning, add the spring onion greens and sesame oil and serve.

GENERAL TSO'S CHICKEN
ZUO ZONG TANG JI 左宗棠雞

Deep-frying is a method I prefer to avoid for everyday cooking, but this is one of the dishes for which I make an exception. When served, it tends to provoke that moment of rapt, intense silence at the dinner table that is one of the tokens of true appreciation. Slices of chicken thigh meat are first deep-fried in a light batter, then tossed in a sophisticated sweet-sour sauce laced with chilli. General Tso's chicken is supposedly a Hunanese dish, but it's virtually unknown in Hunan Province. It was actually invented by Peng Chang-Kuei, a Hunanese exile chef in Taiwan, and cooked by him in his one-time New York restaurant. It has since been taken so much to the heart of Americans living in the northeast that it is now known as the very essence and emblem of Hunanese cuisine. This version of the dish is based on the recipe I learned in Peng Chang-Kuei's kitchen in Taipei.

The dish is usually made with boned chicken leg meat, although you can use breast if you prefer. Do make sure your wok is stable before using it for deep-frying: it's important to use a wok stand with a round-bottomed wok.

4 boneless chicken thighs (about ¾ lb/350g)
6–10 small dried red chillies
Cooking oil, for deep-frying
2 tsp finely chopped ginger
2 tsp finely chopped garlic
2 tsp sesame oil
1 tbsp thinly sliced spring onion greens (optional)

For the marinade/batter
2 tsp light soy sauce
½ tsp dark soy sauce
1 egg yolk
2 tbsp potato flour
2 tsp cooking oil

For the sauce
1 tbsp tomato purée mixed with 1 tbsp water
½ tsp potato flour
½ tsp dark soy sauce
1½ tsp light soy sauce
1 tbsp rice vinegar
3 tbsp chicken stock or water

Unfold the chicken thighs and lay them, skin side down, on a chopping board. (If some parts are very thick, lay your knife flat and slice them across in half, parallel to the board.) Use a sharp knife to make a few shallow criss-cross cuts into the meat; this will help the flavors to penetrate. Then cut each thigh into 1½–1¾ in (3–4cm) slices, an uneven ⅛ in (½cm) or so in thickness. Place the slices in a bowl.

For the marinade, add the soy sauces and egg yolk to the chicken and mix well. Then stir in the potato flour, and lastly the oil. Set aside while you prepare the other ingredients.

Combine the sauce ingredients in a small bowl. Use a pair of scissors to snip the chillies into ¾ in (2cm) sections, discarding seeds as far as possible.

Heat a wok over a high flame. Pour in the deep-frying oil and heat to 350–400°F (180–200°C). Add the chicken and fry until crisp and golden. (If you are deep-frying in a wok with a relatively small volume of oil, fry the chicken in a couple of batches.) Remove the chicken with a slotted spoon and set aside. Pour the oil into a heatproof container and clean the wok if necessary.

Return the wok to a high flame. Add 2–3 tbsp cooking oil and the chillies and stir-fry briefly until they are fragrant and just changing color (do not burn them). Toss in the ginger and garlic and stir-fry for a few seconds more, until you can smell their aromas. Then add the sauce and stir as it thickens. Return the chicken to the wok and stir vigorously to coat the pieces in sauce. Stir in the sesame oil, then serve, with a scattering of spring onion greens if desired.

BRAISED CHICKEN WITH CHESTNUTS
BAN LI SHAO JI 板栗燒雞

Chestnuts are one of China's native crops and have been cultivated there for millennia. They are grown in many parts of the country, but particularly in the north, where they are used in soups, stews and stir-fries, or ground into flour for breads and sweetmeats. Chicken and chestnuts are a classic Chinese combination.

One September morning, I drove out with my friend A Dai into the Zhejiang countryside, through a lush greenness of paddy fields, bamboo groves and lotus ponds, into the tea-bushed hills. Up a rough track we left the van and walked out into the twittering, humming undergrowth. A little further and there was an orchard of chestnut trees, where we plucked the prickly fruits and peeled open and ate, raw, some of the crunchy young nuts. Later, back at A Dai's restaurant, we tasted more of them, stir-fried with ginger and the meat of a young chicken, a tender dish that can only be enjoyed early in the chestnut season. When the nuts are plumper and more mature, they find their way into braises such as this, perfect for a winter's evening. In China, this would be made with a whole chicken, chopped up on the bone, but this quick version is made with boneless meat. Prepare it in advance if you like and reheat just in time for your meal.

4 boneless chicken thighs (about ¾ lb/350g)
½ oz (20g) ginger, unpeeled
2 spring onions, white and green parts separated
3 tbsp cooking oil
1½ tbsp Shaoxing wine

1 cup plus 2 tbsp (300ml) chicken stock or water
1 tbsp brown or sugar
1½ tsp dark soy sauce
7 oz (200g) cooked, peeled chestnuts (canned or vacuum-packed)
Salt

Cut the chicken evenly into bite-sized chunks. Crush the ginger and spring onion whites slightly with the side of a cleaver or a rolling pin. Cut the spring onion greens into neat 1¾ in (4cm) lengths.

Heat the oil in a seasoned wok over a high flame. When it is hot, add the ginger and spring onion whites and stir-fry until you can smell their fragrance. Then add the chicken pieces and fry over a high heat until they are lightly browned: don't move them around too much, but let them rest against the base of the wok so they have the chance to take on a little color. Drain off some of the excess fat at this stage if you wish. Splash in the Shaoxing wine and stir well. Then add all the stock.

Bring the stock to a boil and add the sugar, soy sauce and chestnuts, with salt to taste (¾ tsp should do). Then reduce the heat, cover and simmer for about 15 minutes to allow the chicken to cook through and the chestnuts to absorb some of the flavors of the sauce, stirring from time to time.

Increase the heat to reduce the liquid if you wish and adjust the seasoning if necessary. At the last minute, add the spring onion greens, cover for just a moment to let them feel the heat, then serve.

To cook and peel your own chestnuts
Slice off the bases of the raw chestnuts and blanch them in boiling water for a couple of minutes, then drain. When cool enough to handle, remove their shells and inner skins as far as possible.

CHICKEN LIVERS WITH CHINESE CHIVES
JIU CAI CHAO JI GAN 韭菜炒雞肝

Once, when I was staying in Hangzhou, I went with my restaurateur friend A Dai to a nearby village where a pig was to be slaughtered. We watched three brothers, professional pig-killers, dispatch the animal with a long "willow leaf" knife, stayed for a chat with the farmer over tea and bowlfuls of poached eggs served with sugar, then drove back to town with the meat in the back of the van. That evening, back at A Dai's restaurant, the head chef whipped up two simple stir-fries with the pig's liver and heart and they were both spectacularly delicious.

Here, I've adapted one of his recipes using chicken livers. It takes a few minutes to prepare and cook and would make a good supper for two, with rice and perhaps another vegetable dish. The fast stir-frying method is perfect for chicken livers, which become leathery when overcooked. In Hangzhou, the locals tend not to eat spicy food, but a little ground chilli makes a fine addition to this dish.

5 oz (150g) very fresh chicken livers (and hearts if you have them)
4 oz (100g) Chinese chives
3 tbsp cooking oil
1–2 tsp ground chillies, to taste (optional)

1 tsp light soy sauce
Salt

For the marinade
½ tsp salt
½ tbsp Shaoxing wine

Cut the chicken livers (and hearts, if using) evenly into slices ⅛–⅜ in (½–1cm) thick, and put them in a bowl. Add the marinade ingredients and mix well. Trim the chives and cut into 2 in (5cm) lengths.

Add the oil to a seasoned wok over a high flame, swirl it around, then add the chicken livers (and hearts, if using) and stir-fry to separate the slices. When they have separated and are semi-cooked, remove them from the wok.

Return the wok to the heat and add the chives and chillies, if using. When they are hot and fragrant, return the livers (and hearts, if using) to the wok, with the soy sauce and salt, if you need it, and continue to stir-fry until the livers are barely cooked and still pinkish inside and everything smells delicious. Serve immediately.

STIR-FRIED EGGS WITH TOMATOES
FAN QIE CHAO DAN 番茄炒蛋

When the Chinese of the coastal provinces first encountered the tomato, it reminded them of more familiar fruits and vegetables, which is why it became known as a "barbarian eggplant" or a "Western red persimmon." Here, then, is a recipe for "barbarian eggplant" stir-fried with eggs, which I ate every other day when I lived in Sichuan. It's beautiful, with its vivid mix of red and yellow, and seems much more delicious than the sum of its parts. A fast, simple dish and one of my favorite ways to eat eggs. I've given a recipe for two eggs and two tomatoes, which you can increase by an egg and tomato or two if you please. The potato flour mixture, if added, gives an extra luxuriousness to the juices, but isn't strictly necessary.

2 ripe tomatoes, similar in volume to the eggs
2 eggs
Salt

4 tbsp cooking oil
½ tsp sugar
½ tsp potato flour mixed with 2 tsp water (optional)

Cut each tomato in half, then into sections the size of tangerine segments.

Beat the eggs evenly together with a little salt.

Heat 3 tbsp of the oil in a seasoned wok over a high flame. Add the beaten eggs and swirl them around. Use a wok scoop or a ladle to nudge the edges of the egg towards the center, so the uncooked egg can run out. As soon as the egg has set (it may be a little golden), remove it from the wok.

Return the wok to the high flame with a final 1 tbsp oil if you need it. Add the tomatoes and stir-fry until they are hot and smell cooked and delicious, adding the sugar and salt to taste. Then return the eggs to the wok and mix everything together. Add the potato flour mixture, if using, and serve.

STEAMED EGGS
ZHENG SHUI DAN 蒸水蛋

These simple steamed eggs have a soothing, custardy texture and a very delicate flavor. They are often recommended for small children and the elderly because they don't require chewing. This version of the recipe is based on one from the Zhao Family Teahouse in the Fujianese village of Chengcun, which lies in the heart of oolong tea country. Add some ground pork to the eggs if you like; I prefer to stir-fry it first to make sure it's cooked through. And for a more elaborate dish, combine the beaten eggs with sections of both preserved duck eggs and hard-boiled salted duck eggs, so you have three kinds of egg in a single dish, including the dramatically colored preserved duck eggs. This is an intriguing and rather beautiful dish that I first made myself for an Easter dinner!

2 dried shiitake mushrooms
3 eggs (³/₄ cup/200ml when beaten)
²/₃ cup (150ml) warm chicken stock or water (100–120°F/ 40–50°C)
¼ tsp salt
1 tbsp Shaoxing wine
2 tbsp finely sliced spring onion greens
2 tbsp cooking oil
2 tsp light soy sauce

For the pork (optional)
1 tbsp cooking oil
4 oz (100g) ground pork
1 tsp Shaoxing wine

Soak the dried mushrooms in hot water from the kettle for 30 minutes, until supple, then drain and chop finely.

If using the pork, heat a wok over a high flame. Add the oil, then stir-fry the pork until just cooked, adding the Shaoxing wine and salt to taste. Set aside.

Beat the eggs together very thoroughly. Add the warm stock or water, salt, Shaoxing wine, mushrooms and cooked pork (if using) and mix well.

Pour the egg mixture into a shallow, heatproof bowl. Use a spoon or chopstick to gently remove the froth from the surface. Cover the bowl with plastic wrap or a suitable lid, or secure a piece of wax paper over the top.

Place the bowl in a steamer over boiling water and steam for eight to 10 minutes, until the custard has set.

Remove the cover and scatter the spring onions over the surface of the eggs. Heat the cooking oil until smoking, then ladle it, sizzling, over the spring onions. Finish by pouring the soy sauce over the eggs.

FRESH OYSTER OMELETTE
DAN JIAN SHENG HAO 蛋煎生蠔

Oysters are a favorite ingredient in southern Fujian and Guangdong provinces. This is one of the most delightful ways to eat them, with the plump, succulent mollusks cradled in golden egg and sprinkled with the vivid green of spring onions.

The only tricky bit, if you're not used to it, is shucking the oysters, for which it's best to use a special oyster knife. To shuck, hold each oyster in a wet kitchen towel, with the hinge end poking out of the cloth. Ease the knife gently into the hinge to find the sweet spot of least resistance, then force it in. Twist the knife to force the two shells apart, then run it around the inside of the top part of the shell to allow you to remove the lid. It's best to ask someone to show you how to do this if you haven't tried it before.

If you make this dish with good oysters and free-range eggs, it'll be better than any oyster omelette you'll taste in a restaurant. Make it for a special brunch for someone you love, or serve it with rice as part of a Chinese meal.

Salt
6–8 oysters, freshly shucked
3 eggs
1½ tsp potato flour mixed with 1 tsp cold water

Ground white pepper
2 tbsp cooking oil
4 tbsp finely sliced spring onion greens

Add ¾ tsp salt to the oysters, mix gently, then place in a fine-mesh colander and rinse under the tap, taking care to wash away any fragments of shell. Bring a small panful of water to a boil, add the oysters and blanch for just a few seconds. Drain. (These two steps give the oysters an amazing purity of flavor.)

Beat the eggs, then beat in the flour mixture with salt and pepper to taste.

Add the oil to a seasoned wok over a high flame and swirl it around. Pour in the eggs and swirl the mixture around the base of the wok. Scatter the oysters evenly over the egg mixture and reduce the heat to medium. Tip the wok and use a wok scoop or ladle to allow some of the liquid egg that pools in the center to escape towards the hot metal surface.

When the omelette is golden underneath, scatter with the spring onion greens, then flip to cook the other side. When this side, too, is golden, transfer to a plate and serve.

FISH &
SEAFOOD

In many parts of China, fish ponds and canals were always a part of village life. Carp and catfish fed on weeds and smaller creatures in the water, and provided flesh for the dinner table as part of a sustainable agricultural system. Other freshwater fish came from rivers, lakes and streams, while people living on the coasts had plentiful supplies of sea fish.

In an era when China is suffering the ugly side effects of reckless modernization, it is easy to forget that this was a culture that once prized environmental stewardship. The first duty of a good ruler was always to keep his people well fed. The key to this was a sustainable food system, as the ancient philosopher Mencius (circa 372–289BC) suggested in a statement that could be a manifesto for the modern environmental movement:

Do not disregard the farmer's seasons and food will be more than enough. Forbid the use of fine-meshed nets and fish and turtles will be more than enough. Take wood from the forests at prescribed times only and there will be material enough and to spare. With a sufficiency of grain, of fish and of material, the people would live without anxiety. This is the first principle of Princely Government.

At a time when supplies of sea fish are under strain the world over due to over-fishing, and when fish-farming practices are creating their own environmental problems, it is hard to eat fish with a clear conscience. The best way to do it, perhaps, is to take a leaf from the book of traditional Chinese family dining and make a whole fish an occasional treat, to be shared by a group. This is the way the recipes in this chapter are intended to be used: a whole trout or sea bass, for example, with other dishes, can be shared by at least six people.

Food writers in some Western countries are beginning to champion a revival of carp and other freshwater species as a way of dealing with dwindling ocean fish stocks. If supplies of carp become more available, it will be worth remembering the exciting Chinese repertoire of recipes for it and other freshwater fish. All the recipes in this chapter (bar that for clams) can be adapted to use with many kinds of fish.

Fish are typically served whole on the Chinese dinner table, with guests helping themselves to little pieces of their flesh with chopsticks. When I'm serving guests at home, however, having shown them the whole fish, I often ease the flesh from the spine with a spoon and fork, then lift out and set aside the backbone, head and tail to make things easier. I always remind people, though, that one of the most prized morsels in Chinese terms is the tiny piece of flesh in a fish's cheek (on one occasion in Hangzhou, I was privileged to try a grand old dish made with the cheeks of 200 fish). In some coastal parts of China, it is considered bad luck to turn a fish on a plate as this suggests the capsizing of a fishing boat, so people always remove the backbone to get at the flesh underneath, rather than flipping it over. A whole fish is an essential part of the New Year's Eve feast, because the auspicious phrase *nian nian you yu* is a pun, meaning both "have fish year after year" and "have a surplus year after year."

Some tips on choosing and cooking fish

– Always use the freshest fish you can find: look out for bright eyes, blood-red gills and shiny flesh that bounces back when you poke it with a finger.

– To refine the flavor of a fish and dispel what the Chinese call "off tastes" or "fishy flavors," rub it inside and out with a little salt and Shaoxing wine and place a crushed spring onion and a crushed piece of ginger in its belly. Leave to marinate for 10–15 minutes before cooking, and discard any juices that emerge from the fish.

– When frying a fish in shallow oil, rubbing a little salt into its skin will help keep the skin intact and prevent sticking.

– When steaming a fish on a plate, place a spring onion or two, or a wooden chopstick, beneath its body, to enable steam to circulate between it and the plate.

STEAMED SEA BASS WITH GINGER AND SPRING ONION
QING ZHENG LU YU 清蒸鱸魚

This is one of the easiest dishes to prepare and yet is greeted with more delight at the dinner table than almost any other. The cooking method is typically Cantonese, which is to say that it relies on superbly fresh produce and minimal intervention: the seasonings are there just to enhance the flavor of the fish. The only thing you need to be careful with is the timing, making sure the fish is not overcooked.

Don't worry too much about quantities, just use those I've given as a guide. This recipe will make a farmed sea bass taste splendid, a wild one sublime. You need to steam the fish in a dish that fits into your steamer or wok, with a little room around the edges for steam to circulate. If you can't quite fit the fish, lying flat, in your steamer, you can curl it around, or, in a worst-case scenario, cut it neatly in half then reassemble on the serving plate.

In China, the fish is presented whole. At more informal meals, guests will pluck pieces of fish with their chopsticks, dip them into the soy sauce, and then eat. In more formal settings, a waitress may lift the top fillet from the fish and lay it on the dish, then remove the backbone with attached head and tail. If you do this, don't forget to offer the fish cheeks to your most honored guest before you remove the head!

5 spring onions
2 oz (50g) piece of ginger
1 sea bass, about 1½ lb (700g), scaled and cleaned, but with head and tail intact
Salt
1 tbsp Shaoxing wine
3 tbsp light soy sauce or tamari
4 tbsp cooking oil

Trim the spring onions and cut three of them into 2½ in (6cm) lengths, then into fine slivers. Wash and peel the ginger, keeping the thick peel and any knobbly bits for the marinade. Cut the peeled part into long, thin slivers.

Rinse the fish in cold water and pat it dry. Starting at the head, make three or four parallel, diagonal cuts on each side of the fish, cutting into the thickest part of the flesh near the backbone. Rub it inside and out with a little salt and the Shaoxing wine. Smack the ginger remnants and one of the remaining spring onions with the side of a cleaver or a rolling pin to release their fragrances and place them in the belly cavity of the fish. Leave to marinate for 10–15 minutes.

Pour off any liquid that has emerged from the fish and pat it dry. Tear the last spring onion into two or three pieces and lay it in the center of the steaming plate. Lay the fish over the spring onion (the onion will raise the fish slightly so steam can move around it).

Steam the fish over high heat for 10–12 minutes, until just cooked. Test it by poking a chopstick into the thickest part of the flesh, just behind the head; the flesh should flake away easily from the backbone. When the fish is nearly done, dilute the soy sauce with 2 tbsp hot water.

Remove the fish from the steamer and transfer carefully to a serving dish. Remove and discard the ginger and spring onion from its belly and the cooking juices.

Scatter the fish with the slivered ginger and spring onion. Heat the oil in a wok or small pan over a high flame. When it starts to smoke slightly, drizzle it over the ginger and spring onion slivers, which should sizzle dramatically (make sure the oil is hot enough by dripping a tiny amount over the fish and listening for the sizzle before you pour the rest over it). Pour the diluted soy sauce all around the fish and serve immediately.

VARIATION

Steamed fish fillets with ginger and spring onion
Fillets of fish can be cooked in exactly the same way, adjusting cooking times and quantities accordingly.

SEA BREAM IN FISH-FRAGRANT SAUCE
JI LI JIA XIANG YU 吉利家鄉魚

This is my attempt to recreate, on a domestic scale, a recipe from the Bashu Weiyuan, a splendid little restaurant tucked away on a back street in the center of Chengdu. It's an inexpensive and unassuming place, but the flavors of the food are extraordinary and refreshingly traditional in a city that is changing at breakneck pace. There, where they title the dish "Lucky home town fish," they serve a whole sea bass covered in lavish quantities of fish-fragrant sauce, that famous Sichuanese combination of pickled chilli, garlic and ginger with sweet-and-sour flavors. Here, I've suggested using a smaller fish and more modest amounts of sauce. Use the same sauce to dress a different type of fish, or fillets, blanched razor clams, or steamed scallops. It also goes spectacularly well with deep-fried chicken or tofu.

3 cups (750ml) chicken stock
1 sea bream (³/₄ lb/350g), scaled and cleaned, but with head and tail intact

For the sauce
2 tbsp cooking oil
2 tbsp Sichuan chilli bean paste (or Sichuan pickled chilli paste if you can get it)
1 tbsp finely chopped garlic
1 tbsp finely chopped ginger
³/₄ cup (200ml) chicken stock
1 tbsp sugar
2 tsp potato flour mixed with 1¹/₂ tbsp cold water
1 tbsp Chinkiang vinegar
3 tbsp finely sliced spring onion greens

Heat up the 3 cups (750ml) stock in a wok.

Make parallel cuts ³/₈ in (1cm) apart along each side of the fish, perpendicular to the spine and all the way down to the backbone (this will help the fish to poach quickly and keep it tender). Lay it in the boiling stock, bring the liquid to a boil, then reduce the heat to poach the fish gently. Move the fish around a little if necessary to ensure even cooking. After about two minutes, turn the fish and poach for another two minutes, by which time it should be just tender to the bone: poke a chopstick into the thickest part of the flesh to make sure (it should come away easily from the backbone). Remove the fish to a serving dish and pour off the stock for other uses.

Re-season the surface of the wok, then return to a medium flame with the cooking oil. Add the chilli bean paste and stir-fry for a minute or so until the oil is red and fragrant. Add the garlic and ginger and stir until you can smell their fragrances. Then pour in the ³/₄ cup (200ml) stock and bring to a boil.

Mix in the sugar, then give the potato flour mixture a stir and add just enough to thicken the sauce to a thick, luxurious gravy (you will probably need all of it). Then stir in the vinegar, followed by the spring onion greens. Mix well and ladle over the waiting fish. Serve.

DRY-BRAISED FISH WITH BLACK BEAN AND CHILLI
DOU LA GAN SHAO YU 豆辣乾燒魚

My friend Paul's mother, the daughter of Canadian missionaries, spent her childhood in Sichuan. During the upheavals of early republican China, she and her family made occasional trips back to Canada and had to brave pirates on their way down the Yangtze River to Shanghai. Apparently the joke was that the pirates, lurking in the backwaters, sent spies to watch the passengers on board as they ate, because observing how an individual ate their fish would give them a good idea of the kind of ransom they might fetch. Anyone who preferred the area around the cheeks showed the exquisite taste of the upper classes and was worth kidnapping. Those who favored the delicate flesh near the tail might fetch a good price, while anyone who ate fish indiscrimately might as well be tossed overboard.

What this tells you is what any Chinese person knows, which is that the silky flesh pocketed in a fish's cheeks is the choicest morsel, and the succulent tissue around its lips and eyesockets is also extravagantly delicious. So if you invite Chinese friends for dinner and you'd rather eat the flesh near the backbone, they'll be quietly thrilled.

This recipe uses the favorite Hunanese flavor combination of fermented black beans and chilli.

1 sea bass or trout (1–1¼ lb/ 450–500g), scaled and cleaned, but with head and tail intact
1 tbsp Shaoxing wine
Salt
4–5 tbsp cooking oil
1 tbsp Sichuan chilli bean paste
2 tsp finely chopped garlic
2 tsp finely chopped ginger
1½ tbsp fermented black beans, rinsed and drained
1 tsp chilli flakes
¾ (200ml) chicken stock or water
2 spring onions, green parts only, cut into slivers
¼ red bell pepper, cut into fine slivers
1 tsp sesame oil

Make about four diagonal slashes across each side of the fish, into the thickest part of the flesh. Rub the fish inside and out with the Shaoxing wine and rub a little salt into its belly cavity. Set aside for 10–15 minutes while you prepare the other ingredients.

Pat the fish dry inside and out with paper towels and rub a little salt into its skin. Add 4 tbsp oil to a seasoned wok over a high flame. Then fry the fish in the oil, turning once and tilting the wok to reach the head and tail, until the fish is lightly golden on both sides. Set aside.

Return the wok to the heat with an extra tablespoon of oil, if necessary. Add the chilli bean paste and stir-fry for a few moments until it smells delicious and the oil is reddening. Add the garlic, ginger, black beans and chilli flakes and stir briefly until they also smell wonderful. Then pour in the stock and bring to a boil. Return the fish to the wok and let it simmer in the sauce. Keep tilting the wok and spooning the sauce over the fish. Turn the fish once during the cooking. When the sauce is much reduced and the fish cooked through (poke a chopstick into the thickest part of its flesh, behind the head, to make sure), gently remove it to a serving dish with a spatula or two.

Add the spring onion and red pepper slivers and stir a few times then, off the heat, stir in the sesame oil and scatter the remains of the sauce and seasonings over the fish.

BRAISED TROUT IN CHILLI BEAN SAUCE
DOU BAN YU 豆瓣魚

The first Chinese recipe I ever cooked was a version of this dish from Yan-Kit So's *Classic Chinese Cookbook*. Years later—and having eaten it countless times in the Sichuanese capital Chengdu—it remains one of my favorite fish dishes, and everyone else seems to love it too. The fish lies in a spectacular sauce, a deep rusty red in color, sumptuously spicy and aromatic with ginger and garlic. In Sichuan, they tend to make it with carp. Back home in London, I've made it with sea bass, whole trout and fillets and, more recently, with organic mirror carp. They all taste delicious. (As with many Sichuanese dishes, the soul of the recipe lies in the combination of flavors and you can be flexible about the main ingredient, which is one reason why Sichuanese cuisine travels so well.) I'm particularly happy that the recipe works so well with mirror carp, one of the most sustainable fish and ripe for revival in places such as Britain, where it has long fallen out of favor.

You will probably find that the fish disintegrates slightly during cooking. Don't worry: you can arrange it neatly on the serving plate and pour the sauce over it. And when your guests taste it, if my experiences are anything to go by, they'll be so overcome with rapture that they won't care what it looks like.

1 rainbow trout (about ¾ lb/ 350g), scaled and cleaned, but with head and tail intact
Salt
1 tbsp Shaoxing wine
½ cup (100ml) cooking oil, plus 2–3 tbsp more
2½ tbsp Sichuan chilli bean paste
2 tsp finely chopped ginger
4 tsp finely chopped garlic
¾ cup (200ml) chicken stock
1 tsp light soy sauce, to taste
2 tsp potato flour dissolved in 1½ tbsp cold water
3–4 tbsp finely sliced spring onion greens
1 tsp sesame oil

Make three even, diagonal cuts into the thickest part of each side of the fish, to allow the sauce to penetrate. Rub it inside and out with a little salt, then rub the Shaoxing wine into its belly cavity. Set aside for 10–15 minutes, then drain off any liquid and pat it dry. Rub a little more salt into the skin on both sides (to prevent sticking).

Add the ½ cup (100ml) oil to a seasoned wok over a high flame. When it is hot, slide in the fish and fry on both sides until it is a little golden (it won't be cooked through). You need to turn the fish carefully and tilt it so the oil comes into contact with all the skin. Pour off the oil into a heatproof container and slide the fish on to a plate.

Clean the wok if necessary, then reheat it over a high flame. Add the 2–3 tbsp oil and reduce the heat to medium. Add the chilli bean paste and stir-fry until the oil is red and smells delicious. Add the ginger and garlic and stir-fry until you can smell them. Pour in the stock and bring to a boil. Slide in the fish and cook for five minutes or so, seasoning with soy sauce to taste. Keep spooning the sauce over the fish and tipping the wok so the whole fish is cooked. (If you are using a larger fish, turn it halfway.) Using a wok scoop and fish slice, carefully lift the fish from the sauce and lay it on a serving dish.

Increase the heat, stir the potato flour mixture and add just enough to thicken the sauce to a rich, clingy consistency (do this in stages to avoid over-thickening). Stir in the spring onion, then switch off the heat. Stir in the sesame oil and ladle the sauce over the waiting fish.

VARIATION

Mirror carp in chilli bean sauce
For a 1½–1¾ lb (700–800g) carp, follow the recipe above, but increase the quantities to 2 tbsp Shaoxing wine, 3½ tbsp chilli bean paste, 1 tbsp garlic, 1 tbsp ginger, 1 cup (250ml) stock and 4 tbsp spring onion greens. Cover the wok while simmering so the thicker parts of the fish cook through, raising the lid from time to time to baste with the sauce.

SWEET-AND-SOUR FISH "TILES"
TANG CU WA KUAI YU 糖醋瓦塊魚

The sweet-and-sour sauce made for this dish is dramatically different from the Cantonese version, with its fruity tomato paste sauce. Here, the sauce is made from sugar and Chinkiang vinegar, with the flavors of ginger, garlic and spring onion. In Sichuan, this dish would be made with carp; here I've used whiting instead.

The same sauce can be used to dress deep-fried chicken or tofu.

9 oz (250g) white fish fillet, such as whiting
2 spring onion whites, cut into very fine slivers
Good pinch of very fine slivers of fresh red chilli
2 cups plus 2 tbsp (500ml) cooking oil
1 tbsp finely chopped garlic
1 tbsp finely chopped ginger
2 tbsp finely sliced spring onion greens

For the marinade/batter
2 tsp Shaoxing wine
1/8 tsp salt
1 small egg, beaten
4 tbsp potato flour
1/2 tsp cooking oil

For the sauce
5 tbsp sugar
1/2 tbsp light soy sauce
2 tbsp Chinkiang vinegar
3/4 tsp salt
1 1/4 tsp potato flour
5 tbsp chicken stock or water

Lay the fish, skin-side down, on a board. Holding your knife at an angle to the board, cut the fillet into slices about 1/8 in (1/2cm) thick and place in a bowl. For the marinade, add the Shaoxing wine and salt and mix well. Then mix in the egg and flour to evenly coat. Finally, add the oil. In a separate bowl, mix together all the ingredients for the sauce. Set the spring onion whites and chilli slivers to soak in cold water (this will make them curl up prettily).

Heat the 2 cups plus 2 tbsp (500ml) oil in a seasoned wok over a high flame to about 350°F (180°C). Use chopsticks to drop half the fish slices into the oil, taking care they don't stick together. Deep-fry until lightly golden. Remove from the wok with a slotted spoon and set aside on paper towels to drain. Repeat with the remaining slices. Pile up all the fish slices on a serving dish.

Drain off all but 2 tbsp oil, add the garlic and ginger and stir-fry briefly until they smell wonderful. Give the sauce a stir and pour it into the wok, stirring as it thickens. Add the spring onion greens, mix well and then pour over the waiting fish. Sprinkle with the drained slivered spring onion whites and chilli, and serve.

VARIATIONS

Fish-fragrant fish "tiles"
Pour over a fish-fragrant sauce (see page 138) instead of the sweet-and-sour one here, for a Sichuanese flavor.

Salt-and-pepper fish "tiles"
Instead of a sauce, serve the deep-fried fish with a dip of three parts of salt mixed with one part of ground roasted Sichuan pepper.

SALT-AND-PEPPER SQUID
JIAO YAN YOU YU 椒鹽魷魚

This gorgeous Cantonese preparation can be served as an appetizer or a main course. The fragrant, frilly pieces of squid are embraced by morsels of garlic, chilli and spring onion, with an uplifting sparkle of Sichuan pepper. Incidentally, the "salt-and-pepper" (*jiao yan*), a mixture of one part ground roasted Sichuan pepper and three parts salt, makes a great dip for all kinds of deep-fried and roasted foods, including fish or chicken in batter, roast duck and tofu cubes. (Try it, also, with deep-fried potato chips and roast potatoes.)

2 small squid (1 lb 7 oz/650g uncleaned, 11 oz/300g cleaned)
1 tbsp Shaoxing wine
3 tbsp potato flour
1½ cups plus 2 tbsp (400ml) cooking oil
2 tbsp finely chopped garlic

2 tbsp finely sliced spring onion whites
1–2 tbsp finely sliced fresh red chilli
¼ tsp ground roasted Sichuan pepper, mixed with ¾ tsp salt
2 tbsp finely sliced spring onion greens

Ask your fishmonger to clean the squid, reserving the wings and tentacles as well as the main body. (If you want to do it yourself, gently tug the tentacles, innards and bony blade out of the body. Cut the tentacles away and pull out the beak. Discard the head, innards and beak. Peel the wings from the body of the squid. Peel away and discard the purplish membrane that covers the wings and body. Rinse everything well in cold water.)

Slice open the body of the squid along its length and lay it flat on a board. Then, holding your knife at an angle to the board, score the whole surface in parallel cuts a few millimetres apart. Don't worry if some of your cuts go through to the board: the squid will taste delicious and look appetizing anyway. Then, holding your knife perpendicular to the board, make parallel scores at right angles to the first cuts. You should end up with the whole surface cross-hatched. Do the same with the wings. Then cut the body into bite-sized pieces. Place in a bowl with the wings and tentacles, add the Shaoxing wine and mix well.

Drain the squid as far as possible. Add the flour and mix well. Heat the oil in a wok over a high flame to 350°F (180°C). Add half the squid and deep-fry until lightly golden. Remove with a slotted spoon and drain on paper towels. Repeat with the rest of the squid.

Drain off all but 1 tbsp oil. Add the garlic, spring onion whites and chilli to the wok and stir-fry over a medium heat until they smell wonderful. Increase the heat to high, return the squid with the Sichuan pepper and salt mixture to the wok and stir and toss for a minute. Finally, add the spring onion greens, mix well and serve.

VARIATION

Salt-and-pepper tofu
For a vegetarian version, cut 14 oz (400g) plain white tofu into bite-sized cubes and deep-fry until golden. Toss in fragrant stir-fried garlic, chilli and spring onion whites as above, adding the salt-and-pepper and, finally, the spring onion greens.

CLAMS IN BLACK BEAN SAUCE
CHI ZHI CHAO XIAN 豉汁炒蚬

This Cantonese dish is messy to eat and gorgeously flavored; the home-made black bean sauce is in a different league from the dull bottled versions. Its robust flavors are an equally magnificent match for mussels. Do make sure you don't overcook the clams, or they will become what the Chinese call "old" (tired and leathery).

2 lb 3 oz (1kg) clams, in their shells
3 tbsp cooking oil
2½ tbsp fermented black beans, rinsed and drained
2 tsp finely chopped ginger
1 tbsp finely chopped garlic
1½ fresh red chillies, cut into thin diagonal slices

3 tbsp finely chopped green bell pepper
2 tbsp Shaoxing wine
1 tsp dark soy sauce
1 tsp light soy sauce
Salt (optional)
1 tsp potato flour mixed with 2 tbsp cold water
2 tbsp finely sliced spring onion greens

Rinse the clams thoroughly in cold water. Discard any with broken shells and those that are open and do not close when tapped.

Pour 2 cups 2 tbsp (500ml) water into a lidded saucepan large enough to hold all the clams and bring to a boil. Then add the clams, cover and heat over a high flame for three to four minutes, until all the shells have opened, opening the lid briefly from time to time to stir them. Remove the clams with a slotted spoon and set aside, discarding any that have failed to open. Keep the cooking liquid in the pan.

Heat a seasoned wok over a high flame. Add the oil, followed by the black beans, ginger, garlic, chillies and green pepper, and stir-fry briefly until they all smell wonderful. Pour in ⅔ cup (150ml) of the clams' cooking liquor. Bring to a boil, skim if necessary, then season with the Shaoxing wine and soy sauces and a little salt, if desired.

Give the potato flour mixture a stir and add it to the wok in two or three stages, using just enough to thicken the liquid to the consistency of light cream. Then, off the heat, stir in the clams and spring onion greens and mix everything together. Tip into a dish and serve.

VARIATION

Mussels in black bean sauce
You can cook and serve mussels in exactly the same way: the only difference is that they will take a little longer to open than the clams.

BEANS
& PEAS

Aside from the soy bean, essential as a source of protein and, fermented, as a seasoning, a wide variety of fresh and dried beans are eaten in China, most of them also familiar in the West.

Green, or romano, beans, known as "four-season beans" (*si ji dou*), are magnificent dry-fried the Sichuanese way; fresh peas are brought alive with a tease of chilli and Sichuan pepper; while young soy beans or fava beans—both of them a brilliant emerald green—are delicious steamed or stir-fried. Like the Italians, the people of southern China often cook their beans with a little cured pork for its irresistible umami flavors. And in many provinces, they use pickled or salt-cured vegetables for the same reason, to enhance the delicate savoriness of beans; a perfect marriage, as I hope you'll agree. Some of the healthy, tasty dishes that follow are enough on their own for lunch for one or two people, with just some rice for company and perhaps a dish of stir-fried greens.

Dark red azuki beans, green mung beans and dried yellow peas are the most common legumes. All of them, but especially the former two, are used in sweet pastries and desserts. Split yellow peas, cooked down to a paste, are sold in Sichuanese street markets, to be used as the base of soups like my friend Dai Shuang's. Dried mung beans and soy beans are both sprouted and used as a vegetable; the latter mainly in soups and vegetarian stocks, to which they lend a great savory flavor.

SICHUANESE "DRY-FRIED" GREEN BEANS (VEGETARIAN VERSION)
GAN BIAN SI JI DOU (SU) 乾煸四季豆（素）

A little restaurant near the Music Conservatory in Chengdu used to serve a vegetarian version of Sichuanese dry-fried green beans that was a delicious alternative to the classic dish, which is made with ground pork. They deep-fried their beans, but this is a quick, healthy version in which the beans are blanched rather than cooked in oil. It's incredibly easy to make and wonderfully aromatic; my friend Seema's children are addicted to it and she tells me she cooks it for them on a weekly basis. The preserved vegetable adds a delicious savory kick, but you can omit it if you don't have any in your larder; the beans will be delicious anyway. Leftovers, eaten at room temperature, also taste very good.

Use the same method to cook peas, shelled fava beans, or sliced green or romano beans, adjusting the boiling times accordingly.

¾ lb (350g) green beans
4–6 dried chillies
2 spring onions, white parts only
3 garlic cloves
An equivalent amount of ginger

2 tbsp Sichuanese *ya cai*, snow vegetable or Tianjin preserved vegetable (optional)
Salt
About 3 tbsp cooking oil
½ tsp whole Sichuan pepper
1 tsp sesame oil

Trim the beans and snap them in half.

Snip the chillies in half or into sections with a pair of scissors; shake out and discard as many seeds as possible. Finely slice the spring onion whites. Peel and slice the garlic and ginger. If you are using the Tianjin vegetable, rinse it to get rid of excess salt, then squeeze it dry (the *ya cai* can be used as it comes).

Bring a panful of water to a boil over a high flame. Add salt and a dash of oil to the water. Blanch the beans until tender but not overcooked, then drain thoroughly.

Heat your wok over a high flame. Add 2 tbsp oil, then the chillies and Sichuan pepper; sizzle them briefly until the chillies darken and both spices smell wonderful. Add the spring onion, garlic and ginger and stir-fry for a few moments more until you can smell their fragrances. Add the preserved vegetable, if using, and stir a few times.

Add the blanched beans and stir-fry for a minute or two more, until they are coated in the fragrant oil and chopped seasonings, adding salt to taste. Stir in the sesame oil and serve.

VARIATION

Stir-fried green beans with "olive vegetable"
Yet another take on the blissful theme of beans and preserved vegetables and one of the easiest to make, because the only ingredient that needs chopping is garlic. "Olive vegetable," a dark oily relish made from preserved mustard greens and Chinese "olives" (which are unrelated to the Mediterranean kind), is a speciality of the Cantonese region of Chaozhou. Follow the recipe above, but instead of chillies, Sichuan pepper and the other aromatics, simply stir-fry 2 tsp finely chopped garlic and 4 tbsp "olive vegetable" in 2–3 tbsp oil until fragrant before adding the beans; season with salt to taste.

STIR-FRIED PEAS WITH CHILLI AND SICHUAN PEPPER
QIANG QING WAN DOU 熗青豌豆

On warm, lazy Sichuan evenings, I've often sat with friends at a table under a canopy of wutong trees, drinking beer and picking at a selection of cold dishes, a custom known as *leng dan bei* (loosely translated as "a few cold dishes and a glass of beer"). The titbits on the table might include salted duck eggs, spiced peanuts, cooked meats with a dip of ground chillies, and a selection of stir-fried vegetables: sweet corn with green bell peppers, lotus root, or perhaps this wonderfully easy dish of peas with chilli and Sichuan pepper.

6 dried chillies
9 oz (250g) shelled peas (defrosted frozen peas are fine)

2 tbsp cooking oil
½ tsp whole Sichuan pepper
Salt

Snip the chillies in half with a pair of scissors and discard their seeds as far as possible. If using fresh peas, bring some water to a boil in a saucepan and blanch them for a minute or so. Refresh under the cold tap and drain thoroughly.

Heat a seasoned wok over a high flame. Add the oil, chillies and Sichuan pepper and stir-fry very briefly until you can smell their fragrances and the chillies are darkening but not burned. Then add the peas and stir-fry until hot and fragrant, adding salt to taste. Serve hot or cold.

PEAS WITH DRIED SHRIMP
HUI JIN GOU QING WAN 燴金鈎青丸

The Sichuanese name for this dish translates literally as "golden hooks cooked with green balls" ("golden hooks" is the very apt local word for the little hook-shaped shrimp). The shrimp, ginger and spring onion add a rich savoriness to the peas. Last time I made this dish, I heated up the leftovers with some leftover boiled potatoes, green bok choy and a little extra water for lunch the next day: delicious. You can use the same method to cook shelled fava beans and green soy beans.

2 tbsp dried shrimp
2 spring onions, white
    parts only
1½ oz (25g) piece of ginger,
unpeeled
2 tbsp cooking oil
9 oz (250g) shelled peas
    (defrosted frozen peas are
    fine)

Salt
Ground white pepper
1 tsp potato flour mixed with
    1 tbsp cold water
1 tsp sesame oil

Cover the shrimp in hot water from the kettle and leave to soak for at least 30 minutes before you begin.

Trim the spring onion whites and slightly crush both them and the ginger with the side of a cleaver or a rolling pin. Cut the spring onion whites into a couple of sections.

Heat the oil in a wok over a high flame. Add the spring onions and ginger and stir-fry briefly until they smell wonderful. Add ¾ cup (200ml) water and bring to a boil. Remove the ginger and onion with a slotted spoon and discard. Add the peas and drained shrimp and return to a boil. Add salt and pepper to taste and simmer for two to three minutes, until the peas are hot and have absorbed some of the flavors of the broth.

Give the potato flour mixture a stir and add just enough to the wok to thicken the broth to a lazy, gravy-like consistency. Remove from the heat, stir in the sesame oil and serve.

GREEN OR ROMANO BEANS WITH BLACK BEAN AND CHILLI
JIA CHANG DAO DOU 家常刀豆

Romano beans, or green beans, are known as "knife beans" in China. Sliced and blanched, they are very well suited to the stir-fry treatment, with any of a variety of seasonings. This recipe uses the favorite aromatics of the Hunanese kitchen. Alternatively, stir-fry the blanched beans with a tablespoonful of finely chopped garlic, perhaps with preserved mustard greens or dried chilli, adding salt to taste; or with dried chillies, Sichuan pepper and salt for a Sichuanese flavor.

9 oz (250g) green or romano beans
1 garlic clove
An equivalent amount of ginger
½ fresh red chilli

2 tbsp cooking oil
1 tbsp fermented black beans, rinsed and drained
1–2 tsp ground chillies, to taste
1 tsp light soy sauce
Salt

Trim the beans and cut evenly, on the diagonal, into thin slices (use a green bean cutter if you have one). Peel and slice the garlic and ginger. Cut the chilli, on the diagonal, into thin slices.

Bring a panful of water to a boil and boil the beans for two to three minutes, until just tender. Drain and shake dry.

Add the oil to a seasoned wok over a high flame. Add the garlic, ginger and fresh chilli and stir-fry briefly until fragrant. Add the black beans and ground chillies and, again, stir-fry briefly until fragrant. Add the green beans and continue to stir-fry until hot and sizzlingly delicious, adding the soy sauce, and salt to taste. Serve.

SNOW PEAS WITH CHINESE WIND-DRIED SAUSAGE XIANG CHANG CHAO HE LAN DOU 香腸炒荷蘭豆

Chinese wind-dried sausages are made in a similar way to salamis, by stuffing pork seasoned with soy sauce, sugar, rice wine and other flavorings into lengths of pig's intestine, tying the intestines at sausage-sized intervals, then hanging them up to wind-dry. Although they are sometimes served steamed and sliced as an appetizer, they are more commonly chopped into small pieces and used to enhance the umami taste of other ingredients, such as steamed chicken, or an "eight-treasure" rice stuffing.

In this recipe, they add a rich flavor to snow peas in a swift stir-fry that, served with rice, is enough for a modest meal for two. If you don't have Chinese sausage, you might try using chorizo or an Italian salami instead.

2 Chinese wind-dried sausages
7 oz (200g) snow peas
Salt
1 tbsp cooking oil

A few slices of peeled ginger
Good pinch of sugar
1 tbsp Shaoxing wine

Cut the sausages at an angle into very thin oval slices.

Blanch the snow peas for a few seconds in lightly salted boiling water, then refresh under the cold tap and drain thoroughly.

Heat a seasoned wok over a high flame. Pour in the oil, swirl it around, then add the sliced sausage and ginger and stir-fry until cooked through and fragrant.

Add the snow peas, 1 tbsp water, the sugar, Shaoxing wine and salt to taste, and stir-fry briefly to reheat the snow peas and fuse the flavors. Serve.

HANGZHOU FAVA BEANS WITH HAM
HUO TUI CAN DOU 火腿蠶豆

This beautiful, bright dish is traditionally eaten in Hangzhou around the Beginning of Summer (*li xia*), the seventh solar term of the old agricultural calendar. The date usually falls in early May, when the beans are most tender. It is traditionally made with intense, dark cured ham from nearby Jinhua, but Spanish ham makes a fine substitute (this is a perfect use for the odds and ends left behind after most of the meat has been sliced from a leg of ham).

I know fava beans take time to shell and peel, but for me they are one of the gastronomic highlights of early summer. I like to shell them in the sun on the doorstep, listening to the radio or, if I can, to enlist the help of a guest or a child (I used to love doing this when I was small).

You can use the same method to cook fresh peas, but cut the ham into smaller squares to match the peas. If you wish, add a few square slices of blanched bamboo shoot to make it even more colorful. In China, they steam the ham through before they slice it: this dispels any harsh aspects of its flavor and also fixes its shape, which makes for neater cutting and a more professional appearance. When using Spanish ham that is normally eaten raw, I omit this step.

11 oz (300g) shelled fava beans (just over 2 lb 3 oz/1kg in the pod)
2 oz (50g) Chinese or Spanish cured ham
2 tbsp cooking oil
⅓ cup (75ml) chicken stock or water
¼ tsp sugar
Salt
½ tsp potato flour mixed with 2 tsp cold water (optional)

Boil the beans for three to four minutes in boiling water, then refresh under the cold tap. Unless the beans are very young and tender, pop them out of their skins. (If you wish to take the classic Chinese approach, steam the ham to cook it through at this stage.)

Cut the ham into thin slices, then into ⅜ in (1cm) squares.

Heat a seasoned wok over a medium flame. Add the oil, then the beans and ham and stir-fry for a minute or two until piping hot. Add the stock, sugar and salt to taste and bring to a boil. Reduce the heat and simmer for a minute or so. Stir the potato flour mixture, if using, and use it to thicken the sauce. Serve.

VARIATION

Steamed fava beans with ham

Another spring recipe from Hangzhou that is a cinch to make and pretty, too, with the slices of dark crimson ham laid out over the brilliant beans. It's one that I associate with the Dragon Well Manor restaurant, where I've spent so many happy spring days.

Take 7 oz (200g) shelled fava beans (about 1½ lb/750g in the pod). If they are very young and tender, simply remove what the Chinese call their "eyebrows," the part that connects each bean to the pod; otherwise, peel them completely. Place in a bowl with 1 tbsp Shaoxing wine, 3 tbsp stock and salt to taste. Then lay prettily on top a few thickish, bite-sized pieces of good Chinese or Spanish ham. Place the bowl in a steamer and steam over high heat for about 10 minutes, until the beans are tender, then serve in the bowl, giving the beans a stir before diving in. The ham lends its rich, savory flavors to the juices.

Traditionally, in Zhejiang homes, the bowl of beans is actually laid on top of the rice in the steamer, to allow them to steam together: an economical, old-fashioned method still used in the countryside. If you find peeling fava beans too tiresome, you can use the same method to cook peas or crisp, fresh green soy beans. In Hangzhou, they also cook fresh spring bamboo shoots, sliced thinly, this way.

MASHED FAVA BEANS WITH "SNOW VEGETABLE"
DOU BAN SU 豆瓣酥

This wonderful recipe was explained to me by a lady I met in a Shanghai street market. She told me to use *xue cai* or "snow vegetable," which is a favorite preserve in the Southern Yangtze region, but you could use instead *zha cai* (Sichuanese preserved mustard tuber) or *ya cai* (Sichuanese preserved mustard greens). The preserves turn the mashed beans into something deliciously savory. Some Shanghainese people add less liquid, press the cooked beans into a rice bowl and turn them out on to the serving dish, for a more elegant effect.

Salt
11 oz (300g) shelled fava beans (just over 2 lb 3 oz/1kg in the pod)
3 tbsp cooking oil or lard

3 tbsp finely chopped snow vegetable
1 tbsp finely sliced spring onion greens

Bring a panful of water to a boil. Salt lightly, add the beans and boil for about five minutes, until tender. Plunge into cold water or rinse under a cold tap to cool them quickly. Then pop the beans out of their skins (if they are very small and tender, you can leave the skins on if you don't mind a chunkier mash). Mash the beans coarsely, using either a potato masher in a pan or a cleaver on a chopping board. Boil a little water in a kettle and have it on hand.

Heat a seasoned wok over a medium flame. Add the oil or lard, then the snow vegetable, and stir-fry briefly until fragrant. Add the mashed beans and continue to stir-fry until piping hot, adding enough water from the kettle for a good thick purée, with salt to taste. Finally, add the spring onions, stir a few more times and serve.

VARIATION

Mashed fava beans with cured ham
Simply substitute 1 oz (30g) Spanish or Chinese cured ham, finely chopped, for the snow vegetable. A dish like this thrilled me at the Southern Barbarian restaurant in Shanghai, which is run by artist Feng Jianwen, the husband of an old friend of mine. There, they use the famous cured ham of Yunnan Province (*yun tui*), which vies with Jinhua ham from Zhejiang Province for the position of top Chinese ham, and is prized by chefs all over the country as a flavor-enhancing ingredient. Something marvellous and alchemic occurs in the wok with this dish, the ham serving to intensify the umami flavors of the beans.

FAVA BEANS WITH PRESERVED MUSTARD GREENS
YA CAI CHAO CAN DOU 芽菜炒蠶豆

This is another variation on the theme of beans with preserved vegetables and blissfully easy to make. You can use the same method to cook peas, thinly sliced green or romano beans or green soy beans. I've suggested using Sichuanese *ya cai*, but you could equally well choose Tianjin winter vegetable, or Sichuanese preserved mustard tuber (*zha cai*). If you want, stir-fry a little ground pork in the wok before adding the garlic, to intensify the savory tastes.

11 oz (300g) shelled fava beans (just over 2 lb 3 oz/1kg in the pod)
Salt
3 tbsp cooking oil

1 tsp finely chopped garlic
3 tbsp finely chopped *ya cai* or other Chinese preserved vegetable

Boil the fava beans for three to four minutes in lightly salted water, then refresh under the cold tap. If the beans are young and tender, there is no need to skin them; if their skins are becoming tough, remove them now.

Heat a seasoned wok over a high flame. Add the oil, then the garlic and sizzle for a few seconds, before adding the preserved vegetable. Stir-fry briefly together until they smell delicious (take care not to burn the garlic). Add the beans and stir-fry until everything is hot and fragrant, seasoning with salt to taste. Serve.

VARIATIONS

Fava beans with spring onion
Boil, refresh and drain the beans as in the recipe above. Then stir-fry them with four or five spring onions, finely sliced, a pinch of sugar and salt to taste. It's best to add the spring onion whites at the beginning and the greens just before the wok comes off the heat.

Fava beans with spring onion, Sichuan-style
Use the method for fava beans with spring onion just above, but omit the sugar and sprinkle the finished dish with a little ground roasted Sichuan pepper or Sichuan pepper oil.

STIR-FRIED GREEN SOY BEANS WITH SNOW VEGETABLE
XUE CAI MAO DOU 雪菜毛豆

Young green soy beans, commonly known as edamame, are one of my favorite vegetables, small and exquisite, their color a sweet pea green that brightens up any supper table. You may serve them boiled, in their fuzzy pods, for the pleasure of popping them out and nibbling them with a glass of beer. Otherwise, they can be steamed or stir-fried, or used in colorful "eight treasure" stuffings. I've even had them, dried but still bright green, in mugs of salty green tea in rural Zhejiang Province!

The following dish is one that I enjoyed on a September noon in the Zhejiang hills, when my friend A Dai took me to visit an organic chicken farm. We explored the farm, where healthy-looking chickens pecked around a slope stocked with bamboo, persimmon, camphor and loquat trees, then walked down to the farmhouse for lunch. This recipe, made with "snow vegetable," one of the favorite local preserves, was on the table that day and I've never forgotten it. You can add more or less snow vegetable as you please and you might like to pep it up with a little chilli and Sichuan pepper, to give it a Sichuanese twist. Either version is great served either hot or cold. The same method can be used to cook peas or fava beans.

Salt
9 oz (250g) fresh or defrosted frozen green soy beans (shelled weight)
2 tbsp cooking oil
5 dried chillies (optional)

½ tsp whole Sichuan pepper (optional)
2 oz (50g) snow vegetable, finely chopped
½ tsp sesame oil

If using fresh soy beans, bring a panful of water to a boil, add salt, then the beans. Return to a boil, then cook for about five minutes, until tender. Drain well. (Frozen soy beans are already cooked.)

Heat a seasoned wok over a high flame. Add the oil and swirl it around. If using the spices, add them now and sizzle them very briefly until you can smell their fragrances and the chillies are darkening but not burned. Then add the snow vegetable and stir-fry briefly until fragrant.

Add the beans and stir-fry briefly until everything is hot and delicious, seasoning with salt to taste. Remove from the heat, stir in the sesame oil and serve.

VARIATION

Stir-fried green soy beans
Take 9 oz (250g) fresh or defrosted frozen green soy beans (shelled weight). If they are fresh, boil them as described in the main recipe, then drain. Cut a strip of red bell pepper into small squares about the size of the soy beans. Add 2 tbsp oil to a wok over a high flame. Add the beans and pepper squares and stir-fry until hot, seasoning with salt to taste. Remove from the heat, stir in 1 tsp sesame oil and serve.

STIR-FRIED BEANSPROUTS WITH CHINESE CHIVES
JIU CAI YIN YA 韭菜銀芽

In China, mung beans and soy beans are both commonly sprouted. The thicker, coarser soy bean sprouts tend to be used in soups, while mung bean sprouts, which are those you find in Western supermarkets, are usually stir-fried, as here. They are known in Chinese, rather poetically, as "silver sprouts."

4¼ oz (125g) Chinese chives
4 oz (100g) beansprouts
2 tbsp cooking oil
A few fine slivers of red bell pepper, for color (optional)

Salt
1 tsp Chinkiang vinegar

Trim the chives, discarding any wilted leaves, and cut them into sections to match the beansprouts. Keep the white ends and the green leaves separate.

Bring a panful of water to a boil. Add the beansprouts and blanch them for about 30 seconds to "break their rawness." Drain well.

Heat a seasoned wok over a high flame. Add the oil and swirl it around. Add the chive whites with the red pepper, if using, and stir-fry briefly until fragrant. Add the chive leaves and stir a few more times. Add the beansprouts and stir-fry until everything is hot and fragrant, seasoning with salt to taste. Stir in the vinegar and serve.

VARIATION

Beansprouts with chilli and Sichuan pepper
Blanch the beansprouts as in the recipe above. Then heat oil in a wok, add some halved, deseeded Sichuanese dried chillies and Sichuan pepper and stir-fry until fragrant before adding the beansprouts. Season with salt to taste.

LEAFY
GREENS

Leafy greens are one of the great unsung joys of Chinese eating. Often mentioned only as an afterthought on restaurant menus (usually as "seasonal vegetable"), they are a vital and essential part of the Chinese diet and no supper table is complete without them. There are varieties for almost every season and every region, from the commonest spinach, bok choy and Chinese leaf cabbage, to more exotic specialities such as garland chrysanthemum, wolfberry and purslane leaves. Many of these vegetables are very local, such as the exquisite green and purple rape shoots of Hunan, as subtly pleasing as asparagus, or the tender young alfalfa sprouts and Indian aster leaves adored by the Shanghainese. Often, such greens will simply be stir-fried with a little salt and perhaps ginger or garlic, but they may also be blanched and served cold as a salad, or boiled, braised or steamed.

And when it comes to Chinese-style greens, you can forget the idea that you will eat them only out of duty. Many Chinese recipes for such vegetables are so delicious that for me they are often the highlight of the meal. Chinese or any other kind of cabbage cooked with a handful of dried shrimp is so tasty that it's almost a meal in itself, with a little steamed rice. Something amazing seems to happen in the wok when you cook spinach with ginger and garlic: an everyday vegetable transformed into an irresistible delicacy. Just taste it. And cooking doesn't get much easier than Blanched Choy Sum with Sizzling Oil, but I defy anyone to find a tastier way of serving this everyday

vegetable. (The same method works well for a host of other greens, including non-Chinese varieties.)

Many of these recipes use vegetables that are easily available in markets and supermarkets in the West; others can be found in the fresh produce sections of typical Chinese supermarkets. You'll also find mention of some more unusual varieties that can only occasionally be found in Chinese shops, but are well worth hunting down. And I've also included a few cooking suggestions for vegetable varieties that are rarely found in China, but lend themselves well to Chinese ways of cooking, such as Brussels sprouts and purple-sprouting broccoli. I hope you'll come to regard many of these recipes as basic cooking strategies that can be applied to whatever you find in your kitchen, or have growing in your garden or allotment.

In the long run, I do hope that a wider variety of Chinese leafy greens will become available to people living in the West and will be cultivated locally. Many are easy to grow and particularly nutritious. Supermarkets already stock bok choy and choy sum: why not young rape shoots, purple amaranth and Chinese broccoli?

Tips for stir-frying leafy greens

The wok-seared juiciness of leafy greens stir-fried in the volcanic heat of a professional wok stove is impossible to achieve on a domestic burner, but there are a few ways to make the most of stir-frying your greens at home.

– Most importantly, do not overload your wok: in general, I advise stir-frying no more than 11–12 oz (300–350g) raw greens in one go. Any more than this and you'll find it hard to achieve sufficient heat.

– Before stir-frying raw greens, dry them as far as possible. (You can use a lettuce spinner.)

– Blanch bulky greens or those with thick stems before stir-frying to "break their rawness." This will shrink them to a manageable volume and ensure that thick-stemmed greens are tender. You don't need a lot of water, just enough to immerse the vegetables.

– Always stir-fry in a preheated wok, over the hottest possible flame.

– Season with salt towards the end of the cooking time and stir swiftly to incorporate; if you add salt too early, it will draw water out of the vegetables and they will be less juicy and wok-fragrant.

BLANCHED CHOY SUM WITH SIZZLING OIL
YOU LIN CAI XIN 油淋菜心

This dish of bright, fresh greens in a radiantly delicious dressing uses a common Cantonese flavoring method in which cooked ingredients are scattered with slivered ginger and spring onions, followed by a libation of hot, sizzling oil and a sousing of soy sauce. The hot oil awakens the fragrances of the ginger and onion slivers and the soy sauce gives the vegetables an umami richness. It's one of the quickest and easiest dishes in this book and I can never quite believe how wonderful it tastes.

The same method can be used with many kinds of vegetables, including spinach, lettuce, bok choy, broccoli, Chinese broccoli and purple-sprouting broccoli. Just adjust the blanching time according to your ingredients: you want them to be tender, but still fresh-tasting and a little crisp. At the Wei Zhuang restaurant in Hangzhou, I once had a beautiful starter in which four ingredients—water chestnuts, romaine-type lettuce hearts, peeled strips of cucumber and bundles of beansprouts—had been separately blanched, then bathed like this in hot oil and soy sauce.

11 oz (300g) choy sum
2 spring onions
½ oz (10g) piece of ginger
A small strip of red chilli or red bell pepper for color (optional)

1 tsp salt
4 tbsp cooking oil
2 tbsp light soy sauce diluted with 2 tbsp hot water from the kettle

Bring a panful of water to a boil.

Wash and trim the choy sum. Trim the spring onions and cut them lengthways into very fine slivers. Peel the ginger and cut it, too, into very fine slivers. Cut a few very fine slivers of the chilli or bell pepper, if using.

Add the salt and 1 tbsp of the oil to the water, add the choy sum and blanch for a minute or so until it has just lost its rawness (the stems should still be a little crisp). Drain and shake dry in a colander.

Pile the choy sum neatly on a serving dish and pile the spring onion, ginger and chilli or pepper slivers on top.

Heat the remaining oil over a high flame. When the oil is hot, ladle it carefully over the spring onions, ginger and chilli. It should sizzle dramatically. (To make sure the oil is hot enough, try ladling a few drops on first, to check for the sizzle. As soon as you get a vigorous sizzle, pour over the rest of the oil.)

Pour the diluted soy sauce mixture over the greens and serve.

VARIATION

Purple-sprouting broccoli with sizzling oil
Purple-sprouting broccoli is not a Chinese vegetable, but it tastes spectacular when given the sizzling oil treatment. Blanch 11 oz (300g) broccoli as above, but add a few slices of peeled ginger and a couple of pinches of sugar to the salt and oil in the blanching water. Lay the drained broccoli on a plate and finish with 3 tbsp sizzling-hot oil and 2 tbsp diluted soy sauce, as in the main recipe.

SPINACH WITH CHILLI AND FERMENTED TOFU JIAO SI FU RU CHAO BO CAI 椒絲腐乳炒菠菜

Fermented tofu may be an unfamiliar ingredient, but don't be deterred: almost everyone adores this dish. The tofu, strong, salty and cheesy on its own, melts away into the spinach juices, giving the leaves an irresistible savory gleam and a slightly silken texture. In the Cantonese south of China, this dish is usually made with water spinach, which has crisp juicy stems and long green leaves, but it also works well with regular spinach. Most Cantonese chefs in the West know how to make it, but for some unknown reason they don't tend to put it on English-language menus. I've suggested using the kind of bunched spinach sold in farmers' markets and Chinese or Middle Eastern shops, but you can use the same method to cook baby spinach leaves. (Though I much prefer bunched spinach as it has more body and doesn't shrink quite so much.)

Blanching the leaves before you stir-fry quickly reduces them to a manageable bulk, which makes stir-frying swifter and more even; it's the method I use increasingly at home.

11½ oz (325g) bunched spinach
½ fresh chilli (to taste)
2 cubes of white fermented tofu
¼ tsp sugar
3 tbsp cooking oil
2 tsp finely chopped garlic
Salt (optional)

Wash and trim the spinach and cut the long, leafy stems into thirds. Finely slice the chilli. Mash the tofu with the sugar and some of the juices from the jar to give a liquid the consistency of heavy cream.

Bring a panful of water to a boil and dunk the spinach in it to wilt the leaves. Drain and shake dry.

Pour the oil into a hot, seasoned wok over a high flame and immediately add the garlic and chilli. Stir a couple of times until you can just smell their fragrance, then add the fermented tofu mixture. As soon as the liquid has boiled, add the blanched spinach and stir-fry briskly. When the sauce is incorporated and everything is hot and fragrant, tip the spinach on to a plate and serve. You can add a little salt, but you probably won't need it because of the tofu.

VARIATIONS

Water spinach with fermented tofu
The classic Cantonese version of this dish is made with water spinach rather than regular spinach. Just cut the washed water spinach into chopstickable lengths and follow the recipe above. The taste and texture of this variation are really wonderful.

Spinach with red fermented tofu and ginger
Chefs in eastern China prefer red fermented tofu and ginger to the white fermented tofu, chilli and garlic of the Cantonese version. The method is the same, but the dish has a very different flavor and the juices are prettily pink.

Simple stir-fried spinach
The simplest Chinese stir-fry is a *qing chao*, which literally means an unmixed or "clear" stir-fry and usually involves stir-frying a single ingredient with only salt as a seasoning. A *qing chao* spinach may be an understated kind of dish, but it's a delightful counterpart to rich or spicy foods. Simply blanch the same amount of spinach as in the main recipe, then stir-fry in 3 tbsp oil in a hot wok, adding salt towards the end. This method can be used for beansprouts, pea shoots, snow peas, choy sum, bok choy and Chinese water spinach, or more unusual varieties such as purslane, radish tops and shepherd's purse.

STIR-FRIED GREENS WITH DRIED SHRIMP
BAO XIN CAI CHAO XIA PI 包心菜炒蝦皮

In this dish—which I learned in the kitchen of the Starfish Harbor Restaurant in the eastern city of Ningbo, thanks to the kindness of chef-patron Cui Guangming—crisp-fried dried shrimp lend their marvellous umami taste to the greens and transform them into something extraordinary. It's one of the reasons why I always keep a bag of dried shrimp in the fridge. I've come across variations on the same theme in Beijing and other places.

In Ningbo, the dish was made with *bao xin cai*, a round white cabbage, but I've used the same method in England with Savoy cabbage, choy sum, bok choy, sliced Brussels sprouts and Chinese cabbage, to delicious effect: just make sure you slice them very thinly. I first cooked this particular version in London as part of a nearly vegetarian lunch for a friend. Apart from the greens, we had Pock-marked Old Woman's Tofu (see page 76), Fava Beans with Preserved Mustard Greens (see page 161), brown rice and, as a soup, the rice's cooking water (*mi tang*), followed by fruit and Longjing tea.

You can use the larger dried shrimp if you like, but soak them in hot water for about 30 minutes before cooking.

14 oz (400g) spring greens, or cabbage of your choice
4 spring onions, green parts only
4 tbsp cooking oil or lard

6 tbsp thin dried shrimp (*xia pi*)
2 tbsp light soy sauce
Salt

Discard any fibrous outer leaves and cut out and discard the thick stem of the greens. Shred the leaves. Cut the spring onion greens into thin slices.

Add 3 tbsp of the oil or lard to a seasoned wok over a high flame and swirl it around. Add the shrimp and stir-fry until crisp and fragrant. Remove the shrimp from the wok and set aside.

Return the wok to the stove with the remainder of the oil or lard, add the greens and stir-fry over a high flame until hot, barely cooked and still a little crisp. Return the shrimp, adding the soy sauce and salt to taste (you may not need any salt because of the saltiness of the shrimp and soy). Finally add the spring onions, stir a couple of times, then turn on to a dish and serve.

STIR-FRIED BROCCOLI WITH CHILLI AND SICHUAN PEPPER
QIANG XI NAN HUA CAI 熗西南花菜

The familiar Italian broccoli or calabrese (known in China as *xi nan hua cai*, "flower vegetable from the south west") is a relatively recent import to China, but the Chinese have taken to it with gusto. It is often used as a bright garnish for banquet dishes, and for appetizers or vegetable side dishes. In this Sichuanese recipe, scorched chillies and Sichuan pepper give an everyday vegetable an exciting zing, and the green florets look lovely, too, with their scattering of deep red chilli and pepper. For more formal occasions only the florets are used, but the flesh inside the thick stalks has a wonderful flavor, so for home cooking I recommend peeling them, slicing the jade-like flesh and adding it to the stir-fry. The same dish can also be served cold, as an appetizer, in which case it is usually offered in a much smaller portion.

The same method of stir-frying with chilli and Sichuan pepper, which is known in Sichuan as *qiang*, can be used for many different vegetables, including beansprouts, water spinach, Chinese cabbage, slivered potatoes, and even Brussels sprouts (less fleshy vegetables, or those that are finely cut, do not have to be blanched).

Take care not to blanch the broccoli for too long, or the florets will disintegrate when you stir-fry them.

11 oz (300g) broccoli
5–6 dried chillies, to taste
Salt

4 tbsp cooking oil
½ tsp whole Sichuan pepper
1 tsp sesame oil

Cut the broccoli into florets, and cut larger florets lengthways into smaller pieces. Peel the stalk and slice thickly. Snip the chillies into halves or sections and discard the seeds as far as possible.

Bring a generous 2½ quarts (2½ liters) of water to a boil, add 1 tsp salt and 1 tbsp oil. Add the broccoli and blanch for two to three minutes; it should remain bright and crisp. Drain in a colander.

Add the remaining oil with the chillies and Sichuan pepper to a seasoned wok over a high flame, and stir-fry briefly until the chillies are just beginning to brown (take care not to burn them). Add the broccoli and stir-fry for 30 seconds or so until the florets are coated in the fragrant oil, seasoning with salt to taste. Turn off the heat, stir in the sesame oil, and serve.

VARIATION

Stir-fried broccoli with garlic
Simply substitute two or three garlic cloves, peeled and sliced or finely chopped, for the chillies and pepper, and omit the sesame oil. Fry the garlic very briefly before adding the broccoli: you just want to smell its fragrance, not to brown it.

BABY BOK CHOY IN SUPERIOR STOCK
SHANG TANG BAI CAI MIAO 上湯白菜苗

In recent years I've become completely addicted to this Cantonese way of serving fresh green vegetables. The greens are first blanched, then served in a rich stock, conventionally a *shang tang* or "superior stock" made with chicken, pork bones and ham. In restaurants, the basic dish is often embellished with a scattering of other ingredients, such as chopped salted and preserved duck eggs, mushrooms and chopped shrimp (see variation, right), but at home I like to serve the simpler version, which is a wonderful complement to dryer or more boldly seasoned dishes. You can use this method to cook all kinds of vegetables, including green bok choy, pea shoots, asparagus, Chinese cabbage and fresh mustard greens. I've also used it for spring greens and purple-sprouting broccoli. (If you are using bulkier vegetables, cut them into bite-sized pieces before you begin: bok choy can be quartered lengthways.) This recipe is a great way of using up leftover stock, especially when you don't have enough to make a soup.

Serve the greens in a bowl or a deep serving dish. Encourage your guests to eat the vegetables with their chopsticks, then spoon any leftover stock into their bowls as a soup.

11 oz (300g) baby bok choy or other greens of your choice
1³/₄ cups (450ml) stock, the richer the better (see headnote)
Salt
1 tbsp cooking oil
Ground white pepper

Trim the baby bok choy if necessary. Bring a panful of water to a boil. Heat the stock in a small pan.

Add 1 tsp salt and the oil to the boiling water. Add the bok choy and blanch briefly until barely cooked. Drain and set aside.

Season the stock to taste with salt and pepper. Add the bok choy and return to a boil. Use a slotted spoon to transfer the vegetables to your serving dish or bowl. Pour the stock over the vegetables and serve.

VARIATION

Baby bok choy in superior stock, restaurant style
Blanch the bok choy as in the main recipe and lay it in your serving bowl. Heat 1–2 tbsp oil in a seasoned wok over a high flame. Add any or all of the following: 1 hard-boiled salted duck egg, cut into segments or chopped coarsely; 1 preserved duck egg, cut into segments or chopped coarsely; a few raw large shrimp, chopped coarsely; a couple of mushrooms, sliced or coarsely chopped. Stir-fry briefly, then add the hot stock, return to a boil and season with salt and pepper to taste. Ladle the stock and other ingredients over your waiting vegetables and serve.

STIR-FRIED CHOY SUM
WITH GINGER AND GARLIC
CHAO CAI XIN 家常炒菜心

Choy sum, with its slender, juicy stalks, is easy to stir-fry without a preliminary blanching: all you really need to do in the wok is heat the stalks through and wilt the leaves. This simple method is typical of home cooking in southern China. You can use the same method to cook spinach, or other greens of your choice, blanching them first if you wish.

10 oz (275g) choy sum
2 tbsp cooking oil
2 garlic cloves, peeled
    and sliced

$\frac{1}{3}$ oz (10g) ginger, peeled and sliced
$\frac{1}{4}$ tsp sugar
Salt

Wash the choy sum, then cut into chopstickable sections about 2½ in (6cm) long, keeping the stalks and the leafy parts separate.

Heat a seasoned wok over a high flame. Add the oil, then the garlic and ginger. Stir-fry briefly until you can smell their aromas. Tip the choy sum stalks into the wok and stir-fry until they are hot. Then add the leaves and continue to stir-fry until the stems are tender and the leaves wilted.

Finally, add a tablespoonful of water with the sugar, and salt to taste, stir a few times and serve.

STIR-FRIED CHOPPED CHOY SUM
BO BO CAI XIN 鉢鉢菜心

This is one of those deceptively simple Chinese dishes, and an illustration of the way that a minor variation in cooking method can bring out an entirely different side to the same stir-fried ingredient. Here, the choy sum is blanched, fine-chopped and dry-fried before any seasonings are added; in the finished dish, the leaves are sleek and juicy and wonderfully enlivened by the garlic, ginger and chilli. It's the kind of dish you might find served in a rough clay bowl, in a restaurant specializing in rustic cooking, which is why its Chinese name, *bo bo cai xin*, means "clay bowl choy sum."

You can add a little ground pork or chicken to intensify the flavor if you wish: just follow the first two paragraphs of the recipe, then sizzle the meat in the wok until it has changed color and separated before adding the garlic and ginger.

Salt
1 ½ tbsp cooking oil, plus more for blanching and for seasoning the wok
13 oz (375g) choy sum
1 tbsp finely chopped fresh red chilli
1 tsp finely chopped ginger
1 tsp finely chopped garlic
½ tsp sesame oil
1–2 tbsp chilli oil (optional)

Bring a large panful of water to a boil. Add some salt and a small dash of cooking oil. Add the choy sum and blanch for about 30 seconds to wilt the leaves. Refresh immediately under the cold tap and squeeze out as much water as possible. Chop the choy sum finely and evenly.

Heat a dry wok over a high flame. Add the chopped choy sum and stir it to release any excess water as steam. As the choy sum loses its water, add the chilli and a good pinch of salt. Continue to stir until the surface of the wok is no longer moist and the steam is rising more slowly, then remove the choy sum from the wok and set aside.

Use a thick wad of paper towels to rub the surface of the wok with cooking oil and heat over a high flame to re-season. Then pour in the 1 ½ tbsp cooking oil, swirl it around, then add the ginger and garlic and stir-fry briefly until you can smell their fragrances.

Add the choy sum and stir-fry to incorporate, seasoning with salt to taste. When everything is hot and smells wonderful, remove from the heat, stir in the sesame oil and the chilli oil, if using, and serve.

BOK CHOY WITH FRESH SHIITAKE
XIANG GU XIAO BAI CAI 香菇小白菜

Shiitake mushrooms, commonly known in Chinese as "fragrant mushrooms," have a rich, savory flavor that can enhance the taste of other foods, such as the fresh bok choy in this recipe. For an even more intense flavor, use dried shiitake mushrooms, which should be soaked in hot water for 30 minutes to soften. Rinse them, cover with fresh water, bring to a boil and simmer for at least 20 minutes with a dash of Shaoxing wine, some crushed ginger and spring onion and salt to taste. Leave them to steep in the liquid until you want them.

11 oz (300g) bok choy
6 fresh shiitake mushrooms
¼ tsp sugar
½ tsp potato flour mixed with
   1 tbsp water

Salt
3½ tbsp cooking oil
3 garlic cloves, sliced
An equivalent amount of
   ginger, peeled and sliced

Wash the bok choy, then cut each head lengthways into quarters. Slice off and discard the mushroom stalks and halve the caps. Combine the sugar with the potato flour mixture.

Bring some water to a boil in a saucepan (1 quart/1 liter will do), add ½ tsp salt and ½ tbsp oil, then blanch the bok choy and mushrooms briefly, just until the bok choy leaves have wilted. Drain and shake dry.

Add the remaining 3 tbsp of oil to a seasoned wok over a high flame, swirl it around, then add the garlic and ginger and stir a few times until you can smell their fragrances. Add the blanched mushrooms and bok choy and stir a few times. Finally, add the potato flour mixture with salt to taste, give everything a good stir and serve.

VARIATIONS

The same method can be used to cook all kinds of greens, including choy sum (cut into chopstickable sections), baby bok choy, Shanghai green bok choy, or Chinese leaf cabbage (cut into thick slices).

CHINESE BROCCOLI IN GINGER SAUCE
JIANG ZHI JIE LAN 薑汁芥藍

Chinese broccoli is more like the variety sold in our supermarkets as "brocolini" than the familiar, floreted broccoli or calabrese. It has long, deep green stems, dark leaves and scanty green flower buds. Its flavor has a delicate hint of bitterness and it is particularly good blanched and stir-fried with ginger, as here. I learned this method in the kitchen of the late, great cookbook writer Yan-kit So, at a dinner party where she served it with a sumptuous steamed turbot scattered with preserved winter greens. When I make it, I always think of her.

If you are cooking quite a few dishes, this recipe is a blessing because the broccoli can be blanched an hour or more ahead of time: just make sure you undercook it in this case, so it won't be overdone by the time it's finally heated through for serving. In Cantonese restaurants, they usually thicken the juices with potato flour at the end of the cooking, so they cling to the broccoli stems like a sauce, but if you are not aiming for a professional finish, there is no need to do this at home.

³/₄ lb (350g) Chinese broccoli
Salt
4 tbsp cooking oil
2 tbsp finely chopped ginger

1 tbsp Shaoxing wine
½ tsp sugar
1 tsp potato flour mixed with
    1 tbsp cold water (optional)

Bring a large panful of water to a boil (a generous 2½ quarts/2½ liters will do).

Wash and trim the Chinese broccoli. If the lower parts of the stems are thick and fibrous, peel away their outer skin with a potato peeler.

When the water is boiling, add 1 tbsp salt and 1 tbsp oil, then the Chinese broccoli. Blanch it for a minute or two to "break its rawness." The stems should be just tender, but still crisp. If you are stir-frying them immediately, simply drain the broccoli stems and shake dry in a colander; if you want to serve them later, refresh the stems under a cold tap to arrest cooking before draining well.

When you wish to serve the broccoli, add the remaining oil to a seasoned wok over a high flame, swirl it around, then add the ginger and sizzle briefly until you can smell its fragrance. Splash in the Shaoxing wine and add the sugar. Add the broccoli and stir-fry, adding salt to taste, until it is piping hot. (If you are using broccoli blanched earlier, then cooled, you will need to pour 2–3 tbsp water or stock into the wok and cover it, so the stems reheat thoroughly.)

Remove the stems from the wok and lay them neatly on a serving dish. If you wish to thicken the juices, give the potato flour mixture a stir and add just enough, in stages, to thicken the sauce to a clingy consistency; then pour the sauce over the broccoli and serve. If you do not wish to thicken the juices, simply pour them and the ginger over the broccoli.

CHINESE CABBAGE WITH VINEGAR
CU LIU BAI CAI 醋溜白菜

Chinese cabbage has a mild flavor, with just a hint of mustardy sharpness and, after cooking, a delightfully juicy texture. The following is a Sichuanese version of a simple but satisfying supper dish that is made in many parts of China, in which brown rice vinegar lends its mellow fragrance to the greens. The vinegar is added at the end of the cooking time, to preserve its aroma.

The name of the dish reminds me of a song, to the tune of "Happy Birthday," which my Sichuanese friends Zhou Yu and Tao Ping sung to me once on my birthday in Chengdu: *hancai baicai tudou! Hancai baicai tudou!* It sounds a bit like the words to "Happy Birthday," but means "Amaranth, Chinese cabbage, potatoes! Amaranth, Chinese cabbage, potatoes!"

11 oz (300g) Chinese leaf cabbage
2 tbsp cooking oil
¼ tsp sugar
Salt
2 tsp Chinkiang vinegar
1 tsp potato flour mixed with 1 tbsp water (optional)

Cut the cabbage into ⅜–¾ in (1–2cm) slices. Bring a panful of water to a boil and blanch the cabbage for a minute or two to soften the thicker parts of the leaves. Remove to a colander and shake dry.

Add the oil to a seasoned wok over a high flame, swirl it around, then add the cabbage and stir-fry for a couple of minutes. Add the sugar, and salt to taste. Pour in the vinegar and stir swiftly in. If you are using the flour mixture, add it now and stir quickly to allow it to thicken the juices. Serve.

STIR-FRIED ROMAINE LETTUCE
QING CHAO SHENG CAI 清炒生菜

Since the lettuce entered China from west Asia, probably around 2,000 years ago, the Chinese have grown it more for its stems than its leaves. The most common variety (*qing sun* or *wo sun*) has thick, truncheon-like stems and pointed leaves. Peeled, the stems are crisp and juicy, a pale jade green in color and utterly delicious; the leafy tips, which share the subtle flavor of the stems, are usually stir-fried with a little salt. Stem lettuce can occasionally be found in Western Chinatowns but in my experience, sadly, it's a rarity. The leaves of romaine lettuce, however, stir-fried with a little salt, have a flavor reminiscent of stem lettuce tips and they make a wonderful and easy vegetable dish. If you are not used to eating cooked lettuce, you'll find this dish intriguing, because the heat brings out such a different aspect to its flavor.

1 heart of romaine lettuce (about 9 oz/250g)

3 tbsp cooking oil
Salt

Cut the lettuce heart across its width at 1 in (2½cm) intervals. Wash the cut leaves, then shake dry or (even better) spin in a salad spinner.

Pour the oil into a hot, seasoned wok over a high flame and swirl it around. Add the lettuce and stir-fry until hot and fragrant, but still very crisp, seasoning with salt to taste towards the end. Serve.

TWICE-COOKED SWISS CHARD
HUI GUO NIU PI CAI 回鍋牛皮菜

Chard, known in Chinese as "ox leather greens" or "thick-skinned greens" because of its leathery appearance, is a humble peasant vegetable, so humble in fact that it is traditionally referred to as "pig fodder." In the not-so-distant past, only the desperate would eat it; in Sichuan, at times when meat was hard to come by, it was used as a substitute for pork in that much-loved traditional dish, Twice-cooked Pork (see page 96). Nowadays, with the vogue for rustic food, erstwhile poverty dishes like this have reappeared on restaurant menus, to the bemusement of real peasants.

The following recipe is based on one taught to me by the Chengdu chef Yu Bo, who serves it in an exquisite porcelain dish at his miraculous banquets (the only change I've made is to substitute spring onions for the green garlic leaves, which are hard to find in the West). It's extraordinarily delicious and a marvellous accompaniment to plain steamed rice.

14 oz (400g) thick-stemmed Swiss chard
3 tbsp cooking oil, or 1½ tbsp lard and 1½ tbsp cooking oil
1½ tbsp Sichuanese chilli bean paste
2 tsp finely chopped garlic
2 tsp finely chopped ginger
1½ tbsp fermented black beans, rinsed and drained

½ cup (100ml) chicken stock or water
3 tbsp finely chopped celery (Chinese celery if possible)
2 tbsp finely chopped cilantro
2 tbsp finely sliced spring onion greens

Cut the dark green chard leaves from the stems. Snap each stem into a few pieces, which will allow you to peel away and discard the stringy bits, as you would with celery.

Bring a potful of water to a boil, add the stems and boil for about three minutes, until tender. Add the dark green leaves and boil for another minute or so until they are also cooked. Drain and refresh under cold running water. Squeeze the chard dry, then cut into bite-sized lengths.

Pour the oil into a seasoned wok over a medium flame, swirl it around, then add the chilli bean paste and stir-fry until it smells delicious and the oil is richly red. Add the garlic, ginger and black beans and stir-fry for a few moments more until you can smell their fragrances. Then add the stock, bring to a boil, add the chard and stir until it is piping hot once more.

Finally, stir in the celery, cilantro and spring onion, stir a few times, then serve.

SMOTHERED RAINBOW CHARD WITH GARLIC
MEN CAI HONG CAI 焖彩虹菜

For produce that needs deeper cooking than a simple stir-fry will offer, Chinese cooks often begin by stir-frying their aromatics and main ingredient, then adding a little liquid and covering the wok with a lid to allow the food to cook through. This covered cooking method is known in Chinese as *men*, which expresses it perfectly, because the Chinese character *men* consists of the sign for fire next to the sign that means "stuffy," "stifling" or "tightly covered." The best English translation I've seen of this specializt cooking term is "smothered," so I use it here.

Smothering is a very good way of cooking tougher greens such as rainbow chard, Swiss chard, kale and cavolo nero: you can moisten them with water for a peasant dish or add a little stock for something richer. It's also a very good alternative to stir-frying if you want to make the most of Chinese seasonings without the heat and drama of a stir-fry. My friend Seema, for example, uses this method to cook spinach and other greens, stir-frying a little ginger or garlic (or both) in the bottom of a pan, then adding freshly washed leaves, covering the pan and smothering for a few minutes over a medium heat. The water that clings to the leaves (shaken gently after washing, but not spun) is usually enough to smother them: just keep an eye out to make sure they don't start to catch and brown at the bottom of the pan, adding another tablespoon or so of hot water if necessary. Of course you don't quite get the smoky fragrance of a stir-fry using this method—and the greens will end up softer and somewhat less vibrant in color—but they will still be aromatic and quite juicily delicious. I've never seen rainbow chard in China, although Swiss chard is widely known, so I've no idea what it might be called in Chinese. I've translated the name of the dish literally, in the Chinese characters above, as "rainbow vegetable."

½ lb (225g) rainbow chard
2–3 tbsp cooking oil

2–3 garlic cloves, peeled and sliced
Salt

Trim the chard stems and cut both leaves and stems into chopstickable lengths. Wash them well and shake dry in a colander.

Pour the oil into a seasoned wok over a high flame, swirl it around, then add the garlic and sizzle for a few moments until fragrant but still white.

Add the chard and stir-fry for a minute or two until the leaves are wilting, then season with salt to taste, cover with a lid and cook over a medium heat for five to 10 minutes, until even the stems are tender. (Stir them once or twice to make sure they don't brown and add an extra tablespoonful or so of hot water if necessary to prevent catching.) Serve.

PURPLE AMARANTH WITH RED FERMENTED TOFU
NAN RU XIAN CAI 南乳苋菜

This gorgeous vegetable has deep green, heart-shaped leaves with bright purple hearts and, when it cooks, it colors the juices around it a particularly lovely pink. Its tender stems and young leaves are normally stir-fried, usually with garlic, or simmered in soups. In some parts of China, purple amaranth is traditionally eaten at the Double Fifth or Dragon Boat Festival in the fifth lunar month (the time of this varies, but it is usually in June), perhaps with salted eggs and *zong zi*, glutinous rice cones wrapped in long bamboo leaves. And in the ancient city of Shaoxing, the overgrown stalks of amaranth, which are normally thrown away, are fermented to make an unusual delicacy with a notorious stink and a high, intense flavor that must be tasted to be believed.

For the most common way to cook purple amaranth, with just garlic, see the variation right. The main recipe is a little more unusual, with red fermented tofu giving the vegetable a fragrant, creamy sauce with an almost biscuity flavor. Bunched spinach is a more easily available and delicious alternative to amaranth. Please note that the photograph is of the Purple Amaranth with Garlic variation, as I wanted to show off the vegetable's naturally pink juices.

9 oz (250g) purple amaranth leaves (discard any thick stalks)
3 tbsp cooking oil
2 tsp finely chopped garlic

1 tbsp red fermented tofu, mashed with 1 tbsp liquid from the jar
½ tsp sugar

Blanch the amaranth leaves in a panful of boiling water with 1 tbsp of the cooking oil. Remove the wilted leaves and shake dry.

Pour the remaining oil into a seasoned wok over a high flame, swirl it around, then add the garlic and stir-fry for just a few seconds, until you can smell its fragrance. Add all the amaranth and stir-fry until hot and fragrant, making sure you toss the garlic into the leaves.

Now push the amaranth to one side of the wok and pour the fermented tofu mixture into the space you have created. Stir to heat it, add the sugar, then mix everything in the wok together. Serve.

VARIATION

Purple amaranth with garlic
Blanch the amaranth leaves as in the main recipe and shake dry. Pour 3 tbsp oil into a seasoned wok over a high flame, swirl it around, then add 1 garlic clove, sliced, and stir-fry for just a few seconds until you can smell its fragrance. Add the amaranth and stir-fry until hot and fragrant, seasoning with salt to taste. The purple leaves stain the cooking juices a lyrical pink color: beautiful.

TENDER BOILED VEGETABLES WITH A SPICY DIP

PA PA CAI 炮炮菜

The name of this humble dish has a lovely ring to it in Chinese: it's pronounced *pa-pa-tsai*, which literally means tender-cooked vegetables (*pa* is a Sichuanese dialect term for any food that is cooked to a point of extreme softness). Actually, it's hardly even a dish, but a way of cooking mixed seasonal greens and vegetables that is blindingly easy and surprisingly tasty. I particularly like making *pa pa cai* after a day or two of eating rich food, when I crave something very plain, healthy and nourishing; I might serve it with some plain rice and a few cubes of fermented tofu. *Pa pa cai* is a staple of the rural Sichuanese supper table. In the old days, the vegetables were often cooked in the water beneath the *zengzi*, or rice steamer. Make it with almost any fresh greens and the vegetables you have left over in your fridge or larder: fava beans, carrots, pumpkin, eggplant, bok choy, winter melon, yard-long beans . . . The whole point of *pa pa cai* is, as they say, that it's very *sui yi* ("as-you-please").

According to one Sichuanese chef I know, Yan Baixian, the traditional way to prepare the chillies for the dip is to dry-roast them in a wok until crisp and bronzed then, when they've cooled, to rub them into flakes between the fingers.

Selection of fresh vegetables of your choice (just for an example, try 5 oz/150g Swiss chard, 7 oz/200g new potatoes and 5 oz/150g green beans)
Salt

Ground chillies
Ground roasted Sichuan pepper
Finely sliced spring onion greens
Toasted sesame seeds (optional)

Cut your greens and vegetables evenly into bite-sized pieces. Bring enough water to cover the vegetables to a boil in a saucepan. Add the vegetables and cook until tender: it's best to add vegetables that take longer to cook, such as potatoes, at the beginning, and vegetables that don't take long, such as leafy greens, later on.

Give each person a dipping dish and invite them to add salt, ground chillies, Sichuan pepper, spring onion greens and sesame seeds, if using, to taste.

Serve the vegetables in the pan, or tip them into a serving bowl, with the water. Spoon a little of the cooking liquid into the dipping dishes to make a sauce. Use your chopsticks to dip the greens and vegetables into the dip before eating, then drink the liquid as a soup.

VARIATIONS

An alternative dip, if you want something richer: heat 1–2 tbsp cooking oil in a wok then, over a medium flame, stir-fry 1–2 tbsp Sichuan chilli bean paste until the oil is red and fragrant. Add a little finely-chopped ginger and garlic and/or fermented black beans too, if you like, and stir-fry until it smells rich and wonderful.

SICHUANESE "SEND-THE-RICE-DOWN" CHOPPED CELERY WITH GROUND BEEF
JIA CHANG ROU MO QIN CAI 家常肉末芹菜

Celery is considered to be a very good match for beef, because its herby flavor helps to refine the strong and muscular taste of the meat. Slender Chinese celery, which can sometimes be found in Chinese stores, is even better than the familiar Western kind, because of its superior fragrance. The following dish is typical of Sichuanese home cooking and, with its robust flavor, perfect as a relish to eat with a big bowlful of steamed rice, or for "sending the rice down" (*xia fan*), as they say in China. The celery, jazzed up by the chilli bean paste, should retain a delectable crunchiness in the final dish. You can use pork if you prefer; meat with a little fat will give a juicier result. Chef Zhang Xiaozhong taught me this recipe.

11 oz (300g) celery
3 tbsp cooking oil
4 oz (100g) ground beef
1½ tbsp Sichuan chilli bean paste
1½ tbsp finely chopped ginger
Light soy sauce, to taste (optional)
1 tsp Chinkiang vinegar

De-string the celery sticks and cut them lengthways into ⅜ in (1cm) strips. Finely chop the strips. Bring some water to a boil and blanch the celery for about 30 seconds to "break its rawness." Drain well.

Heat the oil in a seasoned wok over a high flame. Add the ground meat and stir-fry until it is cooked and fragrant, pressing it with the back of your wok scoop or ladle to separate the strands. Then add the chilli bean paste and continue to stir until you can smell it and the oil has reddened. Add the ginger and stir-fry for a few moments more to release its fragrance, then add all the celery.

Continue to stir-fry until the celery is piping hot, seasoning with a little soy sauce, if you wish. Finally, stir in the vinegar and serve.

VARIATION

Stir-fried celery with beef

This is another supper dish that uses celery to balance the flavor of beef. Cut 4 oz (100g) lean beef steak evenly into fine slivers and marinate in a couple of good pinches of salt, ¼ tsp light soy sauce, ½ tsp Shaoxing wine, ½ tsp potato flour, and 2 tsp cold water. Trim and de-string 9 oz (250g) celery sticks and cut into fine slivers to match the beef. Cut a few slivers of red bell pepper too, if you wish, to add color. Blanch the celery and red bell pepper, if using, briefly in boiling water to "break their rawness," then drain well. Heat 3 tbsp cooking oil in a wok over a high flame. Add the beef slivers and stir briskly to separate. Add 1½ tbsp finely chopped ginger, sizzle for a few moments until you can smell it, then add the celery and pepper, if using. Stir-fry until everything is fragrant and piping hot, seasoning with salt to taste. Stir in ¼ tsp Chinkiang vinegar and serve.

STIR-FRIED CELERY WITH LILY BULBS AND MACADAMIA NUTS
XIAN BAI HE CHAO SU 鲜百合炒素

Fresh day lily bulb is a magical, exotic Chinese ingredient, with a delightfully crisp texture. It consists of the bulbs of a plant whose dried flowers are also used in Chinese cooking. The bulbs resemble heads of garlic and can be peeled apart into petal-like flakes. It is particularly lovely in stir-fries like this, which I first tasted in the beautiful surroundings of the China Club in Beijing.

You can use cashew nuts instead of macadamias if you'd rather. Roast your own nuts for a superior crispness (see page 325), or buy them roasted and salted. The lily bulb itself is becoming easier to find in good Chinese groceries but, if you can't get it, the recipe will also work well with just the celery and nuts. It's an utterly beautiful dish, whichever way you look at it.

2 celery sticks (5 oz/150g)
4 oz (100g) fresh lily bulbs
2 oz (60g) roasted macadamia nuts
⅛ tsp sugar
Salt
1½ tbsp cooking oil
4 garlic cloves, halved lengthways

De-string the celery sticks and cut each in half lengthways. Then cut each strip at an angle into diamond-shaped slices. Separate the lily bulb into petal-like sections, discarding any discolored bits; rinse and drain. If you are using roasted, salted macadamia nuts, rub them in a piece of paper towel to get rid of as much salt as possible. Combine the sugar with ¼ tsp salt and 2 tsp water in a small bowl.

Bring some water to a boil and add ½ tbsp of the oil. Add the celery and blanch for about a minute. Add the lily bulb and cook for another 20-30 seconds: both vegetables should remain crunchy. Drain well.

Heat a seasoned wok over a high flame. Add the remaining oil, then the garlic, stir once or twice to release its fragrance (but do not brown it), then add the celery and lily. Stir-fry until everything is piping hot. Pour in the sugar mixture, with a little more salt if you need it, and mix well. Finally, stir in the nuts and serve.

GARLIC
& CHIVES

The pungent vegetables of the Allium family, which include garlic, onions and chives, are one of the pillars of the traditional Chinese diet. Rich in vitamin C and powerfully flavored, they complement the whole grains, legumes and Brassica greens that are the other mainstays of everyday cooking, adding a racy edge to all kinds of meals. Many different varieties and parts of these pungent plants are eaten across the country. Among the most ubiquitous are Chinese green onions, which resemble long spring onions but lack their swelling bulbs, and are an essential aromatic. They have a particular affinity with ginger and garlic. These slender onions are the original Chinese onion, *cong*, cultivated in the country since antiquity; the fat, bulbous onions favored in the West are still known in Chinese as "foreign" or "ocean" onions (*yang cong*).

Chinese chives, also known in English as garlic chives, are radiantly delicious and one of the most important ingredients in simple supper stir-fries and dumpling stuffings. More substantial than the familiar herb chives used in Western cooking, they grow in clumps of long, flat, spear-like leaves and have a deep green color and an assertive garlicky flavor. They rarely play the leading role in a dish, but are used to flatter and enhance ingredients such as firm or smoked tofu, pork, bacon, chicken, beef, lamb, venison, or beaten eggs (apart from eggs, these ingredients will normally be cut into fine slivers to complement the narrow chives). One simple stir-fry of this sort takes a few minutes to make and can serve as lunch for one or two people. Asian-grown Chinese chives are easy to find in Chinese groceries, but I hope before too long that this adaptable vegetable will be cultivated locally and available in mainstream supermarkets.

Aside from the most common garlic chives, the Chinese eat flowering chives—which are sold in bunches of thin stems topped with tiny flower bulbs—and yellow hothouse chives, which are forced to grow in darkness like rhubarb and chicory. Wild garlic (otherwise known as ramsons, or ramps in America) can be a good substitute for Chinese chives in dumpling stuffings and some other recipes, although its fragile leaves wilt more quickly in the heat of the wok, so it's less suitable for stir-frying.

When it comes to garlic, cloves are used whole, sliced, finely chopped or mashed to a paste. They may also be pickled or, in some regions, eaten raw with a lunch of steamed buns or noodles. Another variety of garlic, known in different regions as "garlic sprouts" (*suan miao*), "green garlic" (*qing suan*) and "big garlic" (*da suan*), adds a bright, refreshing pungency to rich dishes such as Twice-cooked Pork and Pock-marked Old Woman's Tofu. With long green leaves and white stems, it resembles Chinese green onions, except its leaves are flat like those of leeks, rather than tubular. It can be hard to find outside China: if you come across it, snap it up.

Garlic stems are also eaten as a vegetable and are happily becoming easier to find in Chinese shops. Juicy, aromatic and beautiful, they are almost irresistible when stir-fried with a little smoked bacon or some sliced mushrooms. They are usually sold in bunches, sometimes with little flower bulbs at their ends. Raw, they have a sharp, aggressive pungency, but they are mellowed by cooking. You can use the green sprouts that emerge from neglected garlic bulbs in your kitchen in stir-fries.

In the old days, when sniffy Englishmen viewed garlic eating as an unsavory continental habit, it's not surprising that Westerners failed to make the most of wonderful possibilities of the Allium family. (Lord Macartney, the leader of the first British diplomatic expedition to China in 1793, dismissed his hosts as "foul feeders and eaters of garlic and strong-scented vegetables.") Now, when people all over the world have woken up to the nutritional richness and sensory pleasures of the vegetable, perhaps it's time for more of us to take to heart some of these delicious Chinese varieties.

STIR-FRIED CHINESE CHIVES WITH PORK SLIVERS
JIU CAI ROU SI 韭菜肉絲

This is one of the most common Chinese supper dishes, a simple stir-fry of slivered pork and fresh, bright chives that is eaten in many parts of the country. It's a meal on its own with rice and perhaps a few stir-fried green leaves or a bowl of soup on the side. You can replace the pork with chicken, beef or lamb if you wish.

4 oz (100g) lean pork
4 oz (100g) Chinese chives
2 tbsp cooking oil
A few fine slivers of red bell pepper for color (optional)
½ tsp light soy sauce
Salt

For the marinade
¼ tsp salt
1 tbsp Shaoxing wine
1 tsp potato flour

Cut the pork evenly into thin slivers. Stir the marinade ingredients with 2 tsp cold water and mix well with the pork.

Trim the chives, discarding any wilted leaves, and cut them into 2½–3 in (6–7cm) lengths, keeping the white and green parts separate.

Add the oil to a seasoned wok over a high flame, swirl it around, then add the pork and stir-fry to separate the slivers. When they have separated but are still pinkish, remove from the wok and set aside.

Return the wok to a high flame, add the chive whites and red pepper, if using, and fry until they are nearly cooked. Add the chive greens and continue to stir-fry until hot and fragrant. Return the pork slivers and stir a few times more, seasoning with the soy sauce, and salt to taste. Serve.

VARIATION

Flowering chives with pork slivers
Replace the chives with flowering chives, snipping off and discarding their flower buds before you cut them into lengths.

CHINESE CHIVES WITH SMOKED TOFU
JIU CAI CHAO XIANG GAN 韭菜炒香乾

In one of the tofu workshops in the old Hunanese village of Zhangguying, where impoverished members of the once-wealthy Zhang clan live amid the grand, drafty halls of their ancestors, they smoke slabs of firm tofu on a grill suspended over a lazy, smoldering pile of wood embers. The tofu, caramel brown on the outside, satisfyingly meaty in texture and darkly aromatic, is one of the staples of Hunanese home cooking. It may be sliced, dressed in chilli oil and eaten cold as an appetizer, or stir-fried with sprightly celery or pungent vegetables as in this recipe. If you're not vegetarian, a few slices of smoked bacon make a scrumptious addition to the dish. And you can, if you prefer, use plain or spiced firm tofu instead of the smoked variety, seasoning either with a little soy sauce as you go.

4 oz (100g) smoked or plain firm tofu
9 oz (250g) Chinese chives, trimmed and washed
2 tbsp cooking oil
Salt
1 tsp sesame oil

Cut the tofu into slices about ¼ in (½cm) thick, then into strips. Cut the chives into lengths to match the tofu.

Add the oil to a seasoned wok over a high flame, swirl it around, then add the tofu strips and stir-fry until tinged with gold. Add the chives and stir-fry until they are piping hot. Season with salt to taste, then stir in the sesame oil and serve.

VARIATION

Flowering chives with smoked tofu
Replace the chives with flowering chives, snipping off and discarding their flower buds before you cut them into lengths.

STIR-FRIED YELLOW CHIVES WITH VENISON SLIVERS

JIU HUANG LU ROU SI 韭黄鹿肉絲

Yellow or hothouse chives are Chinese chives that have been blanched like chicory or forced rhubarb, by growing them in darkness. Fragile and slender, they are a pale, pearlescent yellow and have a bewitching fragrance. In the past, they were considered a luxury food in China and they are still less common than regular chives. Look for them in larger Chinese shops in the West and be aware that they don't keep well; they are best used within a day or two of purchase. A little vinegar brings out their fragrance. Yellow chives, like regular green Chinese chives, are almost always used as the accompanying ingredient in a dish. They are wonderful stir-fried with slivers of any kind of meat, or with beaten eggs.

Venison is a rarity on modern Chinese restaurant menus, but it is one of the grand old delicacies of China and mentioned in written records that date back more than two millennia. Many different kinds of deer are traditionally eaten in China and, although several species are now critically endangered in the wild and hunting them is illegal, some farmed venison is available. Apart from the dark, lean meat of the deer, its tail, tendons, penis and immature antlers are all highly prized as tonic foods. (I had a surprising experience once with a couple of Sichuanese chefs at London's Borough Market: I was showing them a venison stall and all they really wanted to know was what the deer farm did with the penises. At their insistence, I tried to impress upon the rather bemused stall-holder their advice that if the owners dried all their wonderful free-range deer penises and shipped them to China, they could make a fortune.)

5 oz (150g) venison steak
4 oz (100g) yellow or
   hothouse chives
½ fresh red chilli, or ½
   Sichuanese pickled chilli
½ oz (15–20g) piece of ginger, peeled
3 tbsp cooking oil

For the marinade
1 tsp Shaoxing wine
¼ tsp salt
1 tsp potato flour
½ tsp dark soy sauce

For the sauce
⅛ tsp salt
¼ tsp potato flour
½ tsp Shaoxing wine
¾ tsp Chinkiang vinegar
¼ tsp light soy sauce
1 tbsp chicken stock or water

Cut the venison evenly into fine slivers across the grain and place in a bowl. Stir the marinade ingredients with 2 tsp cold water and mix with the venison. Cut the chives into 2½–3 in (6–7cm) sections and the chilli and ginger into slivers. Combine the sauce ingredients in a bowl.

Add 2 tbsp of the oil to a seasoned wok over a high flame and swirl it around. Add the venison slivers and stir-fry to separate. When they are changing color, remove from the wok and set aside.

Return the wok to a high flame with the remaining oil. Add the chives, ginger and chilli and stir-fry for about 30 seconds until hot and fragrant. Return the venison and stir a few times. When everything is hot and the venison just cooked, give the sauce a stir and pour it into the center of the wok. Stir in the sauce, then serve.

VARIATION

Stir-fried yellow chives with chicken or pork slivers
Simply substitute an equal weight of chicken breast or pork for the venison in the recipe above. I like to omit the chillies if I am making the dish with chicken, because I love the pale delicacy of the colors.

GOLDEN CHINESE CHIVE OMELETTE
JIU CAI CHAO DAN 韭菜炒蛋

The Chinese name for this dish is "eggs stir-fried with chives," but it's really a kind of omelette, made in a wok and served in chopstickable pieces. The pungent, garlicky green chives go particularly well with eggs.

I learned to make this simple peasant dish at the Dragon Well Manor restaurant in Hangzhou, where they often serve it to show off their wonderful free-range eggs. You can use the same method to cook eggs with yellow hothouse chives, wild garlic leaves or spring onion greens.

3 eggs, the best and freshest you can get
2 oz (50g) Chinese chives

Salt
2 tbsp cooking oil

Beat the eggs together in a bowl. Chop the chives finely and stir them into the eggs. Add salt to taste.

With a wok scoop on hand, add the oil to a seasoned wok over a high flame, swirl it around, then add the eggs and chives and stir-fry until the eggs are nearly set. Then stop stirring and use the wok scoop to press the eggs into the sides of the wok to brown the bottom. When one side of the omelette is golden, flip it over and fry the other side.

Finally, break it up into chopstickable pieces with your wok scoop and pile up on a serving dish. Don't overcook the omelette; the center should remain light and fluffy.

STIR-FRIED EGGS WITH YELLOW CHIVES
JIU HUANG CHAO JI DAN 韭黃炒雞蛋

Eggs go particularly well with all kinds of oniony vegetables, and yellow chives are no exception. In this recipe, a tiny amount of starch is added to the beaten eggs, to absorb any water that comes out of the chives. You can add a handful of finely sliced spring onion greens in the final throes of cooking if you desire a hint of vibrant color, but I find something lovely in the pale colors of the two main ingredients alone, the delicate gleam of the chives against the golden fluffiness of scrambled egg.

4 eggs
1 tsp potato flour mixed with
  2 tsp cold water
Salt

Ground white pepper
4 oz (100g) yellow chives
3 tbsp cooking oil

Beat the eggs. Give the potato flour mixture a stir and add it to the eggs, with salt and pepper to taste. Cut the chives into 2½ in (6cm) sections and stir them into the eggs.

Heat the oil in a seasoned wok over a high flame. Add the egg and chive mixture and stir-fry until the eggs have just set and the chives are hot and fragrant. Serve immediately.

STIR-FRIED GARLIC STEMS WITH BACON

LA ROU CHAO SUAN TAI 臘肉炒蒜薹

Once you've discovered garlic stems, you'll never look back. The following recipe, which takes about 10 minutes to make, is for a dish I've often eaten in the homes of my Sichuanese friends. It's utterly delicious. The bacon adds a fabulous umami kick to the sweet, pungent garlic and, with rice, it's just about a meal in itself. I generally use smoked bacon, but unsmoked bacon is also fine, as is pancetta or Chinese wind-dried sausage. Add the rinds, if any, to the wok with the bacon for extra richness, then fish them out with chopsticks before serving.

You can use the same method to cook the more slender flowering chives, trimming off and discarding their flower buds before use (they take a little less time to cook than garlic stems).

9 oz (250g) garlic stems
**3 slices bacon, thickly cut if
    possible**
3 tbsp cooking oil
Salt
½ tsp sesame oil

If the bases of the garlic stems are a little fibrous, cut them off and discard. Then cut the stems into 1¾ in (4cm) sections. Slice off the bacon rinds, if necessary, and cut the bacon across the grain into thin strips.

Heat a seasoned wok over a high flame. Add the oil and swirl it around, then add the bacon and its rinds (if using as described in the headnote), and stir a few times to separate the pieces. Add the garlic stems and stir-fry until they are just tender and starting to wrinkle, adding salt to taste. Remove from the heat, remove the bacon rinds (if using), stir in the sesame oil, and serve.

VARIATION

Stir-fried garlic stems with mushrooms
This vegetarian version of the recipe above makes the most of the sumptuous harmony between the flavors of garlic and mushrooms.

Prepare 7 oz (200g) garlic stems as described above and cut the caps of 4¼ oz (125g) button mushrooms into thick slices, discarding their stems. Stir-fry them together in 3 tbsp oil, until the garlic stems are tender and starting to wrinkle and the mushrooms a little golden and marvellously aromatic, adding salt to taste. (Take care not to over-salt: garlic stems do not easily absorb flavors, so the salt will tend to concentrate in the mushrooms.) You can cook Chinese flowering chives with mushrooms in the same way but they take less time to cook than garlic stems, so add them to the wok after stir-frying the mushrooms for a minute or two (trim off and discard their flower buds before you begin).

You may substitute any other kind of mushroom for the button mushrooms, if you fancy. You will find this variation photographed as part of a meal on page 27.

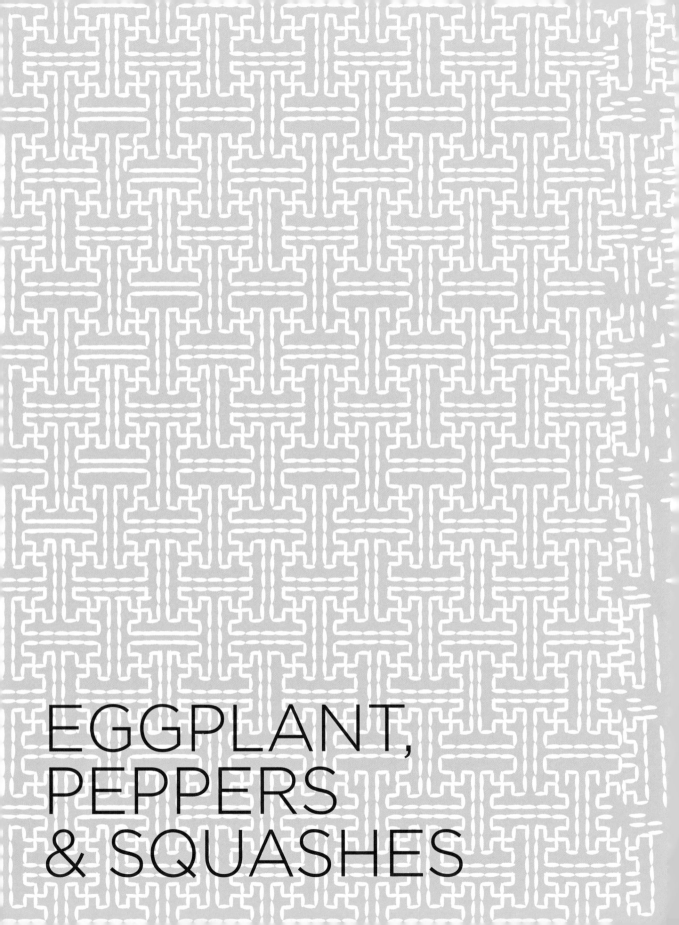

EGGPLANT,
PEPPERS
& SQUASHES

Sleek purple eggplant, fried or grilled, are my most adored vegetable, and Sichuanese Fish-fragrant Eggplant one of my favorite dishes of all times and all places. They are so addictively good that I rarely wish to cook eggplant in any other way but, if you insist, you'll also find in this chapter a couple of rather good recipes from Hangzhou and Shanghai. In general, there is little deep-frying in everyday Chinese home cooking. There are of course exceptions, such as in the case of eggplant, where an encounter with hot oil brings out a divine buttery quality in their flesh. Chinese eggplant are longer and thinner than the common Mediterranean eggplant, with paler purple skin: if you find them fresh in a Chinese shop, do buy them for their delicate color; Mediterranean eggplant, however, can be used equally well in these recipes.

While hot chillies are favored in certain parts of China, other kinds of peppers are used all over the country. Green bell peppers and sweet red bell peppers (often known as "lantern peppers" because of their resemblance to traditional Chinese lanterns) may be stuffed or stir-fried. Often, they are used to provide a bit of color and crunch to a mixture of ingredients in a wok, or simply stir-fried with one other main ingredient, such as pork, beef, or firm tofu.

The Chinese eat a great variety of squashes. Some of them, such as cucumber, which is generally used in cold dishes but may also be stir-fried, are common in the West. Others, less familiar—such as winter melon, fuzzy melon and bitter melon—may be tracked down in Chinese supermarkets, while Chinese cooking methods may be used to prepare slightly different Western varieties, such as zucchini, to delicious effect. One kind of gourd, the waisted calabash, is an ancient lucky symbol and may be dried and carved with intricate designs, or tied with red cord and hung as a decoration. Though it is rarely eaten, it lends its form to some Chinese dishes, such as steamed calabash-shaped dumplings and "calabash eight-treasure duck," a boned duck that is filled with glutinous rice studded with various delicious morsels and tied into a calabash shape before being steamed and deep-fried.

The following section includes recipes for cooking some of the squash varieties that are more easily available. You will also find several cold cucumber dishes in the chapter on appetizers, and some ideas for Chinese winter melon in the soup chapter.

FISH-FRAGRANT EGGPLANT
YU XIANG QIE ZI 魚香茄子

This dish, almost more than any other, expresses for me the gorgeous layering of flavors that is the signature of Sichuanese cooking. Pickled chillies, either on their own or with fermented fava beans in the famous Sichuan chilli bean sauce, give the dish its warmth and luster; garlic, ginger and spring onions add a luxurious kick of flavor and a hint of sweet and sour serves to harmonize all the other tastes. The same sauce, minus the eggplant, can be poured over steamed or deep-fried seafood or chicken; while a similar combination of flavorings can be used to cook slivered pork, or as a dressing for cold, cooked peas or fava beans. They call this complex flavor "fish-fragrant" because it draws on the seasonings used in Sichuanese fish cooking, so it is supposed to recall to those who eat it the taste of fish.

If you prefer not to deep-fry, just salt the eggplant, brush them with oil and shallow-fry them or roast them in the oven, then make a fish fragrant sauce and pour it over them in a serving dish. The eggplant won't absorb the flavors of the sauce quite as well this way, but they'll still be delicious. (If you roast or shallow-fry them, then cook them in the sauce as in the classic recipe, they'll disintegrate, which is why it's better to pour the sauce over.)

Leftovers, if you have any, taste wonderful either hot or cold. Some cooks add ground pork to the dish for extra savoriness but, when it's so delicious as it is, why bother? For me, the beauty of this dish lies in the way it transforms such a humble vegetable into something extraordinary.

1¼ lbs (600g) eggplant
Salt
Cooking oil, for deep-frying (1½ cups plus 2 tbsp/400ml will do if you are using a round-bottomed wok)
1½ tbsp Sichuanese chilli bean paste, or Sichuan pickled chilli paste, or a mixture of the two

If you can get it, Sichuanese pickled chilli paste (without the fava beans) gives a sauce with a brilliant red color and a fresh, almost fruity aspect to its flavor. Some cooks use a mixture of pickled chilli paste (for its bright beauty and fruitiness), and chilli bean paste (for its rich savoriness).

1 tbsp finely chopped ginger
1 tbsp finely chopped garlic
²/₃ cup (150ml) chicken stock
2 tsp sugar
¾ tsp potato flour mixed with 1 tbsp cold water
2 tsp Chinkiang vinegar
4 tbsp finely sliced spring onion greens

Cut the eggplant lengthways into three thick slices, then cut these into evenly sized batons. Sprinkle them with salt, mix well and leave in a colander for at least 30 minutes to drain.

In a wok, heat the oil for deep-frying to 350°F (180°C). Add the eggplant in batches and deep-fry for three to four minutes until slightly golden on the outside and soft and buttery within. Remove and drain on paper towels.

Drain the deep-frying oil, rinse the wok if necessary, then return it to a medium flame. When the wok is hot again, add 3 tbsp of oil. Add the chilli bean paste and stir-fry until the oil is red and fragrant, then add the ginger and garlic and continue to stir-fry until you can smell their aromas. Take care not to burn these seasonings; remove the wok from the heat for a few seconds if necessary to control the temperature (you want a gentle, coaxing sizzle, not a scorching heat).

Add the stock and sugar and mix well. Season with salt to taste if necessary. Add the fried eggplant to the sauce and let them simmer gently for a minute or so to absorb some of the flavors. Then stir the potato flour mixture, pour it over the eggplant and stir in gently to thicken the sauce. Add the vinegar and spring onions and stir a few times, then serve.

HANGZHOU EGGPLANT
ROU MO QIE ZI 肉末茄子

When I told the Hangzhou chef Hu Zhongying that I was interested in local home cooking, he took me into the kitchens of his restaurant, the Hangzhou Jiujia, and asked one of the chefs there to demonstrate this everyday dish, in which tender eggplant are flavored with a rich, fermented sauce and a scattering of ground pork. It's wonderful, even for a loyal fish-fragrant eggplant devotee like me. Vegetarians can use the same method, omitting the pork and substituting water or vegetarian stock. (Please note that the photograph shows the vegetarian version of this dish.) In China, they never salt their eggplant before frying, but I find that this Mediterranean method gives a better, less oily result.

14 oz (400g) eggplant
Salt
Cooking oil, for deep-frying
    (1½ cups/350ml will do)
2–3 oz (50–75g) ground pork,
    ideally with a little fat
2 tsp finely chopped ginger
1 tbsp sweet fermented sauce
2 tbsp chicken stock

1 tbsp Shaoxing wine
1 tsp light soy sauce
½ tsp dark soy sauce
½ tsp sugar
¼ tsp potato flour mixed with
    2 tsp cold water
2 tbsp finely chopped spring
    onion greens

Cut the eggplant lengthways into ¾ in (2cm) slices, then cut the slices into ¾ in (2cm) strips. Cut these into 2–2½ in (5–6cm) lengths. Sprinkle with a little salt, mix well and leave in a colander to drain for 30 minutes or so.

Heat the oil for deep-frying to 350–400°F (180–200°C). Shake the eggplant dry and deep-fry, in a couple of batches, until slightly golden. Remove with a slotted spoon and set aside on paper towels.

Drain the deep-frying oil, rinse the wok if necessary, then return it to a high flame. When the wok is hot again, add 1–2 tbsp oil, swirl it around, then add the pork and stir-fry over a medium flame until the meat has lost its pinkness and the oil has cleared again. Add the ginger and stir to release its fragrance. Add the fermented sauce and stir until it smells delicious, too. Add the stock, Shaoxing wine, soy sauces and sugar, return the eggplant, and mix well.

Toss the eggplant in the sauce, then give the potato flour mixture a stir and pour it into the center of the wok, moving briskly to stir it in. Add the spring onions, stir a few times, then serve.

SHANGHAI HOME-STYLE EGGPLANT
JIA CHANG QIE ZI 家常茄子

I've often picked up cooking tips through the generosity of shoppers in Chinese markets, who have taken the trouble to help me identify all the produce on display and explained how they like to cook the different ingredients. This recipe was a gift from a lady shopper in a Shanghai market. It's terribly easy and very good to eat. I've given quantities for a single eggplant, because it's the kind of dish you might want to rustle up for lunch for just a couple of people, but you can double them if you wish.

1 decent-sized eggplant (11 oz/300g)
Salt
1 cup plus 2 tbsp (300ml) cooking oil
4 tbsp chicken stock or water
½ tbsp light soy sauce
½ tsp dark soy sauce
1 tsp sugar
A few slices of peeled ginger
1 spring onion, green parts only, finely sliced

Cut the eggplant in half lengthways, then into three sections. Now cut each section lengthways into about three chunky strips. Sprinkle lightly with salt, mix well and leave to drain in a colander for 30 minutes or so.

Heat a wok over a high flame. Add the oil and heat to 350°F (180°C). Add the eggplant in a couple of batches and deep-fry until tender and golden. Set aside to drain on paper towels.

Combine the stock, soy sauces and sugar in a small bowl.

Pour all but 1 tbsp oil into a heatproof container and return the wok to a high flame. Add the ginger and sizzle briefly until you can smell its fragrance. Give the stock mixture a stir and pour it into the wok. Return the eggplant and stir briskly until the liquid has largely evaporated. Then stir in the spring onions and serve.

STIR-FRIED GREEN PEPPER WITH PORK SLIVERS
QING JIAO ROU SI 青椒肉絲

Stir-fried green pepper with slivered pork is one of the most common supper dishes in many parts of China. In Sichuan, they like to use long, thin-skinned green peppers with a spicy edge to them, but you can use bell peppers instead if you'd rather. The same recipe works with beef, lamb or chicken slivers. The optional egg white in the marinade gives the meat a more silky texture.

4 oz (100g) lean pork
Salt
1 green pepper (see headnote)
A few slivers of red bell pepper for color (optional)
3 tbsp cooking oil
1 tsp sweet fermented sauce
1 tsp light soy sauce

For the marinade
½ tsp Shaoxing wine
¼ tsp light soy sauce
½ tsp potato flour
1 tbsp egg white or cold water

Cut the pork evenly into fine slivers and place in a small bowl. Add the marinade ingredients with a couple of good pinches of salt, and mix well.

Cut the green pepper lengthways into quarters, discard the seeds and membranes and cut evenly into thin slivers to match the pork.

Heat the wok over a high flame without any oil. Add all the peppers and dry-fry them until they are hot, fragrant and a little supple, then set aside. Return the wok to the heat with the oil, add the pork and stir-fry to separate the slivers. Then add the sweet fermented sauce and stir a few times until you can smell it. Return the peppers, add the soy sauce, and salt to taste, and stir-fry until everything is incorporated. Serve.

VARIATION

Stir-fried green pepper with firm tofu
Use firm tofu, cut into thin strips, instead of meat. Omit the marinade and the sweet fermented sauce and simply season with salt and light soy sauce to taste.

STIR-FRIED CUCUMBER WITH WOOD EAR
HUANG GUA MU'ER 黄瓜木耳

Stir-fried cucumber can be a revelation if you've never imagined eating it hot. This recipe, a simple marriage of sliced cucumber and frilly cloud or wood ear mushrooms, is a Sichuanese supper dish taught to me by Chef Zhang Xiaozhong. Add a little pork if you like (see variation, right). And if you have neither pork nor mushrooms, sliced cucumber simply stir-fried on its own, with a little salt, can be really wonderful, bringing out a whole new side to this familiar vegetable.

A handful of wood ear mushrooms (about 4 oz/100g, after soaking)
4 oz (100g) cucumber
1 spring onion, trimmed
1 Sichuanese pickled chilli or ½ fresh red chilli
2 tbsp cooking oil
1 tbsp peeled, sliced garlic
1 tbsp peeled, sliced ginger
Salt
Light soy sauce, to taste
¼ tsp potato flour mixed with 1 tsp cold water

Pour hot water from the kettle over the mushrooms and leave to soak for 30 minutes.

Cut the cucumber section lengthways into thin slices. Lay these flat on a chopping board and, holding the knife at an angle, cut them into diamond-shaped slices. Drain the wood ears and, if they are large, break them into bite-sized pieces. Cut the spring onion and pickled or red chilli on the diagonal into "horse ears."

Heat a seasoned wok over a high flame. Add the oil, then the garlic, ginger, pickled chilli or red chilli and the spring onion and stir-fry briefly until you can smell their fragrances. Then add the cucumber and mushrooms and stir-fry until everything is piping hot.

Add 1 tbsp water, season with a little salt and light soy sauce to taste, then pour in the flour mixture, stirring vigorously as you do so. Stir a couple of times more, then serve.

VARIATION

Stir-fried cucumber with pork and wood ear
Cut 3 oz (75g) lean pork into thin slices. Marinate in a couple of pinches of salt, 2 tsp Shaoxing wine, ½ tsp potato flour and 1½ tsp cold water. Stir-fry the pork slices briefly to separate them before you add the garlic and other seasonings, then proceed as in the main recipe above.

SWEET AND SOUR ZUCCHINI
TANG CU YI DA LI GUA 糖醋義大利瓜

It was one of those evenings when I wanted to make something quick for supper but seemed to have nothing very promising in the refrigerator or larder. In the end, I rounded up some mushrooms, some eggs, a fading tomato and a couple of zucchini that were a little past their best. I put some rice on to cook, stir-fried the mushrooms with garlic and the eggs with the tomato, then peeled and cut the zucchini and gave them a sweet-and-sour stir-fry treatment.

The zucchini dish turned out to be so delicately pleasing that I've been making it deliberately ever since. The zucchini are tender but not overcooked and the understated sweet-sour flavor is delightful. Zucchini are not generally available in China, although in the south they stir-fry the flesh of young green pumpkins to similar effect.

2 zucchini (11 oz/300g)
Salt
2 tbsp cooking oil

2 garlic cloves, finely sliced
½ tsp sugar
1 tsp Chinkiang vinegar

Cut the zucchini in half lengthways, then cut each half into about three sections. Thinly slice each section lengthways and place in a bowl. Add ½ tsp salt, mix well and set aside for 30 minutes or so. When you are ready to cook, drain the slices and squeeze them to get rid of excess water.

Heat a wok over a high flame. Add the oil, then the garlic, and stir-fry for a few seconds until you smell its fragrance. Add the zucchini and stir-fry until they are hot and just cooked, but still a little crisp. Add the sugar and vinegar, with salt to taste, stir a couple of times, then tip on to a dish and serve.

VARIATION

Zucchini slivers with garlic
Cut the zucchini evenly into thin slices, then into slivers. Salt them and squeeze as in the recipe above. Stir-fry the zucchini with the garlic only, as above, omitting the sugar and vinegar. This is how the Sichuanese often cook young green pumpkins.

STEAMED FUZZY MELON WITH GROUND PORK STUFFING
QING ZHENG NAN GUA 清蒸南瓜

One evening in Chengdu my Chinese teacher, Yu Weiqin, served us a whole little squash stuffed with ground pork that had been steamed until tender. It was so lovely to eat that I have never forgotten it. Fortunately she showed me how to make it and I've recreated it at home using the squash that I can buy here. Use the same method to cook zucchini and other varieties of squash, store-bought or home-grown: the stuffing is fabulous.

1 dried shiitake mushroom
Small piece of ginger, unpeeled
4 oz (100g) ground pork with a little fat
½ egg
1 tbsp finely chopped spring onion greens
½ tsp sesame oil
1 tsp potato flour
Salt
Ground white pepper
Around 14 oz (400g) fuzzy melon

Soak the dried mushroom for 30 minutes in hot water from the kettle. Crush the ginger with the side of a cleaver or a rolling pin, then put it in a glass with cold water to cover.

When the mushroom is soft, chop it finely. Place the pork in a bowl and add 1 tbsp of the ginger-soaking water and all the other stuffing ingredients, including salt and pepper. The stuffing should be slightly over-salted, to balance the blandness of the melon.

Trim off both ends of the fuzzy melon. Cut the rest into round 1 in (2½ cm) sections and hollow out their pulpy centers. Arrange the sections in a shallow heatproof bowl that will fit into your steamer. Fill the centers of the sections with the ground pork mixture.

Steam over high heat for 30 minutes, until the pork is cooked through.

SILK GOURD WITH GREEN SOY BEANS
QING DOU SI GUA 青豆絲瓜

I first tasted this dish after a wet morning's fishing in a lake in the Zhejiang countryside. We went out, three of us, in a wobbly wooden punt (a flat-bottomed boat) and when we were in the middle of the lake it started to drizzle. The fisherman cast his net from one end of the punt and pulled in a few fish that he stored in the watery hold. Soon the rain came more steadily and the sky and water were the same soft grey, almost indistinguishable. We paddled back to the shore and lit a fire in the kitchen to warm ourselves up as the fisherman finished preparing our lunch.

He turned out to be an astoundingly good cook, offering us an unforgettable red-braised pork, poached free-range chicken with a soy sauce dip, braised catfish with ginger, stir-fried river shrimp and this sumptuous stew of silk gourd and soy beans. The silk gourd has a soft, juicy texture and the beans and ham give the dish a rich umami savoriness. Vegetarians may omit the ham and perhaps add a little sweet red bell pepper for color. I suspect the same recipe would also work excellently with zucchini.

1 silk gourd (about 1¹/₄ lb/500g)
1½ oz (45g) Chinese or Spanish ham, or 3 slices of bacon
4 oz (100g) shelled green soy beans

2 tbsp cooking oil
½ tbsp Shaoxing wine
²/₃ cup (150ml) chicken stock
Salt
1 tsp potato flour mixed with 1 tbsp cold water (optional)

Peel the silk gourd (I use a potato peeler), then roll-cut into chunks (see page 20). Cut the ham or bacon into small, bite-sized slices. If you are using fresh soy beans, boil them for about five minutes until tender (the frozen kind are already cooked and simply need defrosting).

Heat a seasoned wok over a high flame, then add the oil and swirl it around. Add the ham or bacon and sizzle for a few seconds until you can smell it. Then add the beans, stir-fry for 30 seconds or so, and add the silk gourd. Continue to stir-fry until everything is piping hot, then add the Shaoxing wine and next the stock.

Bring to a boil, season with salt to taste, then cover and simmer gently for about three minutes. Lastly, if you wish to thicken the sauce, give the potato flour mixture a stir, add it to the wok and stir as the sauce thickens.

VARIATION

Silk gourd with garlic
Heat a wok, add oil then sliced garlic and stir-fry briefly until the garlic is fragrant. Add roll-cut silk gourd and stir-fry until hot. Pour in some stock, bring to a boil, season with salt to taste, then cover and simmer for a few minutes. Thicken the sauce with potato flour as above if you wish.

RUSTIC STEAMED SQUASH WITH SPICY BLACK BEAN SAUCE
XIANG CUN NAN GUA 鄉村南瓜

In rural China, bowls of seasoned ingredients are often steamed over rice in the same pot, to economize on fuel. This is my attempt to recreate one such dish served by my chef friend Lan Guijun in his Village Cook restaurant in Chengdu. He used a pumpkin, but the same method also works very well with butternut squash.

3 tbsp cooking oil
2 tbsp Sichuan chilli bean paste
1 tsp finely chopped ginger
1 tsp finely chopped garlic
1 tbsp fermented black beans, rinsed and drained
½ tsp sugar
1¼ lb (500g) butternut squash or pumpkin
2 spring onions, green parts only, finely sliced

Heat a seasoned wok over a high flame. Add the oil, swirl it around, then add the chilli bean paste. Reduce the heat to medium and stir-fry gently until the oil is red and fragrant. Add the ginger, garlic and black beans and stir-fry until you can smell their fragrances. Stir in the sugar, then put everything into a small dish and set aside.

Peel the squash or pumpkin and discard the pulp and seeds. Cut evenly into slices about ⅛ in (½cm) thick. Lay the slices neatly in a china bowl. Spoon the prepared spicy sauce over the squash or pumpkin, place the uncovered bowl in a steamer and steam at high heat for about 15 minutes, until the vegetable is tender. Scatter with the spring onions and serve in the steaming bowl.

ROOT
VEGETABLES

In China, only the desperate consider potatoes, sweet potatoes and other roots to be staple foods. For everyone else, they are made into seasoned dishes to be eaten with rice or noodles. Potatoes have a much lesser role in Chinese cooking than they do in many Western cuisines. They may be added to a meat stew, or cut into slivers or slices and stir-fried, but even mashed potato (on the rare occasions when it is served) is normally accompanied by rice. In many parts of China, the vegetable is still known as "foreign taro" (*yang yu*), because of its relatively recent introduction into the Chinese food system.

Carrots are sometimes eaten, but almost invariably to add a little color to other ingredients rather than as the main event: they too are commonly known as "barbarian radishes" (*hu luo bo*), a reference to their foreign origins. More widely used than either potatoes and carrots are two ancient Chinese crops: daikon and taro. The radish may be eaten raw as a salad, pickled, stir-fried, or added to soups and stews; taro, with its silky, milky texture, is usually boiled, steamed or braised, though it may also be fashioned into deep-fried dumplings.

STIR-FRIED POTATO SLIVERS
WITH CHILLI AND SICHUAN PEPPER
QIANG TU DOU SI 熗土豆絲

In Sichuanese cuisine, this is the most common method of cooking potatoes, yet it seems revolutionary to many Westerners because the potatoes remain a little crunchy when they are served. If you've never seen the dish before, you may find it hard to believe that it's actually made from potatoes. In restaurants, the potato slivers are usually rinsed in cold water, which washes away some of their starch, but Chinese friends who cook potatoes this way at home often don't bother. If you don't rinse them, they will become a little sticky as you stir-fry them—not so elegant, but delicious.

You can make this with any kind of potato, the taste and texture of the final dish varying according to the type. Don't worry if your slivers are not as fine or even as those in the photograph, they'll still taste wonderful.

4–5 dried chillies
14 oz (400g) potatoes
Salt

2 tbsp cooking oil
½ tsp whole Sichuan pepper
½ tsp sesame oil (optional)

Snip the chillies in half and discard their seeds as far as possible.

Peel the potatoes. Take one and cut a thin slice from one side. Lay the rest of the potato on its now-flat side on your board, and cut into slices, as thin and as even as possible. Spread the slices out in an overlapping line, then cut them into very fine slivers. Repeat with the other potatoes. If you are not cooking them immediately, cover them in slightly salted cold water so they don't discolor and shake them dry in a colander before cooking.

Heat a seasoned wok over a high flame, then add the oil and swirl it around. Swiftly throw in the chillies and Sichuan pepper and stir-fry briefly until the spices smell wonderful and the chillies are darkening but not burned, then add the potatoes. Continue to stir-fry for a few minutes, until the potatoes are hot and no longer taste raw, but retain a little crispness, adding salt to taste. (If you have cut very fine slivers, you can do this over a high flame; if your slivers are not very fine, reduce the heat and stir-fry for a little longer.)

Remove from the heat, stir in the sesame oil, if using, then serve.

VARIATIONS

Stir-fried potato slivers with spring onion
If you prefer not to use chilli and Sichuan pepper, you can stir-fry the potato slivers in unseasoned oil, adding salt to taste and a small handful of finely sliced spring onion greens just before you take the wok off the heat (the spring onions only need to be stir-fried for a few seconds, until you can smell their fragrance). Then add the sesame oil and serve. This is a most delectable variation.

Stir-fried potato slivers with green bell pepper
Omit the chilli and Sichuan pepper and stir-fry the potato slivers with a handful of green pepper slivers in unseasoned oil, adding salt to taste and a small handful of finely sliced spring onion greens just before you take the wok from the heat. Use about one-fifth of the amount of green bell pepper slivers as potato slivers.

Stir-fried potato slivers with vinegar
Rinse the potato slivers in water and shake them dry. Stir-fry them with a few slivers of green pepper, for color. Season with salt and a little light soy sauce and add 1–2 tsp Chinkiang vinegar towards the end of the cooking time.

STIR-FRIED MASHED POTATO WITH PRESERVED MUSTARD GREENS
SUAN CAI CHAO TU DOU NI 酸菜炒土豆泥

Mashed potatoes are eaten as an occasional side dish in China and they are usually served almost soupy, with a lot of added stock and scattered with spring onion. This version comes from the Wolong nature reserve in the mountainous borderlands of Sichuan, where I came across a young chef, Peng Rui, who had studied at the same Chengdu cooking school as me. Peng Rui took me foraging in the hills and we spent some time cooking in the tiny restaurant he ran with his mother. One day he decided to cook up a potato feast, an eccentric idea in China, where potatoes are normally considered to be a peripheral and rather unexciting food. He made dry-fried potato strips with chilli and Sichuan pepper; fine, crisp-fried "pine-needle potatoes" with a sprinkling of white sugar; deep-fried, sweetened potato balls; potato pancake with spring onion; and this fabulous potato mash with salted mustard greens, a sort of Chinese bubble-and-squeak. We ate all this with a rich stew of red-braised beef. And rice, of course.

The mixture of potatoes and preserved vegetables was so good that I've often made it since with leftover potatoes. Peng Rui cooked it in a wok, but you can of course make it in a flat-bottomed frying pan if you prefer. I have a feeling these potatoes would go very well with duck. Roast duck and preserved mustard greens, after all, are a classic Chinese combination that tends to show up in fried rice and noodle dishes. Just before serving the dish you may, if you wish, sprinkle the cooked potatoes with a little ground roasted Sichuan pepper.

12 oz (350g) leftover cooked
   potatoes
2½ oz (60g) Sichuanese
   ya cai or "snow vegetable"
3 tbsp cooking oil or lard
Salt
Ground white pepper
2 tbsp finely sliced spring
   onion greens

Mash the potatoes if they are not already mashed. Chop the preserved vegetable, if not already chopped.

Heat a seasoned wok over a high flame, then add the oil or lard and swirl it around. Add the preserved vegetable and stir-fry briefly until it smells delicious. Add the potato and fry until hot and fragrant, seasoning with salt and pepper to taste. You can either stir-fry constantly, adding some stock or water if you like a more runny consistency, or leave the potato to brown before turning it in the wok.

Add the spring onions, stir-fry for a few moments longer and serve.

PENG RUI'S POTATO SLIVER BING
PENG RUI TU DOU BING 彭鋭土豆餅

Bing is a word that originally referred to all kinds of foods made from wheat flour; nowadays it is used to describe edible things that are round and flattish, from the mandarin pancakes used to wrap Peking duck, to squidgy deep-fried sweet potato balls, steamed "lotus leaf" buns and flatbreads.

In this recipe, which I learned on that distant afternoon in the Wolong nature reserve with young chef Peng Rui, potato slivers are fried into a golden pancake and scattered with Sichuan pepper to serve.

9 oz (250g) potatoes
3 tbsp finely sliced spring onion greens
Salt

3 tbsp cooking oil
About ¼ tsp ground roasted Sichuan pepper

Peel the potatoes, cut them into thin slices, then fine slivers. Place them in a colander, rinse under the cold tap, then shake dry. Mix in the spring onion greens and salt to taste.

Heat a seasoned wok or frying pan over a high flame. Add the oil and swirl it around, then spread the potatoes out around the hot surface. Reduce the heat and fry gently until the outside is golden and the potato slivers inside are cooked but still a little crunchy. Flip the potato cake over: the easiest way to do this is to loosen it with a spatula, invert a dinner plate over the wok or pan, then quickly turn the wok over so that the potato cake ends up on the plate. Then slide the potato cake back into the wok or frying pan, and continue to cook until the other side is golden.

Serve with a sprinkling of ground Sichuan pepper, to taste.

MUSHROOMS

Many of the less developed regions of China produce magnificent wild mushrooms, which can be a highlight of visits to rural areas. Yunnan Province is particularly famed for its fungi which, dried, are now exported all over the world. But I've also had exotic and delicious varieties in other regions, such as the gelatinous, glassy little "ground ear" mushrooms served in a remote roadside restaurant in Guizhou, or the lyrically beautiful "eggs" of the phallic bamboo pith fungus that are gathered in the bamboo forests of southern Sichuan. Some of these more unusual mushrooms can be found, dried, in Chinese groceries abroad, but in fact even the most ordinary kinds taste divine when stir-fried the Chinese way with a little garlic and spring onion.

The most commonly used fresh mushrooms in southern China tend to be the oyster, enoki, shiitake and button mushrooms, which are often wokked with garlic and a little stock to bring out their umami flavors. A little chicken or pork, or a spoonful of lard or chicken fat, is a marvellous addition to mushroom dishes of this sort. Wood or cloud ear mushrooms are also common, although more often cooked as an accompaniment than as a dish in their own right. Tasteless, they are prized for their slippery-crisp texture and dark color, which can be a pretty contrast to green vegetables.

STIR-FRIED OYSTER AND SHIITAKE MUSHROOMS WITH GARLIC
SU CHAO SHUANG GU 素炒雙菇

Stir-fried mushrooms with garlic and spring onion are one of the dishes I most frequently cook: this simple method seems to produce a dish that is delicious out of all proportion to its ingredients. You can use any mixture of mushrooms you like, or indeed a single variety—button and enoki mushrooms are also very good—but I find oyster and shiitake a particularly happy combination.

Lard or chicken fat adds another, irresistible dimension (use lard instead of regular cooking oil, or add a spoonful of chicken fat towards the end of cooking to intensify the flavors of the mushrooms). Sometimes I'll use goose fat if I have some, or add a little of the fat that has solidified at the top of a potful of Red-braised Pork (see page 94). And don't throw away the layer of fat that solidifies in a roast chicken pan or at the top of a stock; it keeps well in the refrigerator and is a perfect addition to stir-fried mushrooms.

10 oz (275g) oyster mushrooms
5 oz (150g) fresh shiitake mushrooms
2–3 tbsp cooking oil or lard

3 garlic cloves, sliced
¾ cup (200ml) chicken stock
Salt
2 spring onions, green parts only, finely sliced

Clean the oyster mushrooms if necessary and tear or cut lengthways into bite-sized pieces. Trim off and discard the shiitake stalks and slice their caps.

Heat the wok over a high flame. Add the oil or lard and swirl it around before adding the garlic, which should be stir-fried very briefly until you can smell its fragrance. Then add the mushrooms and stir-fry for a couple of minutes until they have somewhat reduced in volume. Then pour in the stock and bring to a boil. Continue to stir until the mushrooms are tender and the stock has been largely absorbed, adding salt to taste. Then add the spring onions, stir a few times so they feel the lick of heat, then serve.

STIR-FRIED OYSTER MUSHROOMS WITH CHICKEN
PING GU JI PIAN 平菇雞片

This gentle, understated dish was one I often enjoyed at a small restaurant near Sichuan University. The subtle savoriness of the chicken marries beautifully with the mushrooms and garlic. You don't need much chicken, actually: just half a breast would be enough to make the dish. And lard, if you have it, will magically enhance the flavors.

1 chicken breast, without skin (5 oz/150g)
1 spring onion
7 oz (200g) oyster mushrooms
3 tbsp cooking oil or lard
A piece of ginger, about the size of a large clove of garlic, peeled and sliced
2 garlic cloves, sliced

Salt
Ground white pepper

For the marinade
½ tsp salt
1 tsp Shaoxing wine
1 tsp potato flour

Lay the chicken breast on a chopping board and, holding your knife at a right angle to the board, cut it into thin slices. Place in a bowl. Add the marinade ingredients with 2 tsp cold water and mix well.

Holding your knife at a steep angle, cut the spring onion into ⅜ in (1cm) diagonal "horse-ear" slices, keeping the white and green parts separate. Clean the oyster mushrooms if necessary and tear or cut lengthways into bite-sized pieces, discarding any hard bits at the base of their stalks.

Heat a seasoned wok over a high flame. Add 1 tbsp of the oil or lard, swirl it around, then add the mushrooms and stir-fry for a couple of minutes until nearly cooked. Set aside.

Reheat the wok over a high flame, then add the remaining oil and swirl it around. Add the chicken and stir-fry to separate the slices. When the slices are separating but still pinkish, add the ginger, garlic and spring onion whites and continue to stir for a few moments until you can smell their fragrances. Then return the mushrooms and stir to incorporate, adding salt and pepper to taste. Finally, stir in the spring onion greens, then serve.

VEGETARIAN "GONG BAO CHICKEN"
GONG BAO JI DING (SU) 宮保雞丁

At the Baoguang Temple, an hour away from Chengdu, if you walk through the grand courtyard just within the entrance gates, past the racks of burning incense and candles and slip off to the right, past the tea house garden with its shady trees and bamboo chairs, you'll find another, smaller courtyard. At the far side of this are a few tables and chairs and a hatch, hung with wooden slats bearing the names of classic Sichuanese dishes. There is twice-cooked pork, dry-fried eels, crispy-skin fish and even shark's fin but, because this is a Buddhist monastery, none of them contain any meat or fish at all. The restaurant at the Baoguang Temple is one of the best exponents I know of the Buddhist vegetarian style of cooking, where vegetable ingredients are cunningly engineered to mimic the appearance, aromas and tastes of meat. The "eel" is made from dried shiitakes; the "fish" from mashed potato in tofu skin.

This recipe, in which meaty portobello mushrooms take the place of chicken, is in the same style, although it does include the garlic and onion that are frowned on in monasteries, so it's not strictly Buddhist. It takes a little time to make, but it's worth it because, frankly, everyone should have the chance to taste Gong Bao chicken, even vegetarians.

3 large portobello mushrooms (11 oz/300g)
8–10 Sichuanese dried chillies
3 garlic cloves
An equivalent amount of ginger
5 spring onions, white parts only
About ¾ cup (200ml) cooking oil
1 tsp whole Sichuan pepper
3 oz (75g) roasted peanuts

For the marinade
¼ tsp salt
1½ tbsp potato flour

For the sauce
3 tsp sugar
⅛ tsp salt
¼ tsp potato flour
½ tsp dark soy sauce
2 tsp light soy sauce
3 tsp Chinkiang vinegar

Bring a panful of water (about 2 quarts/2 liters) to a boil. Trim the mushrooms and cut into ⅜–¾ in (1–2cm) cubes. Blanch the mushroom cubes in the boiling water for about a minute, until partially cooked. Drain, refresh under the cold tap and shake dry. Add the marinade ingredients and mix well.

Cut the chillies in half and shake out and discard the seeds as far as possible. Peel and thinly slice the garlic and ginger. Cut the spring onion whites into ⅜ in (1cm) sections. Combine the sauce ingredients in a small bowl with 1 tbsp water and mix well.

Heat the oil in a seasoned wok to about 300°F (150°C). At this temperature, you should see small movements in the oil and the surface will tremble slightly. Add the mushrooms and fry for 30–60 seconds until glossy, stirring gently. Remove with a slotted spoon and set aside. Drain off all but about 2 tbsp of the oil.

Return the wok to the heat with the chillies and Sichuan pepper and sizzle briefly until the chillies are darkening but not burned and the oil is wonderfully fragrant. Add the ginger, garlic and spring onions and stir-fry briefly until you can smell them. Then return the mushrooms and stir into the fragrant oil. Give the sauce a stir and add it to the wok, stirring swiftly as it thickens. Finally, stir in the peanuts and serve.

SOUPS

For most Chinese people, soup is an essential part of a meal. Sometimes it is served as an appetizer, but more often it is offered alongside other dishes, or towards the end of the meal. In restaurants, the soup may be served in individual bowls, while at home, a great bowlful of soup—the equivalent of a Western tureen—will be placed on the table with a serving spoon so everyone can help themselves.

While the soups served in Chinese restaurants abroad tend to be the dense, somewhat heavy soups that the Chinese call *geng* (a soup thick with finely cut ingredients), most Chinese meals include a very lightly seasoned broth (known as a *tang*) to refresh the palate after the other dishes. In a Sichuanese home, this might be as simple as a broth made by simmering pickled mustard greens in water, with a few bean thread noodles added at the end.

Traditionally, the soup might be the only liquid served with a meal, which is perhaps why Chinese people always talk of "drinking" soup rather than "eating" it. The way to consume a typical home-cooked soup is to ladle some into your empty rice bowl after you've eaten your fill of the other dishes. Then use your chopsticks to eat the solid pieces of food from the soup and drink the liquid from the lip of the bowl. Where the soup contains pieces of meat or poultry, they may be dipped into a little dish of soy or chilli bean sauce before eating.

Although Chinese soups are generally eaten as part of a Chinese meal, as described, many of them also work well as Western appetizers.

Because the soups that follow are intended to be shared, portion sizes are inexact, but as a general rule a soup of 6 cups (about 1½ liters) will serve up to six people.

SOUP OF SALTED DUCK EGGS, SLICED PORK AND MUSTARD GREENS JIE CAI XIAN DAN ROU PIAN TANG 芥菜鹹蛋肉片湯

This refreshing, savory soup is an everyday Cantonese classic: a light broth dense with leafy greens and enlivened by scrumptious morsels of pork and salted egg. Many Chinese chefs in the West know how to make it, but it's rarely listed on English language menus. Chicken can be substituted for the pork, while vegetarians will enjoy the soup with a vegetarian stock and no meat at all.

Don't be alarmed by the instruction to "cut the yolks into small pieces": the process of salting the duck eggs transforms the yolk into a golden, waxy sphere which can be cut with a knife, while the white remains runny.

5 oz (150g) pork tenderloin
2 salted duck eggs
11 oz (300g) preserved mustard greens
½ oz (20g) piece of ginger
6⅓ cups (1½ liters) chicken stock
3 tbsp cooking oil
Salt

For the marinade
½ tsp salt
½ tbsp Shaoxing wine
1½ tsp potato flour

Cut the pork into thin slices and put in a bowl. Stir the marinade ingredients with 1 tbsp water and mix well into the pork. Set aside.

Break the eggs and drain the whites into a cup, keeping the solid, waxy egg yolks in the shell. Cut the yolks into small pieces. Slice the mustard greens across into ⅜–¾ in (1–2cm) ribbons. Peel and slice the ginger.

Bring the stock to a boil in a saucepan.

Heat a wok over a high flame. Add the oil, followed by the ginger and stir-fry briefly until fragrant. Then add the greens and stir-fry until they are wilted, fragrant and half-cooked. Pour in the stock and bring to a boil. Add the egg yolk, separating the pieces if they stick together. Use chopsticks to drop slices of pork into the soup.

Boil for a couple more minutes until the greens are tender and the pork cooked, then reduce the heat and drizzle in the egg whites. When they have set into frothy strands, taste the soup, adding a little salt if necessary, pour into a deep bowl and serve.

VARIATION

Winter melon and salted duck egg soup
Salted duck egg is also an exquisite match for winter melon, lending a thrilling intensity of flavor to its delicate, pale green flesh.

Peel 2 lb (900g) winter melon, then cut away and discard its soft, seedy center. Cut the flesh into bite-sized slices ⅛–⅜ in (½–1cm) thick. Peel and cut into slivers a ⅓ oz (15g) piece of ginger. Break 3 salted duck eggs into a bowl. Remove the yolks and chop them into small pieces. Sizzle the ginger in 2 tbsp cooking oil in a seasoned wok, add the melon and stir-fry for a minute or two. Then add 6⅓ cups (1½ liters) stock, bring to a boil and simmer until the melon is nearly cooked. Add the egg yolks, stirring so they don't stick together. When the melon is cooked, scatter the egg whites into the soup. Taste the liquid and add a little salt if you want. Serve as soon as the wisps of egg white have set.

SOUR-AND-HOT MUSHROOM SOUP
SUAN LA SHAN ZHEN TANG 酸辣山珍湯

I've never been crazy about the sour-and-hot (or hot-and-sour) soups they serve in Chinese restaurants in the West, but I adore the subtler southern Chinese versions, of which this is one. I like to make it with a good chicken stock, but if you use a vegetable stock the recipe is entirely vegetarian.

The soup is floaty with slivered mushrooms, tofu and exotically lovely day lily flowers, its light mushroomy broth enlivened by Chinkiang vinegar and a good kick of white pepper. Feel free to vary the variety of mushrooms as you please. A few slivers of leftover chicken, added to the broth, would make a nice addition for meat eaters. You'll need a deep pot or tureen to serve this soup.

4 dried shiitake mushrooms
Small handful of dried day lily flowers (optional, but nice)
1 qt (1 liter) stock of your choice (see headnote)
1/3 oz (15g) piece of ginger, peeled
3 oz (75g) fresh shiitake mushrooms
3 oz (75g) oyster mushrooms
2 oz (50g) enoki mushrooms

8 oz (225g) plain white tofu
1 tbsp cooking oil
2 tsp light soy sauce
1/4 tsp dark soy sauce
Salt
2 1/2 tbsp Chinkiang vinegar
1/2 tsp ground white pepper
1 tsp sesame oil
2 tbsp finely sliced spring onion greens

Soak the dried shiitake and lily flowers (if using) in hot water from the kettle for at least an hour before you begin.

Set the stock in a pan to heat up before you begin cooking.

Cut the ginger into fine slivers. Trim off and discard the stalks of the soaked mushrooms and thinly slice the caps. Discard the stalks of the fresh shiitake and cut the caps into 1/8–3/8 in (1/2–1cm) wide strips. Cut the oyster mushrooms lengthways into similar thin strips. Gently pull apart the clumped enoki mushrooms. Cut the tofu into strips of a similar size to the mushrooms (it may disintegrate slightly, but don't worry about this).

Heat the oil in a seasoned wok over a high flame. Add the ginger and sizzle for a few moments until fragrant. Then add the dried and fresh mushrooms and lily flowers (if using) and stir-fry until the mushrooms are about half-cooked and smell wonderful. Pour in the heated stock and bring to a boil. Add the tofu and stir gently. Season the soup with the soy sauces, and salt to taste (a good salty flavor is a necessary base for a sour-and-hot soup).

Reduce the heat to a simmer, add the vinegar and pepper and continue to simmer for 30 seconds or so to fuse the flavors. Remove from the heat, stir in the sesame oil, then ladle or pour the soup into a deep pot or tureen. Scatter the spring onions over the soup and serve.

FAVA BEAN AND SNOW VEGETABLE SOUP
DOU BAN XUE CAI TANG 豆瓣雪菜湯

This is a simple soup from Shanghai, where fava beans are a seasonal treat and snow vegetable is one of the most ubiquitous preserves. The sour-juicy vegetable is wonderful with the delicate, savory beans. Sichuanese pickled mustard greens may be used instead of the snow vegetable, if that's easier. And if you have any leftovers of a roasted or poached chicken, do shred them and add them to the soup.

2 tbsp cooking oil
4¼ oz (125g) snow vegetable, chopped
7 oz (200g) shelled, skinned fava beans
6⅓ cups (1½ liters) chicken stock
A few slices of tomato, for color
Salt

Heat the oil in a wok over a high flame. Add the snow vegetable and stir-fry until hot and fragrant. Add the beans, stir a few times, then pour in the stock.

Bring to a boil and simmer gently for 10 minutes or more, until the preserved vegetable has lent its gentle, aromatic sourness to the soup and the beans are tender. Add the tomato slices and simmer briefly to heat through. Season with salt to taste, and serve.

VARIATION

In Sichuan, one of the most popular everyday soups is a quick brew of pickled mustard greens in stock, with a skein of slippy, transparent bean thread noodles for mouthfeel and a handful of sliced spring onion greens for color. With its clean, slightly sour taste, it makes a refreshing conclusion to a spicy Sichuanese meal. To prepare this soup, simply fry 4¼ oz (125g) sliced mustard greens in a little oil, add 6⅓ cups (1½ liters) of stock and a good handful of pre-soaked bean thread noodles and bring to a boil. Season with salt and white pepper, garnish with finely sliced spring onion greens and serve.

FRIED EGG AND TOMATO SOUP
FAN QIE JIAN DAN TANG 番茄煎蛋湯

This simple, vividly colored soup is typical of the domestic supper table in many parts of China and it's one of the soups I ate most frequently when I lived in Chengdu. Feel free to substitute other greens—spinach or pea shoots perhaps—for the bok choy, if you wish.

3 eggs
Salt
3 ripe, red tomatoes
2 heads of green bok choy
6⅓ cups (1½ liters) chicken stock

3 tbsp finely sliced spring onion greens
3 tbsp cooking oil
Ground white pepper

In a small bowl, beat the eggs with a little salt. Slice the tomatoes and cut the bok choy into chopstickable pieces. Bring the stock to a boil in a pan. Put the spring onion greens into a serving bowl.

Add the oil to a seasoned wok over a high flame and swirl it around. Pour in the eggs and swirl them around too. Let them set into an omelette. When the underside is golden, flip it over and brown the other side. Remove the omelette from the wok and set aside.

Add the tomatoes and bok choy to the hot stock, return to a boil, add the omelette and cook briefly until the vegetables are tender, seasoning with salt and white pepper to taste.

Pour the soup over the spring onions in the serving bowl. Invite your guests to use chopsticks to tear off pieces of omelette as they serve themselves soup.

DAI SHUANG'S YELLOW SPLIT PEA SOUP DAI SHUANG PA WAN DOU TANG 戴雙豌豆湯

This is a recipe explained to me by Dai Shuang, the wife and business partner of Chengdu chef Yu Bo, as we strolled through a market not long ago. She was giving me tips on how to use various kinds of produce, including the cabbages and fat stem mustards that were then in season. We passed a stall that was selling *pa wan dou*, a coarse, dull yellow paste made from split peas that is used as a base for soups.

The following is Dai Shuang's family recipe for split pea soup, a version of which they serve in the restaurant as part of their now-legendary 40-course banquets. They serve it in a grand tureen, augmented by little dishes of peanuts, fried dough twists, crisp soy beans, pea leaves and chrysanthemum petals, to be cast into the hot silky liquid. It is a soft, soothing soup, with a stirring hint of ginger. At home, the serving is less grandiose, but the flavors equally pleasing.

11 oz (300g) yellow split peas, soaked overnight in plenty of cold water
½ oz (25g) piece of ginger, unpeeled
2 spring onions, white parts only
3 tbsp lard or cooking oil
¾ tsp whole Sichuan pepper
Up to 6⅓ cups (1½ liters) chicken stock or water
Salt

To serve
A good handful of pea shoots
4 tbsp finely sliced spring onion greens
Handful of Fried or Roasted Peanuts (see page 325)
Small handful of Chinese fried dough twists (*ma hua*) or croutons (optional)

Rinse the soaked peas, place in a saucepan with plenty of water to cover and bring to a boil. Boil vigorously for 10 minutes, then reduce the heat and simmer for about 30 minutes until the peas are completely cooked and starting to disintegrate. Strain, reserving the water. (This step can be done in advance.)

Smack the ginger and spring onion whites hard with the side of a cleaver or a rolling pin, to break them open (without smashing them to smithereens!). Heat a wok over a high flame. Add the lard or oil, followed by the ginger and spring onion and stir-fry until the oil is wonderfully fragrant. Add the Sichuan pepper and sizzle for a few moments more until you can smell its aroma. Then use a slotted spoon to add the peas to the wok and stir them in the fragrant oil for a minute or two. Now measure and add the remains of the pea cooking water to the wok, with enough stock or water to make up about 6⅓ cups (1½ liters) in total. Season with salt to taste.

Put the pea sprouts in a serving bowl and pour the hot soup over them. Scatter the other ingredients on top and serve immediately.

SOUP WITH VEGETABLES AND MEATBALLS
YUAN ZI TANG 丸子湯

I remember, one warm evening, walking with a friend through the tranquil old lanes of central Chengdu a year or two before they were demolished. We came across a woman sitting at a low bamboo table in the street, eating her supper. I couldn't help gazing at the simple meal laid out in front of her, which consisted simply of a lovely looking soup of meatballs and winter melon and a bowl of rice. I still have a photograph, taken by my friend, of myself bending down towards the seated lady, and a detailed description, written down in my notebook, of what she was eating.

This soup is so easy to make and so delicious to eat. You can use any vegetable you like as an accompanying ingredient: beansprouts, Chinese cabbage, tomatoes, choy sum or winter melon. If the vegetable you choose takes a few minutes to become tender, such as Chinese cabbage, cook it before you add the meatballs; if it cooks almost instantly, like pea sprouts or choy sum, add it when the meatballs are just about ready. If you want to make this into a one-dish meal, like the lady in the old lanes, use your chopsticks to pluck out the meatballs and vegetables and eat them with your rice, then drink the soup from your empty rice bowl. Served like this, with rice, it will easily feed two people.

For the meatballs
1 dried shiitake mushroom
A small piece of ginger
4 oz (100g) ground pork with a little fat
½ egg, beaten
1 tbsp finely chopped spring onion greens
½ tsp sesame oil
1 tsp potato flour
Salt
Ground white pepper

For the soup
6⅓ cups (1½ liters) chicken stock
1¼ lb (500g) winter melon, or other vegetable of your choice (the exact quantity is not critical)
2 tbsp finely sliced spring onion greens

Soak the dried mushroom for 30 minutes in hot water from the kettle. Crush the ginger, then put it in a glass with cold water to cover.

When the mushroom is soft, chop it finely. Place the pork in a bowl, and add 1 tbsp of the ginger-soaking water and all the other meatball ingredients, seasoning with salt and pepper. Mix vigorously, stirring in one direction (this is supposed to give the meat a better texture). You will end up with a nice soft meatball mixture.

Bring the stock to a boil over a high flame. Peel the winter melon, then cut away and discard the soft, seedy section in the center. Cut the rest of the melon into ⅛–⅜ in (½–1cm) slices. Add the winter melon (or any other prepared vegetable) and simmer until tender. Season with salt and pepper to taste.

Reduce the heat to a gentle simmer, then add the meatballs. The Chinese way is to take a small handful of paste in your left hand (if you are right-handed), make a fist, then gently squeeze the paste up through the hole made by your thumb and index finger. Use the other hand to scoop off walnut-sized balls of paste, and drop them into the soup. If you prefer, you can use a couple of teaspoons to mold the meatballs.

Simmer gently for about five minutes until the meatballs have risen to the surface and are cooked through. (If using tomatoes or greens that cook quickly, add them at this stage and let them heat through.)

Turn the soup into a warmed serving bowl and scatter with spring onion greens.

TARO AND ARUGULA SOUP
YU TOU WA WA CAI 芋頭娃娃菜

This is a variation of a simple and rustic Hunanese dish that is traditionally made with very young and tender radish sprouts, known locally as "baby vegetables" or *wa wa cai*. In my Hunanese *Revolutionary Chinese Cookbook*, I suggested using watercress as an easily available substitute, but my mother has since come up with an even better version, made with arugula. The peppery arugula is a delightful alternative to the *wa wa cai*, while the taro gives the soup a soft, silky consistency: comfort food, Hunanese style. You could use another green vegetable if you wish. I suspect the tender tips of nettles, picked with rubber gloves, would also work well.

I've suggested boiling the taro before you peel them, as their skins contain an irritant (neutralized by cooking) that will make your hands itch like crazy. If you insist on peeling them raw, make sure you wear rubber gloves.

1³/₄ lb (800g) taro
6¹/₃ cups (1¹/₂ liters) chicken stock or water
3 tbsp cooking oil
7 oz (200g) arugula leaves

Salt
Ground white pepper
3 spring onions, green parts only, finely sliced

Wash the taro, place in a saucepan, cover with cold water and bring to a boil. Reduce the heat and simmer until tender (about 20 minutes). When the taro is cool enough to handle, peel and rinse.

Cut the taro into slices about ³/₈ in (1cm) thick, put them in a pan with the chicken stock or water and simmer for 20–30 minutes. This step can be done some time in advance of your meal.

When you are ready to eat, heat a wok over a high flame. Add the oil, then the arugula, and stir-fry until just wilted. Then add the soupy taro mixture, bring to a boil and season with salt and pepper. Simmer for a couple of minutes to allow the flavors to meld, then turn into a serving bowl or tureen. Scatter with the spring onions.

SIMPLE CHICKEN SOUP
QING DUN QUAN JI 清燉全雞

As in many other cultures, a simple stewed chicken, served in its own rich broth, is a Chinese tonic and pick-me-up. Find a good chicken—preferably an old free-range hen—and the flavor of the soup will be almost miraculous: I've never forgotten a chicken soup I ate in rural Hunan, made with an old hen that had spent its life pecking around my friend Fan Qun's farm.

The ingredients used in the basic soup are minimal: just the bird and water with a little rice wine, ginger and spring onion to refine its flavor. You can, though, add other ingredients if you wish: dried mushrooms of any kind, first soaked in hot water to plump them up and cooked with the chicken, or perhaps some fresh greens added just before you serve the dish. Many Chinese people would add tonic herbs such as Chinese angelica, milk vetch root or a handful of scarlet gouqi berries (you can buy selections of mixed herbs intended for use in tonic soups in larger Chinese supermarkets). The berries are normally added for the last few minutes of cooking time, so they don't lose their color or disintegrate.

If you cook the chicken in a clay pot, you can bring it straight to table; otherwise, the whole, cooked chicken is normally transferred to a deep tureen and the broth poured over.

To serve, give each guest some chicken meat and some soup in a small bowl, or scoop out the chicken and serve it separately, with small dipping dishes of tamari or light soy sauce for the meat. Any leftovers will give you a glorious bowlful of Stewed Chicken Noodles the next day (see page 284). You can, of course, use exactly the same method to cook a chopped or cut up chicken, or just a chicken leg or two if you are cooking for a small number of people. Other birds, such as ducks, pheasants and pigeons, can be cooked in a similar way. This recipe makes a larger quantity than the other soups in this chapter and will serve six to eight people.

1 chicken, about 3¼ lb (1½kg) (preferably a mature, free-range hen)
½ oz (25g) piece of ginger, unpeeled
2 spring onions, white parts only
1 tbsp Shaoxing wine
Salt
Ground white pepper (optional)

For best results, start by blanching the chicken for a few minutes in boiling water to allow any impurities to rise to the surface, then rinse it thoroughly under the tap. Smack the ginger with the side of a cleaver or a rolling pin to crush it slightly.

Place the chicken in a saucepan or a large clay pot with a lid: the pot should be large enough to hold it without too much space around (the flavors of the soup will be faint if there is too much water). Cover the bird with cold water and bring to a boil.

Skim the liquid, then add the ginger, spring onion whites and Shaoxing wine. Cover the pan or pot with a lid and simmer very gently for two to three hours, with the surface of the liquid just murmuring, until the bird is tender and the broth rich and delicious.

Remove and discard the ginger and spring onion. Season with salt and white pepper, if desired, to taste, simmer for another 10 minutes, then serve.

RICE

In May the landscape is intensely green. The terraced paddies follow the curves of the hills, their watery surfaces glistening silver in the sunlight, pricked by narrow spears of seedling rice. Whole mountainsides are rimmed and ribbed with these incredible fields. Viewed close-up, the water quivers with the feet of water boatmen and the kicks and wriggles of half-seen creatures. Out of the red clay banks spring chilli plants, their tiny white flowers peering out from the leaves. Every spare inch is sown with crops: broad leaves of pumpkins sprawl in one corner; in another fava bean runners cling to bamboo poles. Tight little hedges of tea plants run along the slopes, mulberry trees stand here and there, and the whole landscape twitters with insects.

Rice not only shapes the scenery in southern China, it is the foundation of the diet. Most meals, including breakfast, are based on rice (wheaten noodles, dumplings and breads only play a supplementary role). Someone from the south of China, deprived of rice for a few days, is likely to feel the same pangs as an Englishman forced to live without potatoes. The word for "cooked rice" (*fan*) crops up in many contexts, including the old-fashioned greeting "have you eaten your rice yet?," and expressions as disparate as those for restaurant (*fan guan*, "rice building"), livelihood (*fan wan*, "rice bowl") and a greedy eater (*fan tong*, "rice bucket"). Once you have your rice, the rest of your diet is negotiable. You might have a plethora of rich and delicious dishes if you can afford them, or simply a couple of cubes of fermented tofu and some pickled vegetables: in both cases, the purpose of the other dishes is to "send the rice down" (*xia fan*).

Glutinous and non-glutinous, long-grained and short-grained rices are all eaten. Glutinous rices, including black glutinous rice that has a dark purple color when cooked, are most often used in snacks and sweet dishes, while rarer varieties such as the purple rice of Yunnan Province and the reddish blood rice (*xue nuo*), grown in just a few parts of the country, are eaten either as local delicacies or as an exotic banquet treat.

Plain white rice, which is typically boiled, then left to steam gently in a covered pot (or these days in an electric rice cooker), is the most common form. For more casual meals, and especially for breakfast, thick rice congees or runny rice gruels may be served. Rice can also be soaked then ground with water to make noodles or dumpling wrappers. Brown, unpolished rice is almost never eaten in China, despite its vast superiority in nutritional terms. (I love brown rice and increasingly serve it with Chinese food for simple suppers at home.)

In the past, children were told to eat up every grain of rice in their bowls, not only out of respect for the farmers who produced it, but because any future spouse would have a pock mark on their face for each discarded grain. There is still no excuse to throw away leftover rice, because there are so many wonderful things to do with it. You may stir-fry it with an egg and spring onions to give a fragrant bowlful that can be a meal in itself. You may reheat it with water or stock, adding greens or titbits of meat or fish to make "soaked rice" (*pao fan*), a delicious soupy brew that can be eaten on its own or with other dishes. Cook your soaked rice for longer, until the grains rupture and form a smooth mass, and you have congee (*zhou*), a particular favorite in the Cantonese south, that can be jazzed up with all manner of added ingredients. Or just reheat leftover rice quickly with a lot of water to make "watery rice" or rice gruel (*xi fan*), which, eaten with fermented tofu, pickles, boiled eggs, steamed buns and any leftovers you have, is the staple of the Sichuanese breakfast table. In China, all these are invariably made with white rice, but I like them with brown rice too.

In rural households, rice may be boiled before being turned into a perforated bamboo pot for a final steaming. In this case, the careful economy of the traditional kitchen extends to the boiling water beneath the steamer (*mi tang*, "rice soup"). Milky in appearance and with a silken mouthfeel, it may be drunk as a soup, or boiled up with odds and ends of vegetables. This broth, once a poverty dish designed to save every last nutrient, is now a fashionable treat in "rustic" restaurants. It is best made with the cooking water from less polished or even brown rice.

When cooking rice, it is vital to remember that leftovers should be cooled then refrigerated as quickly as possible, definitely within four hours (rice left sitting in warm temperatures can cause food poisoning). It's best not to keep cooked rice for more than three days.

PLAIN WHITE RICE
BAI MI FAN 白米飯

The most common method for cooking rice is to boil it in a measured amount of water, until the surface of the rice is almost dry and punctuated by little round holes, then to cover the pot and leave it to cook very gently for 12–15 minutes. At the end, you should have a potful of fluffy white rice with a delicious golden crust on the bottom. This crust is traditionally adored, especially by children; try to divide it fairly among your guests!

Deciding exactly how much rice to cook can be tricky: when I'm entertaining, I find sometimes I'm left with substantial amounts of uneaten rice at the end of the evening; while on other occasions I have to run out and cook some more during dinner. In general, I prefer to err on the side of generosity and find the quantities suggested in this recipe, which yields enough for two or three rice bowlfuls for each of four people, a decent compromise. You may well find you have some leftovers: use them to make fried rice or soupy rice the following day.

Different varieties of rice require slightly different cooking times and absorb varying quantities of water. Some, notably short-grained and brown rices, benefit from a prior soaking. Thai fragrant rice, also known as jasmine rice, is the one I normally use.

3 cups (600g) Thai fragrant rice

Rinse the rice well in a colander under the tap. Place in a saucepan with 4½ oz (1.1 liters) of water and bring to a boil over a high heat. Give the rice a good stir to remove any grains sticking to the base of the pan, then continue to boil for a few minutes until the surface of the rice is dry and covered in little round "breathing" holes.

Cover the pan tightly, reduce the heat to a minimum and continue to cook for 12–15 minutes, until tender.

VARIATIONS

Traditional steamer rice (*zeng zi fan*)
Bring your rice to a boil in plenty of water, then simmer for seven to eight minutes, until nearly cooked but still a little hard and starchy in the center of each grain. Then strain (reserving the water to use as a rice "soup," if desired), put in a bamboo steamer—or a regular steamer lined with clean muslin—and steam over a high flame for about 10 minutes, until fragrant and fully cooked.

Pot-sticker rice served with rice "soup"
Another method is to cover the rice with plenty of water and boil it vigorously for seven to eight minutes, until partially cooked but still a little hard in the center. Then strain off and reserve the cooking water to use as a soup. Brush a little cooking oil over the base of the pan and return the rice. Cover with a tight-fitting lid and cook on the lowest possible heat until tender. (Chopped root vegetables such as potatoes, sweet potatoes and taro may be boiled and slow-cooked along with the rice, another old rural strategy for making the rice go further that is now enjoyed in "rustic" restaurants.) If you are making rice "soup," do not rinse the rice before cooking and use less highly polished rices if available: you want as much starch and flavor in the water as possible. Serve the rice with the soup.

PLAIN BROWN RICE
CAO MI FAN 糙米飯

The word used to describe brown rice in Chinese, *cao*, means rough, coarse, crude, or even inferior. The unpolished grain is almost never eaten in modern China, even in restaurants that make a point of offering other coarse staples such as sweetcorn and sweet potatoes. I can't actually remember a single occasion on which I've been offered brown rice to eat in China. Nonetheless, as most people know, it is far healthier than its refined white equivalent, in which most of the nutrients have been polished away to leave just a starchy kernel.

When it comes to entertaining, I have to admit that I'm still a rice snob and serve plain white rice as an elegant background to the flavors of other dishes. For simple home meals, however, I find I'm increasingly cooking brown rice to serve with Chinese dishes. Quite apart from its superior nutritional value, I love its juicy chewiness and taste and find it keeps me full and satisfied for longer. Here, then, is what I find the best method for cooking it. The pre-soaking really helps to give a perfect texture.

If you don't have time to pre-soak your rice, or forget to, as I often do, you can also cover the rice in plenty of water, bring to a boil and simmer for about 30 minutes. I find it more difficult to achieve a perfect texture this way: you need more water for the longer cooking time if you are to avoid boiling the pan dry and, in my experience, the rice can end up a little soggy. In this case, I make a virtue of necessity, deliberately using more water than I need, then, when the rice is tender, straining off the silky liquid to be served as a "soup" at the end of the meal. I then cover the rice pan and heat it very gently until the remnants of water are absorbed. This quantity of rice serves about four people.

3 cups (600g) short-grain brown rice

Soak the rice in cold water for at least two hours.

Drain the rice and place it in a saucepan with 5 cups (1.2 liters) of water. Bring to a boil, then half-cover the pan, reduce the heat and simmer for 25 minutes, keeping an eye on it to make sure it does not boil dry.

Remove from the heat, fluff up with a fork, cover and leave for 10 minutes before serving.

EGG-FRIED RICE
DAN CHAO FAN 蛋炒飯

This is one of the simplest fried rices and a brilliant way of making leftovers into a satisfying meal. The following recipe gives an understated rice that can be served with Chinese dishes. If you want to make it into a one-dish meal, I suggest you use three eggs instead of two and season it more heavily with salt and soy sauce. Breaking the rice down into small clumps before you cook it will make the stir-frying quicker and easier.

When making fried rice, it is vitally important to use rice that has cooled completely (it is best to use rice cooked the previous day). If you try to stir-fry wet rice, the final result will be soggy and lack the marvellous fragrance that is the joy of this type of dish. For a more robust dish, use leftover brown rice instead of white.

This recipe serves two.

2 large eggs
1½ cups (300g) cooked, cooled rice (¾ cup/150g when raw)
2 tbsp cooking oil

Salt
Light soy sauce, to taste
4 spring onions, green parts only, finely sliced
1 tsp sesame oil

Beat the eggs together in a small bowl. Break the rice up as far as possible.

Heat the oil in a seasoned wok over a high flame. Add the eggs and swirl them around to cover the base of the wok. When the eggs are half-cooked but still a littly runny on top, add all the rice and stir-fry vigorously, mixing everything together and breaking up any clumps of rice with your wok scoop or ladle.

Continue to stir-fry for a few minutes until the rice is piping hot and fragrant, seasoning with salt and soy sauce to taste. Add the spring onions and stir a few times until you can smell their fragrance. Stir in the sesame oil and serve.

VARIATIONS

Green fried rice
Beat a single egg and stir it into 1 scant cup (200g) cooked, cooled rice. Finely chop a few handfuls of spinach. Heat 2 tbsp cooking oil in a seasoned wok over a high flame, add the eggy rice and stir-fry until the grains have separated out and it smells delicious, adding salt to taste. Finally, add the chopped spinach and continue to stir-fry until the rice has acquired a greenish color. Serve.

Soy sauce-fried rice
Omit the egg and stir-fry leftover rice on its own, adding a rich soy sauce such as tamari to taste. The soy sauce will give the rice a pale brown luster and a good savory flavor.

YANGZHOU FRIED RICE
YANG ZHOU CHAO FAN 揚州炒飯

The city of Yangzhou in eastern Jiangsu Province is one of the ancient centers of Chinese gastronomy and the heartland of what is known as Huaiyang Cuisine. Strangely, only one of its dishes is widely known in the West and that is Yangzhou fried rice, which is on the menu of almost every overseas Cantonese restaurant. A colorful mixture of fragrant rice with diced meat, seafood and vegetables, it traditionally includes a little sea cucumber and crab meat as well as fresh bamboo shoots. Many versions, even some of those cooked up in Yangzhou itself, make this dish as a simple fried rice, but the classic recipe, upon which mine is based, includes an injection of chicken stock that adds an extra deliciousness. I have omitted hard-to-find ingredients, such as sea cucumber.

I first wrote this recipe for a Chinese New Year's feature in a magazine. One friend told me afterwards that it had been such a hit with her children that she had been making it almost once a week ever since, so I've included it here in her honor.

Don't worry if you don't have every ingredient: the key is to have a tempting selection of colors and tastes amid the rice. There's no need to weigh them exactly; just aim to have a small pile (about 3 tbsp when chopped) of each.

Yangzhou fried rice can be served as part of a special Chinese meal, or as a whole meal in itself, perhaps with simply a salad or a lightly cooked green vegetable on the side (Spinach in Ginger Sauce, see page 64, would be perfect).

This quantity serves four as a main dish, or more as part of a Chinese meal.

½ oz (25g) raw pork fillet
½ oz (25g) ham or salami
½ oz (25g) cold, cooked chicken
2 dried shiitake mushrooms, soaked in hot water for 30 minutes, stalks discarded
½ oz (25g) bamboo shoot (optional)
3 spring onions, green parts only
1 egg, plus 1 egg yolk (optional)
Salt

Ground white pepper
5 tbsp cooking oil
½ oz (25g) small peeled shrimp, fresh or frozen, cooked or uncooked
½ oz (25g) fresh or frozen peas, peeled fava beans or cooked green soy beans
2 tsp Shaoxing wine
¾ cup (200ml) chicken stock
3 cups (600g) cooked, cooled Thai fragrant rice (1½ cups/ 300g when raw)

Cut the pork, ham or salami, chicken, soaked mushrooms and bamboo shoot, if using, into small dice. Finely slice the spring onion greens. Beat the egg with salt and pepper to taste (add an extra yolk if you wish to give the cooked egg an intense yellow color).

Heat 2 tbsp oil in a seasoned wok over a high flame. Add the raw pork and shrimp and stir-fry briefly, until the pork is pale. Add the ham, chicken, mushrooms, peas or beans and bamboo shoot, if using, and continue to stir-fry for a minute or two, until everything is hot and sizzling. Add the Shaoxing wine, then pour in the stock and bring to a boil. Season with salt to taste, then pour into a bowl.

Rinse and dry the wok. Return it to the heat with the remaining oil. When the oil is hot, add the beaten egg mixture and swirl around the base of the wok. When the egg is half-cooked, add all the rice and stir-fry, using your ladle or wok scoop to break up any lumps.

When the rice is very hot and smells delicious (it will make a popping sound around the edges at this stage), add the bowlful of prepared ingredients in their stock sauce. Mix well and continue to stir-fry for another 30 seconds or so, seasoning with salt or pepper if you wish. Finally, stir in the spring onion greens and serve.

SHANGHAINESE RICE WITH SALT PORK AND BOK CHOY
XIAN ROU CAI FAN 鹹肉菜販

This is a typically Shanghainese supper dish, made with salt pork and Shanghai green bok choy. I first ate it in the wonderful Fu 1088 restaurant, which occupies an old mansion in the French Concession. There, it was served in a black clay pot. My Shanghainese lunch companion said it reminded her of her childhood, when she ate it often, but she thought her family's version was made with salted mustard greens rather than fresh bok choy, or perhaps with a mixture.

Anyway, it's a delicious and terrifically simple dish. Don't pay too much attention to the quantities; you can add more or less meat and vegetables as you please. Use Shanghainese salt pork if you have it (soak it for five to ten minutes in hot water if it's very salty, then rinse), or pancetta, or bacon. Just make sure the meat is fatty rather than lean, as the fat helps to flavor the rice. I'm sure this method would also work well with other green vegetables, particularly broccoli and kale. And of course you can make it with Chinese preserved mustard greens too, rinsing them before use if they are very salty. If you are eating this instead of plain steamed rice with a few Chinese dishes, you don't need to salt it. If you are eating it as a one-dish meal, add salt to taste.

This recipe serves two to three.

2 oz (50g) salt pork, pancetta or bacon
11 oz (300g) Shanghai green bok choy

2 tbsp cooking oil or lard, plus a little more if you are using a clay pot
1 cup (200g) Thai fragrant rice, rinsed

If you are using a clay pot, heat it with a little water over a very low flame, or warm it in an oven, so it won't crack. Bring a kettle to a boil.

Cut the meat into very fine dice. Coarsely chop the bok choy.

Heat the oil or lard in a wok over a high flame. Add the pork and stir-fry briefly until it is cooked and fragrant. Add the rice and stir-fry until it smells delicious. Then add the bok choy and stir-fry for another minute or so.

If you are using a clay pot, pour off the water used to warm it, dry the inside of the pot and rub it with a little oil or lard. Place the rice mixture in the clay pot (if using), and add enough hot water from the kettle to just cover the rice. Bring to a boil, then cover with a lid and cook over a very low flame for about 20 minutes, until the rice is cooked and a golden crust is developing at the bottom of the pot. (If you are using a rice cooker, simply put the rice mixture into the cooker, cover with water and set it to cook.)

Serve the rice with some nice bits of *guo ba* (the golden crust at the bottom of the pot).

VARIATION

The same ingredients can be used to make a fine fried rice: simply stir-fry the salt pork and greens as described above, add some cooked, cooled rice and stir-fry until wonderfully fragrant, seasoning with salt to taste.

SOUPY RICE WITH PORK AND GREENS
SHANG HAI PAO FAN 上海泡飯

"Soaked" or soupy rice (*pao fan*) is cooked rice that has been reheated in water or stock, but not long enough for the grains to disintegrate as in a congee. You may add to it any ingredients you like: chicken, fresh pork, salt pork or bacon, with greens or other vegetables in any proportions you like. I often make it as a way of using up leftovers, not only of rice (white or brown), but any odds and ends I might have in the fridge: orphaned vegetables, cold cooked beans, the remains of a roast chicken . . . At one of my favorite restaurants in Chengdu, they heat up yesterday's rice in chicken stock and add plenty of sliced greens before serving for a very rich "soaked rice."

All the quantities and even the ingredients in this recipe are extremely flexible. The following amount of rice is enough for two. You will see two bowlfuls of soupy rice in the background to the photograph of Chicken Livers with Chinese Chives, page 127.

2 dried shiitake mushrooms
A slice or two of bacon
5 oz (150g) Shanghai green bok choy
1–2 tbsp cooking oil
4–5 slices of peeled ginger

1 scant cup (200g) cooked, cooled rice
4 cups (1 liter) chicken stock
Salt
Ground white pepper

Soak the mushrooms for 30 minutes in hot water from the kettle, until soft.

Remove and discard any rinds from the bacon and cut into slivers. Cut the mushrooms into slivers and slice or chop the bok choy.

Heat the oil in a wok over a high flame. Add the bacon and stir-fry until fragrant. Add the ginger, stir a couple of times, then add the mushrooms. Stir a few more times, then add the greens and stir-fry until wilted. Add the rice and stock and bring to a boil.

Simmer for a couple of minutes, season with salt and pepper to taste and serve (if you are serving the rice, Chinese-style, with a selection of other dishes, you probably won't wish to add salt).

CONGEE
ZHOU 粥

All cultures and all individuals have their comfort foods. In China, one Jin Dynasty official is said to have become so consumed with longing for the water shield soup and ground perch of his native region that he abandoned his post and returned home. But perhaps the most universal of comfort foods is rice congee, which is like a caress of the mouth and stomach, as soothing as baby food. At its simplest, it is just rice cooked slowly, in plenty of water, until the grains dissolve into a voluptuous, satiny mass. Because of this long, lazy cooking, the Cantonese like to say that someone who spends hours talking on the phone is "making telephone congee."

Plain congee can be made with water or stock: chicken stock is particularly good. Eat it on its own, with fermented tofu or other relishes, or with any Chinese dishes. For a more nutritious congee, cook the rice with pre-soaked mung beans, peanuts or dried lotus seeds. Plain congee made with water is the perfect antidote to gastronomic excess, and recommended for invalids. In the Cantonese south, where congee is dearly loved, they add all kinds of ingredients: one restaurant I visited in Hong Kong offered nearly 60 kinds. They had a vast potful of plain congee in the kitchen, and a cabinet full of ingredients to be added to it in a smaller pan. This recipe serves four.

³/₄ cup (150g) Thai fragrant rice

½ tsp salt
2 tsp cooking oil

Rinse and drain the rice. Mix it with the salt and oil and set aside for 30 minutes. Rinse and drain.

Bring 2½ cups (2.4 liters) of water to a boil in a thick-bottomed pan over a high flame, add the rice, return to a boil, partially cover the pan and simmer gently for about an hour and a half, stirring occasionally. The rice grains will burst open; by the end of the cooking they will have largely melted into the water to form a soft porridge.

The congee can be eaten plain (good if you are feeling delicate), or with seasonings and other ingredients of your choice.

VARIATIONS

Congee with other seeds and grains
The congee can be cooked with many other seeds and grains: in this case omit the oil and salt, cook the rice for an extra 30 minutes and season with sugar before eating if desired. Mung or azuki beans, as well as lotus seeds, should first be soaked overnight, then cooked with the rice. Peanuts and walnuts, as well as black glutinous rice (which will color the congee a deep purple) can simply be cooked with the rice. Dried Chinese dates and wolfberries may be added towards the end of cooking time.

Congee with pork ribs, preserved duck eggs and ginger
Blanch pork ribs, chopped into bite-sized pieces, for a few minutes to remove any bloody juices, then rinse well. Cook them with the rice. Half.an hour before serving, add chopped preserved duck eggs and slivers of ginger. Scatter it with ground white pepper and finely sliced spring onion greens and mix well before eating.

Dandelion leaf congee
My Sichuanese friends Yu Bo and Dai Shuang recently served me a congee made with dandelion leaves, added towards the end of the cooking time . . . a rather lyrical spring version on the congee theme.

Congee with chicken and shiitake mushrooms
Soak some dried shiitake mushrooms in hot water from the kettle for 30 minutes. Slice some raw chicken and marinate in a little soy sauce, finely chopped ginger, cooking oil and potato flour mixed with water. Slice off and discard the mushroom stalks and slice the caps. Add the mushrooms and chicken to your hot congee and boil for about five minutes. Cover and leave to steep for another 10 minutes or so before serving with a garnish of spring onion greens, sesame oil and pepper.

RICE-COOKED VEGETABLES AND RICE-COOKED PORK
FAN WU CAI 飯焐菜

One of the traditional ways of cooking rice in China is in a *zengzi*, a bamboo or wooden steamer. The rice is boiled for a few minutes to "break its rawness," then tipped into a *zengzi* and steamed until cooked. In the countryside, it was common to cook other food over the rice, inside the *zengzi*. One way of doing this is to place the cut ingredients with oil and seasonings in a bowl, then lay the bowl directly on the rice, or on a bamboo frame suspended over it. Another way, known as *fan wu*, is to steam food directly on the rice.

I first encountered this in Hangzhou, at the Dragon Well Manor, a restaurant specializing in artisanal foods and old-fashioned cooking methods. There, I ate *fan wu* eggplant, the whole vegetables steamed directly on the rice, then torn and served with a dip of rich soy sauce and garlic. I also tasted *fan wu* pork belly: thick slices of meat, served again with a dip of soy. I was smitten both by their tastes and by the economy and simplicity of the cooking method, which works equally well with an electric rice cooker.

Because of the unadorned nature of food cooked this way, fine ingredients are essential. If you have a garden, it's a wonderful way of enjoying the subtle flavors of freshly gathered vegetables.

Thai fragrant rice

Thin Chinese eggplant, whole and washed

or

Mediterranean eggplant, cut lengthways into quarters or small pieces, depending on size

or

Water bamboo (wild rice stem), peeled and quartered

or

Very tender, fresh bamboo shoots, peeled and sliced

or

3/8 in- (1 cm) thick slices of raw pork belly, with skin if you please

or

Whatever you like (obviously it must require no more cooking time than the rice)

To serve

A really good soy sauce (I prefer an organic tamari)

Finely chopped garlic, to taste

If making traditional steamer rice, follow the instructions on page 254, but lay your ingredients directly on the rice before steaming.

If using an electric rice cooker, measure the rinsed rice and water into the rice cooker. Lay the food on top. Steam.

To serve, remove the food from the rice and lay neatly in a dish. Dress with soy sauce and garlic if desired, or serve the soy sauce and garlic separately, in a dipping dish.

The photograph opposite shows *fan wu* eggplant with a soy-and-garlic dressing, and thick slices of belly pork with a dip.

NOODLES

In southern China, noodles are often eaten at lunchtime, perhaps in a small restaurant near a place of work, or for a quick and casual meal at home, or a late-night snack. When I was a student at Sichuan University, I used to eat noodles for lunch almost every day at Mr. Xie's legendary noodle shop; later, living in Hunan, I ate soupy rice noodles for breakfast, with pickled chilli relish on the side. And "long-life noodles," so-called because of their auspicious length, are a traditional birthday food across China.

Many Chinese noodle dishes, in common with Italian pastas, make fantastic last-minute meals. If you keep some dried noodles and a few basic seasonings in your larder, and some spring onions in your refrigerator, you'll be able to rustle up several of the recipes in this chapter in only about 15 minutes. And although some of the recipes may look startlingly simple, I hope you'll find the flavors extraordinary.

In restaurants, fresh wheat or rice noodles are most commonly served, while some specializt shops offer buckwheat noodles that are made from scratch on the spot. At home, dried noodles are the first recourse of the busy cook in search of almost instant sustenance. Most Chinese supermarkets sell a variety of dried noodles made with wheat, rice, or buckwheat, as well as transparent pastas made from sweet potato and mung bean starch, among others; many also keep fresh rice or wheat noodles in the refrigerator. I tend to keep in stock dried noodles made both from wheat flour and from a mixture of wheat and buckwheat flours, as well as dried bean thread noodles. For making noodle soups, I like to keep packages of home-made stock in my freezer, but you can use canned or powdered stock if you prefer (just take care with seasoning if you are using a ready-made stock that is already salty).

If you don't eat wheat, do use rice noodles instead of wheat noodles in these recipes. Fresh rice noodles simply need a quick blanching to heat them up; dried rice noodles should be soaked in hot water until supple before using.

In China, "dry" noodles—that is, noodles that are not served in a broth—are almost invariably served with a soup, to refresh the palate. This soup might be as simple as a bowl of stock with a few spring onion slices, or a broth with wisps of beaten egg or tender tofu with strands of seaweed. One Chinese tradition I enjoy is to use the silky water used for cooking noodles (*mian tang*) as a soup, perhaps with a little sliced spring onion and a tiny slug of sesame oil. Chinese noodles for "dry" noodle dishes are often rinsed after cooking, to get rid of any starchiness that will make them stick together.

Soup noodles are the perfect one-dish meal, with their filling, starchy staple, refreshing broth, delicious seasonings, and whatever you like to add in the way of meat, fish, tofu or vegetables as a topping.

SPICY BUCKWHEAT NOODLES (WITH OR WITHOUT CHICKEN)
SUAN LA QIAO MIAN 酸辣蕎麵

Buckwheat is mainly grown in cold, mountainous areas, especially in northern China. In Sichuan, where the bitter or Tartary variety is favored, it is usually eaten in the form of noodles. This recipe is one of my old favorites and was taught to me by Liu Shaokun, who runs a small pickling and preserving factory at his restaurant on the outskirts of Chengdu. His storerooms contain ranks of waist-high pickle jars, some filled with scarlet pickled chillies, others with dark salted mustards, still others lit up with a glorious paste made from pickled chillies, rapeseed (canola) oil and salt. Liu Shaokun's restaurant specializes in old-fashioned rustic cooking, including his own wind-dried winter sausages, steamed and served with a dried chilli dip; braised turtle with radishes; chicken or fish with pickled vegetables; twice-cooked pork with salted greens; and old-fashioned soups of alfalfa leaves and other greens boiled in rice cooking water.

This dish is usually served cold, but will also taste good hot if you can't wait that long. It serves two people as a snack, or more as part of a spread of cold dishes.

5½ oz (160g) dried buckwheat noodles
A little cooking oil
1 tbsp light or tamari soy sauce
2 tbsp Chinkiang vinegar
½ tsp sugar
Salt, to taste
4 tbsp chilli oil (with its sediment, if desired)
1–2 tsp finely chopped garlic, to taste
3 tbsp finely sliced spring onion greens
A little cold, cooked chicken meat, torn into shreds (optional)
2 tsp finely chopped fresh red chilli, plus a few chilli slices to serve

Bring a pan of water to a boil and cook the noodles to your liking. Rinse in cold water and shake dry. If you want to eat the noodles cold, sprinkle a little plain oil on them and mix well with chopsticks, before spreading the noodles out to cool (the oil will stop them from sticking together).

Place the noodles in a deep bowl and add all the other ingredients, except the chilli slices. Mix well, turn on to a serving dish and top with the chicken shreds (if using) and the sliced chillies.

MRS. YU'S SWEET AND SPICY COLD NOODLES
YU LAO SHI LIANG MIAN 余老師涼麵

When I was a student at Sichuan University, I took private classes in Chinese with a teacher named Yu Weiqin. With my limited vocabulary of the time, I struggled to keep up with our fascinating discussions about sexual politics and social mores in China, but revelled in the lunches and dinners she cooked for me from time to time, because Teacher Yu is a marvellous cook. Sometimes she would conjure up a bowlful of fried rice studded with morsels of her homemade wind-dried sausage; sometimes she would invite my roommate and me for supper and whip up a dozen dishes. This was one of her regular offerings, cold noodles and beansprouts tossed with an improbable array of seasonings.

You can make this with any cold noodles, but I prefer the kind Teacher Yu used to use: simple Chinese flour-and-water noodles, which you can buy fresh or dried from Chinese supermarkets. You can add shredded chicken if you wish (it's a great use for leftovers), or a sprinkling of toasted sesame seeds. The noodles should be cooled and dried before use, so you need to start a couple of hours in advance of your meal.

This makes enough to serve two people as an appetizer or a snack on its own, or more if served alongside other dishes as part of a Chinese meal.

5 oz (150g) beansprouts
7 oz (200g) dried noodles, or 11 oz (300g) fresh noodles
A little cooking oil
2 tbsp light soy sauce or tamari
2 tsp Chinkiang vinegar
2 tbsp runny sesame paste (optional)
3 tsp sugar
2 tsp finely chopped garlic
¼ tsp ground roasted Sichuan pepper
2 tbsp finely sliced spring onion greens
2–4 tbsp chilli oil, with its sediment, to taste
½ tsp sesame oil
1 tsp toasted sesame seeds
Some leftover chicken meat, shredded (optional)

Bring a large panful of water to a boil over a high flame. When boiling, plunge in the beansprouts and blanch for a minute or so, until barely cooked and still a bit crisp. Remove the beansprouts to a colander with a slotted spoon and cool quickly under the cold tap. Shake dry.

Cook the noodles in the boiling water. When they are done, turn them into a colander and rinse under the cold tap. Shake out as much water as possible. Pour over ½–1 tsp cooking oil and mix it in thoroughly with clean hands or chopsticks: this helps prevent the noodles from sticking together. Then spread them out on a tray in a well-ventilated place for an hour or two to dry. (Some people use an electric fan to dry the noodles more quickly and effectively.)

Place the noodles in a serving bowl with the beansprouts. Just before serving, add all the other ingredients and top with the chicken, if using. Mix well with a pair of chopsticks before eating.

HO FUN RICE NOODLES WITH MUSHROOMS
GAN CHAO SU HE 乾炒素河

This is a vegetarian version of a noodle dish that was a staple of the *dai pai dong* street stalls, once a mainstay of Hong Kong life and now a dying breed. The original dish, *gan chao niu he*, is made with beef, but this mushroom variation is also delicious. Eat it as a main dish at lunchtime, or serve it with other dishes as part of a Chinese meal. The cooking method is based on one I learned at Kin's Kitchen in Hong Kong, with the kind permission of restaurant owner Lau Kin Wai. For the original beef recipe, see variation, right.

This serves three as a main dish, or six with other dishes as part of a Chinese meal.

4 dried shiitake mushrooms
5 oz (150g) white mushrooms, or others of your choice
3 spring onions
1 lb (450g) fresh *ho fun* rice noodles
4 tbsp cooking oil
3 garlic cloves, peeled and sliced
4 tsp light soy sauce
½ tsp dark soy sauce
Salt
7 oz (200g) beansprouts
Ground white pepper

Soak the dried mushrooms in hot water from the kettle for at least 30 minutes. Then slice off and discard the stems and slice the caps. Slice the mushrooms very thin. Trim the spring onions and separate the green and white parts. Smack the whites with the side of a cleaver or a rolling pin to loosen the fibers. Cut the greens into two or three sections, then lengthways into slivers. Cover the noodles in warm water, leave for a minute or so, then use your fingers to separate them gently (some will break: don't worry). Shake dry in a colander.

Heat 2 tbsp oil in a seasoned wok over a high flame, add the garlic and shiitake and stir-fry briefly until you can smell the garlic. Then add the other mushrooms and stir-fry over a medium heat until just cooked, seasoning with 2 tsp of the light soy sauce and ¼ tsp of the dark soy sauce, with salt to taste. Remove from the wok and set aside. Return the wok to a high heat with another 1 tbsp oil, add the beansprouts and stir-fry until hot but still crisp. Set aside.

Return the wok to a high heat with 1 tbsp oil and the spring onion whites and sizzle briefly until you can smell their fragrance. Add the noodles and stir-fry until hot, adding the remaining light and dark soy sauces, with a couple of pinches of ground white pepper. Add the mushrooms and beansprouts and stir-fry until all is piping hot and smells delicious, seasoning with a little salt if you need it. Finally, add the spring onion greens, stir a few times and serve.

VARIATION

Ho fun rice noodles with beef
Instead of the mushrooms and garlic in the recipe above, use 7 oz (200g) trimmed steak, cut into thin, bite-sized pieces. Place the beef in a bowl, add ½ tsp sugar, ¼ tsp salt, ½ tsp dark soy sauce, 1 tsp light soy sauce, ¾ tsp potato flour and 2 tsp cold water and mix well. Follow the recipe, but instead of stir-frying the fresh mushrooms, stir-fry the beef until nearly cooked; set aside. Fry the beansprouts as above. Finally, stir-fry the noodles, adding the beef instead of the mushrooms. If you wish, stir in a handful of Chinese yellow chives, cut into sections, with the spring onion greens.

SHANGHAI NOODLES WITH DRIED SHRIMP AND SPRING ONION OIL
KAI YANG CONG YOU MIAN 開洋蔥油麵

This deceptively simple dish is packed with flavor and totally irresistible, a southern Chinese equivalent of the Italian *spaghetti all'aglio, olio e peperoncino*, in which a seemingly tiny amount of seasonings makes a whole bowlful of pasta taste delicious. With a simple cucumber salad or some other light and refreshing side dish, it is a perfect lunchtime snack. The origins of this recipe are said to lie near the City God Temple in Shanghai, where it was cooked up by one of the street vendors who gathered there to serve visiting pilgrims. For this dish, you need the more substantial dried shrimp rather than the paper-thin ones (see Glossary, page 340).

This recipe serves two people.

2 tbsp dried shrimp
2 tsp Shaoxing wine
7 oz (200g) dried noodles of your choice, or 11 oz (300g) fresh noodles
4 spring onions
5 tsp light or tamari soy sauce, to taste
Salt (optional)
6 tbsp cooking oil

Place the dried shrimp in a small bowl with the Shaoxing wine and just enough hot water from the kettle to cover them. Set aside for 30 minutes. Bring a large panful of water to a boil for cooking the noodles. Smack the spring onions lightly with the side of a cleaver to open up the white parts slightly, then cut them evenly into 2½–3 in (6–7cm) sections. Pour the soy sauce into your serving bowl with a little salt, if you like.

Heat the oil in a wok over a high flame. Add the spring onions and stir-fry until they are turning a little golden. Drain the shrimp, add them to the wok and continue to stir-fry until the spring onions are well-browned and wonderfully fragrant, but not burned. Then set aside this fragrant oil, with the spring onions and shrimp.

Boil the noodles to your liking, then drain them well and place them in the serving bowl. Put the spring onions, shrimp and their fragrant oil on top. Mix everything together very well with a pair of chopsticks before eating.

ZHAJIANG NOODLES
ZHA JIANG MIAN 炸醬麵

"Fried sauce noodles," or *zha jiang mian*, is a Beijing speciality that is now popular all over the country. The classic version uses hand-pulled noodles, a rich sauce of ground pork cooked with sweet fermented wheat paste and a selection of fresh, crisp vegetables, all mixed together at the table. It's a whole meal in one bowl and absolutely delicious. This version of the recipe was taught to me by Jia Suxiang, in her kitchen in Beijing.

The meat sauce can be made in advance and refrigerated or frozen until you need it.

This recipe serves two people.

2 tbsp cooking oil
1 tsp whole Sichuan pepper
2 star anise
4¼ oz (125g) finely chopped or coarsely ground belly pork
2 tbsp finely chopped ginger
1 tbsp Shaoxing wine
5 tbsp sweet fermented sauce
Salt, to taste
7 oz (200g) dried Chinese wheat flour noodles, or 11 oz (300g) fresh noodles

To serve, any or all of the following
Small section of cucumber
1 celery stick
1 small carrot
Some Chinese cabbage
1 small piece of purple-hearted Chinese radish (*xin li mei*)
Good handful of beansprouts
Handful of cooked green soy beans or peas
A few slices of red chilli (optional)

Add the oil to a seasoned wok over a high flame and swirl it around. Immediately add the Sichuan pepper and star anise and stir-fry for a few moments until they smell delicious. Then remove the spices with a slotted spoon, leaving the fragrant oil in the wok.

Add the pork and stir-fry until it has become pale, pressing the meat with the back of your ladle or wok scoop to help separate it out into little morsels. Then add the ginger and stir-fry until you can smell it. Add the Shaoxing wine, stir once or twice, then add the sweet fermented sauce. Stir-fry for a few moments more until it smells rich and delicious, then cover the pork generously with water. Bring to a boil, then simmer over a low heat for about 15 minutes, until the sauce is dark and luxuriantly thick. Season with a scattering of salt (the sauce should be intensely-flavored and seem on its own a little over-salted, because it will be used to flavor the bland noodles).

When you wish to eat, bring a pan of water to a boil. Cut whichever you are using of the cucumber, celery, carrot, cabbage and radish into fine slivers. Blanch the beansprouts and all the vegetables except for the cucumber in the boiling water; they should remain a bit crisp. (It is best to blanch each vegetable separately, using a slotted spoon to remove them from the water.) Refresh the blanched vegetables immediately under a cold tap and drain well. Reheat the pork sauce.

Cook the noodles, rinse briefly under the tap, shake dry, then divide between two serving bowls.

Add some of each of your vegetables to the bowls. Top with the pork sauce. Stir everything together with chopsticks before eating, scattering with chilli slices, if you like.

HANGZHOU BREAKFAST NOODLES
CONG YOU BAN MIAN 蔥油拌麵

This is an utterly simple noodle dish that I came to adore in Hangzhou, where I ate it for breakfast many times in a travellers' hostel at Manjuelong, the village on the outskirts of the city that is famous for its osmanthus flowers. Eat it on its own, or with a couple of eggs, fried on both sides and served on a separate dish with a drizzle of soy sauce as seasoning. This recipe serves two people.

4 spring onions, green parts only
7 oz (200g) dried noodles of your choice, or 11 oz (300g) fresh noodles
5–6 tbsp cooking oil, plus more if cooking eggs

1–2 tbsp light or tamari soy sauce, to taste, plus more if cooking eggs
2 eggs (optional)

Bring a panful of water to a boil. Finely slice the spring onion greens.

Boil the noodles to your satisfaction. Drain them and divide between two serving dishes. Scatter over the spring onions.

Heat the oil over a high flame until sizzling hot. (Test it by ladling a few drops on to the spring onions: if it sizzles furiously, the oil is ready. Do not overheat the oil.) Ladle the oil over the spring onions on both piles of noodles. Pour the soy sauce over the noodles and serve.

If using the eggs, fry them on both sides until golden and serve on a separate dish, with a dash of soy sauce as seasoning.

Stir the noodles together with chopsticks before eating.

XIE LAOBAN'S DAN DAN NOODLES
NIU ROU DAN DAN MIAN 牛肉擔擔麵

This legendary recipe comes from a small noodle shop in Chengdu that was erased a few years ago when the whole neighborhood around Sichuan University was redeveloped. It was a tiny place on the ground floor of an old wooden house, tiled in white, with a few tables spilling out into the street, but it sold the best Dan Dan noodles in the city and arguably the world. Before it was demolished, I managed to coax the proprietor, Mr. Xie, into giving me his recipe, and this is it. Somehow, this dish more than any other sums up for me the story of Chengdu street food and the atmosphere of the now-demolished old city. "Dan Dan" refers to the shoulder poles that old-fashioned street vendors once used to transport their stoves, ingredients, bowls and chopsticks around town.

This recipe serves two people. I've given instructions for making one big bowlful, but you can assemble it in two separate serving bowls in the traditional manner, if you prefer.

1 tbsp cooking oil
3 Sichuanese dried chillies, snipped in half, seeds discarded
½ tsp whole Sichuan pepper
½ oz (25g) Sichuanese *ya cai* or Tianjin preserved vegetable
4 oz (100g) ground beef
2 tsp light soy sauce
Salt
7 oz (200g) dried Chinese wheat flour noodles, or 11 oz (300g) fresh noodles

For the sauce
¼ tsp ground roasted Sichuan pepper
2 tbsp sesame paste
3 tbsp light soy sauce
2 tsp dark soy sauce
4 tbsp chilli oil with its sediment
Salt, to taste

Add the oil to a seasoned wok over a medium flame and swirl it around. Immediately add the chillies and Sichuan pepper and stir-fry briefly until the oil is spicy and fragrant. Take care not to burn the spices. Add the *ya cai* and continue to stir-fry until hot and fragrant. Add the meat and increase the heat to high, splash in the soy sauce and stir-fry until the beef is brown and a little crisp, but not too dry. Press the beef against the wok with your scoop or ladle as you go, to encourage it to separate into little morsels. Season with salt to taste. When the meat is cooked (it should only take a couple of minutes), remove the mixture from the wok and set aside.

Place the sauce ingredients in a serving bowl and mix well.

Cook the noodles. Turn into a colander, rinse and drain, then place in the serving bowl. Sprinkle with the meat mixture, give the noodles a good stir until the sauce and meat are evenly distributed, and serve.

VARIATION

Vegetarian dan dan noodles

This tastes stupendous. Soak one large dried shiitake mushroom in hot water for 30 minutes. Slice off and discard the stalk and finely chop the cap. Snip 3 dried chillies in half or into sections, discarding the seeds as far as possible. Heat 1 tbsp cooking oil in a seasoned wok over a medium flame. Add the chillies and ½ tsp whole Sichuan pepper and sizzle until fragrant, taking care not to burn them. Add ½ oz (25g) Sichuanese *ya cai* or Tianjin preserved vegetable and the mushroom. Stir-fry until they smell wonderful, seasoning with 2 tsp light soy sauce and 1 tsp dark soy sauce. Remove from the wok. Prepare the bowls with the sauce in the main recipe, add the cooked noodles and then your vegetarian topping. Mix well before eating.

CLASSIC DAN DAN NOODLES
DAN DAN MIAN 擔擔麵

Addicted as I am to Mr. Xie's Dan Dan noodles (see page 279), I have to admit that this classic recipe is also glorious. As with the other version, it serves two people, either in one big bowl to share, or in two separate bowls. If you wish, you can blanch a handful of leafy greens in the noodle cooking water and add to the bowl, as shown in the photograph.

3 tbsp cooking oil
4 oz (100g) ground pork
2 tsp Shaoxing wine
1 tsp sweet fermented sauce
1 tsp light soy sauce
Salt
7 oz (200g) dried Chinese wheat flour noodles, or 11 oz (300g) fresh noodles

For the sauce
³/₄ cup (200ml) chicken stock (or noodle cooking water)
2 tsp light soy sauce
¼ tsp salt
1 tsp Chinkiang vinegar
2–4 tbsp chilli oil with its sediment, to taste
4 tbsp finely sliced spring onion greens
5 tbsp Sichuanese *ya cai*

Put the oil in a seasoned wok over a medium flame and swirl it around. Add the meat and stir-fry until it changes color. Add the Shaoxing wine, stir a few times, then add the sweet fermented sauce and stir-fry until you can smell it. Season with the soy sauce, and salt to taste, and press the meat against the wok with your scoop or ladle to encourage it to separate out into little morsels. When the meat has separated and is fragrant but still juicy, remove from the wok and set aside.

Bring a panful of water to a boil and, in a separate pan, reheat the stock, if using.

Boil the noodles to your liking in the water. While they are cooking, place all the sauce ingredients except for the stock in a serving bowl.

When the noodles are ready, drain them in a colander (reserving some of the cooking water if you are not using stock). Add the stock or noodle cooking water to the sauce. Place the noodles in the bowl, top with the pork and serve. Before eating, give the noodles a good stir until the sauce and meat are evenly distributed.

CHEF CHEN DAILU'S SPICY SESAME NOODLES CHEN SHIFU HONG YOU SU MIAN 陳師傅紅油素麵

This is a recipe taught to me by Chef Chen Dailu of the wonderful Chengdu snack restaurant Long Chao Shou. I was interviewing him for a feature for *Saveur* magazine and I asked him to tell me about his favorite food. To my surprise, he came up with this scrumptious but blindingly simple vegetarian recipe.

This serves two people.

2 tsp sesame paste
1 tbsp light soy sauce
½ tsp dark soy sauce
½ tsp Chinkiang vinegar
1 tsp finely chopped garlic
Good pinch of ground, roasted Sichuan pepper, or a dash of Sichuan pepper oil
1½ tbsp chilli oil with sediment

7 oz (200g) Chinese wheat or buckwheat noodles
Handful of pea shoots, green bok choy or choy sum leaves (optional)
1 tbsp finely chopped spring onion greens

Combine all the ingredients—except for the noodles, greens, if using, and spring onions—in a serving bowl and mix well.

Cook the noodles. If you are using the greens, toss them into the cooking water for the last minute to blanch them. Drain the noodles and greens and add to the serving bowl. Scatter with the spring onions, mix well and serve.

BASIC NOODLE SOUP
QING TANG MIAN 清湯麵

Think of this as a master recipe that will enable you to make many different kinds of soup noodles. The basic process—arranging some seasonings in a bowl, ladling in some hot stock and adding freshly cooked noodles—is common to a multitude of recipes. The flavor, of course, depends on the quality of your stock: with a rich, homemade chicken stock, the basic noodle soup alone will be most satisfying, regardless of any topping.

You might like to crown your noodles with a spoonful of yesterday's red-braised beef or stewed chicken, simply reheated; with some juicy ground pork, pre-fried in a wok with a few seasonings; a few pieces of poached or stir-fried seafood; stir-fried mushrooms or another straightforward stir-fry that takes your fancy. If you keep small packages of stock in your freezer, this is an incredibly quick dish.

The recipe serves two.

7 oz (200g) dried noodles, or 11 oz (300g) fresh noodles
2½ cups (600ml) chicken stock
Salt
Ground white pepper
4 tsp lard, rendered chicken fat or cooking oil
½ tsp sesame oil
2 spring onions, green parts only, finely sliced
Handful of bok choy, choy sum, pea shoots, lettuce leaves or other greens

Bring a pan of water to a boil for the noodles. Set the noodles to cook in the boiling water. Reheat the stock in a separate pan

In each of two deep serving bowls, place ¼ tsp salt, a generous pinch of pepper, 2 tsp lard or oil, ¼ tsp sesame oil and half the spring onions.

When the noodles are nearly cooked to your liking, divide the hot stock between the two bowls. Then use a slotted spoon to dunk the greens in the boiling water to wilt. Scoop out the greens and divide them between the bowls. Do the same with the noodles, mix well, and serve.

VARIATIONS

Ground pork noodle soup
Stir-fry some ground pork, preferably from the shoulder, adding a dash of Shaoxing wine. Add a little stock and salt and pepper to taste and simmer until tender to make a meat sauce. Spoon this over your plain noodle soup and mix well before eating.

Mushroom noodle soup
A vegetarian version of ground pork noodle soup: stir-fry finely chopped mushrooms of your choice with garlic and salt to taste. Spoon them over your plain noodle soup and mix well before eating.

FRIED EGG AND TOMATO NOODLES
FAN QIE JIAN DAN MIAN 番茄煎蛋麵

This easy and colorful dish was one of my regular lunches as a student in China: simple, nourishing and delicious. There, they would always fry the eggs on both sides until they were golden and their yolks just set, but you can leave the yolks runny if you prefer. Eggs and tomatoes are a particularly delicious combination, but the noodles are good with a fried egg alone.

This recipe serves two.

2 bowls of Basic Noodle Soup (see page 283), with or without the blanched greens
2 tbsp cooking oil
2 eggs
1 tomato, sliced
Salt

When your noodles are ready and sitting appealingly in their bowls of soup with green leaves, heat a seasoned wok over a high flame. Add the oil and swirl it around. Separately, fry each egg on both sides until golden, scoop it out and lay it on a bowl of noodles.

Return the wok to the stove over a high flame, add the tomato and stir-fry until the slices are hot and tender but still intact, adding salt to taste. Divide the tomatoes between the bowls of noodles. (This dish looks pretty if you place your blanched greens, if using, on one side of the egg and the tomatoes on the other.)

VARIATIONS FOR EASY SOUP NOODLES

Noodles with mixed mushrooms
Stir-fry some mushrooms (see page 234) and add them to a bowlful of Basic Noodle Soup.

Stewed chicken noodles
Top your Basic Noodle Soup with some of the chicken from the Simple Chicken Soup (see page 251), having used the soup as your noodle broth. (Add a few reconstituted dried shiitake mushrooms to the chicken as it cooks to make this even more delicious.)

Braised chicken with shiitake mushrooms on noodles
Use any leftovers from this dish (see page 121) as a Basic Noodle Soup topping.

Red-braised pork or beef noodles
Top Basic Noodle Soup with a spoonful of reheated, leftover Red-braised Pork (see page 94) or Red-braised Beef (see page 108).

Slow-cooked beef brisket noodles
Use leftovers from this dish (see page 110) as a Basic Noodle Soup topping.

BUCKWHEAT NOODLES WITH RED-BRAISED BEEF
NIU ROU QIAO MIAN 牛肉蕎麵

This is my attempt to recreate a fabulous noodle dish served at a little snack shop called Granny Wang's Buckwheat Noodles, which has a branch just opposite the Qingshiqiao food market in the center of Chengdu. At this modest but glorious little eaterie, they make their own buckwheat noodles on the spot, using an old-fashioned wooden press to shoot strings of buckwheat paste directly into a wok of boiling water. (They also make bouncy, transparent sweet potato noodles and the best *ye'er ba*—leaf-wrapped glutinous rice dumplings—I can remember having eaten.)

For this recipe, you will need to make some red-braised beef in advance, or have some leftovers hanging around in the refrigerator or freezer. At Granny Wang's, they serve the noodles topped with red-braised beef with dried bamboo shoots; Red-braised Beef with Tofu Bamboo, with or without the tofu, see page 108, also works very well. You can use pure buckwheat noodles if you wish, but they tend to fall apart during cooking if they are not freshly made, so I tend to use wholewheat noodles with buckwheat, which are more elastic and which I buy in a wholefood shop or a Chinese supermarket.

Vegetarians can make the same dish without the beef: just increase the quantities of celery and chilli oil and cover the noodles in the serving bowl with some of their piping hot cooking water. A handful of crisp, fried peanuts or a sprinkling of toasted sesame seeds makes a delicious addition to this vegetarian version. This recipe serves two.

Good ladleful of leftover Red-braised Beef (see page 108), with or without the tofu "bamboo"
1 cup plus 2 tbsp (300ml) chicken stock (or noodle cooking water)
1 tbsp light or tamari soy sauce
2–3 tbsp chilli oil with its sediment

7 oz (200g) dried wholewheat noodles with buckwheat
¼ tsp ground roasted Sichuan pepper, or to taste
3 tbsp finely sliced spring onion greens
Handful of finely chopped celery, including leaves (Chinese celery is best, if you can get it)

Bring a large pan of water to a boil. Bring the leftover beef to a boil, then simmer gently to heat through. Reheat the stock, if using. Put the soy sauce and chilli oil into a serving bowl.

Cook the noodles, then shake dry in a colander, retaining some of the cooking water if you wish to use it instead of stock. Briefly rinse the noodles under the cold tap.

Pour the stock or noodle-cooking water into your serving bowl. Add the noodles and top with the beef stew. Scatter with the Sichuan pepper, followed by the spring onions and celery. Mix well before eating.

FUCHSIA'S EMERGENCY MIDNIGHT NOODLES
FU XIA FANG BIAN MIAN 扶霞方便麵

A physiological peculiarity I've inherited from my mother and grandmother is an inability to sleep without eating a starchy snack in the evening. If I've been out and haven't eaten enough starchy foods at dinner, I come home ravenous and in need of a midnight feast. In these circumstances, my top two choices for a nibble are melted cheese on toast and spicy Sichuanese noodles. The exact noodle recipe is different each time: sometimes I desire more chilli oil; in hot weather I might add more refreshing vinegar. Here, anyway, is one version, but feel free to improvise. I also eat these noodles for breakfast or lunch with a fried egg or two on top.

This recipe serves two people.

7 oz (200g) Chinese dried wheat or buckwheat noodles, or 11 oz (300g) fresh noodles
2 spring onions, greens part only, finely sliced

For the sauce
3–4 tbsp tamari soy sauce
2 tbsp Chinkiang vinegar
4 tbsp chilli oil with its sediment
1 tsp sesame oil

Optional extras
An egg or two for each person
Spoonful of "olive" vegetable

Combine all the sauce ingredients in a serving bowl.

Cook the noodles. Rinse, drain and put in the serving bowl. Scatter with the spring onions. Mix well before eating.

If desired, top with eggs, fried on both sides, and a spoonful of "olive" vegetable, as shown in the photograph.

DUMPLINGS

The English word "dumpling"—used as a blanket term for everything from the balls of dough cooked in European stews to an ethereal Cantonese steamed titbit in the shape of a goldfish—doesn't do justice to the astonishing wealth of little buns and pastries eaten in China. A Cantonese dim sum menu may hint at the possibilities of this splendid side of Chinese food culture, with its translucent steamed dumplings pinched into pretty shapes and its slithery sheets of rice paste wrapped about juicy shrimp, but the Cantonese south is just one region of China. Every part of this vast country has its own tradition of "small eats" (*xiao chi*) and the dainty pastries known as *dian xin*, (literally "touch the heart"), made with wheat, rice and other starches, which can be stuffed or wrapped, then steamed, baked, deep-fried, pan-fried or boiled. One single restaurant in the old northern capital Xi'an, home of the terracotta army, serves 300 different kinds of dumpling!

Of course many of these pastries are very difficult to make and are served mainly in specializt restaurants. Yet dumplings are also part of home cooking, especially in northern China, where a family get-together to wrap and eat boiled crescent dumplings (*shui jiao*) is a traditional part of New Year celebrations. In this chapter I've brought together a few classic recipes that are not too difficult and are extremely rewarding. These snacks are also great fun to make and eat as a team effort with friends or family. The resulting dumplings can be served as an appetizer, a snack or—in the case of the wontons and Northern boiled dumplings—a main meal.

SICHUANESE WONTONS IN CHILLI OIL SAUCE
HONG YOU CHAO SHOU 紅油抄手

Of all Chinese dumplings, wontons are the simplest to make, if you buy ready-made wrappers. They cook in minutes and have a delightfully slippery mouthfeel. In Sichuan, the source of this recipe, they are known as "folded arms" (*chao shou*). Some say this is because the raw dumplings look like the folded arms of a person sitting back in relaxation; others that it's because of the way they are wrapped, with one corner crossed over the other and the two pinched together. The basic wontons can be served in a host of different ways and this Chengdu version is one of my favorites, with its sumptuous, heart-warming sauce.

Wonton skins can be bought fresh or frozen in most Chinese food shops; they should be very thin and supple. If you want to take the easiest option in wrapping the dumplings, you can simply fold them in half, on the diagonal, to make a triangle. Otherwise, wrap into the classic "water caltrop" shape (see page 295), as professional cooks and market vendors do across China. (The water caltrop is an exotic-looking aquatic nut with a pair of horns.) This recipe makes 15–20, enough for four as an appetizer, or two for lunch. If you use fresh ingredients and make more than you need, the surplus can be frozen and cooked straight from the freezer.

½ oz (20g) piece of ginger, unpeeled
5 oz (150g) ground pork
½ egg, beaten
1 tsp Shaoxing wine
½ tsp sesame oil
Salt
Ground white pepper
3 tbsp chicken stock
3 tbsp finely sliced spring onion greens
7 oz (200g) package of wonton wrappers
Flour, to dust

To serve
3–4 tbsp sweet aromatic soy sauce (see page 322), or 3–4 tbsp light or tamari soy sauce with 1½–2 tsp sugar
5–6 tbsp chilli oil, with its sediment
2–4 heaped tsp crushed garlic
2 tbsp finely sliced spring onion greens

Crush the ginger with the flat of a cleaver or a rolling pin and put it in a cup with just enough cold water to cover. Place the pork, egg, Shaoxing wine and sesame oil in a bowl with 1½ tsp of the ginger water and salt and pepper to taste. Stir well. Mix in the stock, 1 tbsp at a time. Finally, add the spring onion greens.

Fill a small bowl with cold water. Take a wonton wrapper and lay it flat in one hand. Use a table knife or a small spatula to press about 1 tsp of the pork mixture into the center of the wrapper. Dip a finger into the cold water, run it around the edges of the wrapper and fold it diagonally in half. Press the edges tightly together and lay on a flour-dusted tray or large plate. (If you want to make a "water caltrop" shape, please see the photos on pages 294–95.)

Bring a large pan of water to a boil over a high heat. While you are waiting for the water to boil, prepare three or four serving bowls. In each bowl, place 1 tbsp sweet aromatic soy sauce (or 1 tbsp tamari soy sauce and ½ tsp sugar), 1½ tbsp chilli oil with sediment and ½–1 heaped tsp of crushed garlic, to taste.

When the water has come to a boil, drop in the wontons. Stir gently to make sure they do not stick together. When the water returns to a rolling boil, pour in a small cup of cold water to calm it down. Repeat this one more time. When the water has come to a boil for the third time, the wontons should be cooked through (cut one open to make sure). Remove the wontons with a slotted spoon, drain well, and divide between the prepared serving bowls. Scatter each bowl with some of the spring onion greens. Serve immediately, stirring everything together before digging in.

TO FORM "WATER CALTROP" WONTONS

If you are right-handed, lay a wonton wrapper in the palm of your left hand and use a table knife or bamboo spatula to press about 1 tbsp filling into the center of the wrapper.

Fold the wrapper in half so the opposite corners meet.

Smear a little more of the filling on to one corner of the triangle you have made. Using both hands, gently squeeze the edges of the dumpling as you bring the two corners together.

Lay the dry corner on to the corner that has been moistened by the filling, and press firmly together to seal the dumpling.

Place the finished dumplings on a flour-dusted plate or tray.

For an easier method, simply fold the wrapper in half over the stuffing, bringing the opposite corners together and pressing firmly all around the edges, as in the recipe method on page 292.

HANGZHOU WONTONS IN SOUP
XIAN ROU XIAO HUN TUN 鹹肉小餛飩

The West Lake of Hangzhou is dreamily beautiful in any season. On wet spring days the banks are lush and green, weeping with willows, and the islands and distant shores dissolve in the mist. In summer, the glittering surface of the lake is criss-crossed by wooden boats, and the golden pinnacle of the Lei Feng tower gleams in the sun. The city is known for the elegance and refinement of its cooking, and this popular snack, though easy to make, is a lovely example of Hangzhou cuisine. The slippery wontons are served in a broth all floaty with shrimp, seaweed and spring onions: refreshing and soothing at the same time.

This recipe serves four as a snack or appetizer, two for breakfast or lunch.

One quantity of wontons (see page 292), stuffed and wrapped

To serve
1 egg
A little cooking oil
3–4 cups (750ml–1 liter) clear stock
1–2 tbsp papery dried shrimp
4–8 tbsp finely sliced spring onion greens
2 tsp cooking oil or lard
Salt
Ground white pepper
4 good pinches of dried laver seaweed

Beat the egg in a small bowl. Heat an oiled frying pan over a high heat, then allow to cool slightly before adding a little fresh cooking oil. Pour in the egg and swirl it around to form a thin yellow pancake. When it is just cooked but not browned, remove it from the pan. When cool, cut it into 1/8 in (1/2 cm) ribbons.

Bring a large pan of water to a boil over a high heat. Bring the stock to a boil in another saucepan and keep it hot. Prepare your serving bowls: in each of four bowls place a generous pinch of dried shrimp, 1–2 tbsp sliced spring onion greens, 1/2 tsp oil or lard, and salt and pepper to taste. Break the laver seaweed into small pieces and distribute it among the bowls. (If you are cooking for two, redistribute the seasonings into two bowls accordingly.)

When the water has boiled, cook the wontons in it (follow the instructions on page 292). Just before they are ready, divide the hot stock between the bowls. Distribute the wontons among the bowls and garnish with a few ribbons of egg. Serve.

NORTHERN-STYLE BOILED DUMPLINGS
SHUI JIAO 水餃

These crescent-shaped boiled dumplings, more substantial than wontons, are one of the staple foods of northern China. They are invariably eaten at Chinese New Year, when whole families gather to make them on an impromptu production line. Their wrappers are made from a simple flour-and-water dough, and they can be stuffed with almost anything. The most common filling is seasoned ground pork mixed with cabbage or chives, but Chinese Muslims use ground lamb, while vegetarians may choose stir-fried eggs and chives, or tofu and vegetables. And instead of cabbage or chives, you may mix the pork with any vegetable: shredded radish, fennel tops, pumpkin and wild garlic are wonderful. Crisp vegetables that contain a lot of water, such as Chinese cabbage and radish, are best blanched or salted before you begin, so the dumplings don't become soggy.

Making your own wrappers isn't difficult, but requires a little practice; ready-made wrappers—thin rounds of pale wheaten dough—are available in many Chinese food shops. They are less sticky than the homemade version, so you'll need to moisten their edges with a wet finger to seal. And if you can, ask a Chinese friend to show you how to roll the wrappers and wrap the dumplings: it's by far the easiest way to learn.

To learn how to make your own wrappers, see page 303.

Serve the steaming dumplings with bottles of Chinese brown vinegar and soy sauce and a jar of chilli oil or dried chillies. Provide each guest with a dipping dish and let them mix their own seasonings. You might also prepare one or two vegetable dishes from the cold dishes chapter (see pages 32–73) to eat with them.

I have to admit that when I tested these with pork and wild garlic, the dumplings were so delicious—and I was so hungry—that I ate them all myself, but this should serve two for lunch, or four as an appetizer.

Small piece of ginger, unpeeled
4 oz (100g) ground pork with a little fat
½ small egg, beaten
1 tsp Shaoxing wine
1 tbsp chicken stock
½ tsp sesame oil
Salt
4 oz (100g) Chinese chives, yellow chives, or wild garlic

7 oz (200g) pack of round dumpling wrappers (about 18 wrappers)

To serve
Chinkiang or Shanxi vinegar
Light or tamari soy sauce
Chilli oil or ground chillies (optional)

Crush the ginger with the flat of a cleaver or a rolling pin and place in a cup with just enough cold water to cover.

Put the pork in a bowl and add the egg, Shaoxing wine, stock, sesame oil and salt to taste, with 1 tbsp of the water in which you have soaked the ginger. Mix well (I find this easiest by hand). Finely chop the chives or wild garlic and add them to the pork. Mix well. Set a large pan of water to boil.

Fill a small dish with cold water and have it on hand. Lay a dumpling wrapper in your hand and place about 1 tbsp of the pork mixture in its center, pressing the mixture into the wrapper. Dip your finger in the dish of water and run it around the edge of the wrapper. Then seal the wrapper with a few little pleats (see page 302). Lay the dumpling on a tray or a large plate. Wrap the remaining dumplings.

Drop some of the dumplings into the boiling water and cook them for four to five minutes. Each time the water comes back to a rolling boil, add a small cup of cold water to calm it down, so the dumplings do not fall apart. (You should do this a couple of times before the dumplings are cooked.) When they are cooked, remove the dumplings with a slotted spoon and place in a serving dish.

FILLING VARIATIONS

Use these to stuff wontons, Northern-style boiled dumplings, or pot-stickers. If you wish, use other ground meats—beef, lamb or chicken—and season them the same way. Ground beef is particularly good with finely chopped cilantro or celery (blanch the latter for 30 seconds and squeeze dry, before mixing with the meat).

Chinese cabbage and ground pork

Use 7 oz (200g) Chinese leaf cabbage instead of the chives or garlic in the recipe on page 298. Finely chop the cabbage, add ¾ tsp salt and scrunch the salt into the leaves with your hands. Leave for at least 30 minutes, then squeeze out the water that emerges before using. Add to the seasoned ground pork. You can adapt this recipe for other crisp, watery vegetables such as green bok choy or Asian radish instead of cabbage. If using Asian radish, cut it into very thin slices, then into fine slivers, before salting.

Fennel tops and ground pork

Use 4 oz (100g) finely chopped fennel tops instead of the chives in the recipe on page 298 (discarding the thicker stalks and using only the fronds). Add to the seasoned ground pork.

Scrambled eggs and chives

Trim and finely chop 4 oz (100g) Chinese chives, yellow chives or wild garlic. Beat together 2 eggs with salt to taste, then stir-fry in a wok until just cooked through. Turn the eggs on to a board and chop finely. Combine the eggs and chives and use this as your stuffing (1–2 tbsp papery dried shrimp make a delicious addition). Because this stuffing lacks the stickiness of one made with ground meat, be extra careful in moistening and sealing the edges of the dumplings.

SERVING VARIATIONS

Dumplings in chilli oil sauce

This scrumptious Sichuanese version simply uses the seasonings described for Sichuanese Wontons in Chilli Oil Sauce (see page 292) to dress the boiled dumplings. This variation is shown in the photograph opposite. Frankly, it's irresistible. This snack is the speciality of the Zhong Boiled Dumplings restaurant (*zhong shui jiao*) in Chengdu, which is named after a late 19th-century street vendor called Zhong Xiesen. I used to pass this restaurant every day on my way to and from cooking school and would often have to stop for a bowl of spicy dumplings.

Sour-and-hot boiled dumplings

Serve the dumplings in a bowl of stock seasoned to taste with salt, soy sauce, Chinese brown vinegar and chilli oil. Scatter with chopped cilantro and/or finely sliced spring onion greens.

TO MAKE NORTHERN-STYLE WRAPPERS

Put 2⅓ cups (300g) all-purpose flour on to a work surface and make a well in the center. Pour in about ⅔ cup (180ml) cold water and draw in the flour to make a stiff but pliable dough. Knead for several minutes until smooth and elastic, then cover with a damp tea towel and leave to rest for about 30 minutes. On a lightly floured board, roll the dough into a couple of sausages ¾–1 in (2–2½cm) in diameter.

Use a knife to cut the dough into 1 in (2cm) pieces, giving the sausage a half roll between cuts (to stop it from getting flatter with each cut).

Lay each piece cut end-up on the board and flatten with your palm, to make convex discs.

Roll the discs into flat wrappers about 3 in (7cm) in diameter. The best way to do this (for someone right-handed) is to cradle the far edge of a disc in the fingers of your left hand while you roll from near edge into the center, turning the disc between rolling movements. You will end up with a slightly curved disc that is thinner at the edges than in the center. Lay the wrappers on a board.

TO FORM THE DUMPLINGS

Use a table knife or a bamboo spatula to press about 1 tbsp of the filling into the center of the wrapper. Dip a finger into cold water and run it along the upper edge of the wrapper.

Bring the opposite edges of the wrapper towards each other. If you are right-handed, lay the dumpling in your left hand. Pinch the wrapper together at the right end, then use the fingers of both hands to pleat the far edge of the wrapper against the near edge, pressing the two edges firmly together after each pleat. The easiest way to learn to do this is to ask a willing Chinese friend to show you how.

For a simpler method, without pleating, simply squeeze the opposite edges together around the plumpness of the filling.

Lay the dumplings on a flour-dusted plate or tray.

FRESH SPRING ROLLS
CHUN JUAN 春捲

It was April and my first day back in Chengdu for more than a year. My friends Yu Bo and Dai Shuang invited me for supper and, because of the season, they said I really had to eat spring rolls. "Spring rolls," as eaten in Sichuan and many other parts of China, are nothing like the golden, deep-fried rolls found on almost every Chinese restaurant menu in the West. Lighter, healthier and altogether more pleasing, they consist of pale wheaten pancakes traditionally served with a salad of slivered spring vegetables and wrapped up at the dinner table. In Sichuan, the vegetables are often given a feisty mustard oil dressing, and other dishes, hot or cold, may be served as additional fillings.

On that Chengdu evening, our simple supper of spring rolls turned out to be an exquisite little feast. Alongside a stack of the alabaster pancakes were a mustardy salad of "three silken threads" (slivers of carrot, stem lettuce and Asian radish), thinly sliced cooked pork and toon tree shoots (the tender young leaves of the Chinese toon tree) tossed in chilli oil, blanched wolfberry plant leaves with a sour-hot dressing, shredded chicken in chilli oil sauce, and a stir-fry of yellow chives with pork slivers, each served on an elegant porcelain dish. We filled the pancakes with a couple of chopstickfuls of any dish we fancied, rolled them up and ate.

Spring rolls evolved out of the "spring platters" (chun pan) that were served to mark li chun, the first day of spring. These were delicate assortments of fresh and finely cut seasonal vegetables to be enjoyed as a contrast to the meaty excesses of the New Year's festival season. No one is sure when thin pancake wrappers became part of this custom, but there are written descriptions of Tang Dynasty spring platters that included not only vegetables (such as lettuce, radish and yellow chives), but accompanying "spring pancakes" (chun bing). Fried spring rolls of the kind that are so popular outside China seem to have been first mentioned a few hundred years later, in a Yuan Dynasty description of pancake roll stuffed with sugared fruits and nuts and finely chopped lamb. They are still much less popular in China than the fresh, unfried rolls.

In Chengdu, the pancakes are made and sold in the open markets for a few months, until the weather turns warm and humid, at the end of April or thereabouts. Women sit or stand over blackened griddles, holding a fluid, mobile ball of dough in their hands. They roll the dough lightly over the heated surface, where a thin, moon-like circle of the paste adheres. It takes a few seconds to cook. They turn it over for a moment, then place it on the stack of pancakes. Often the pancake vendors sell a selection of slivered vegetables too—radish, carrot, cilantro, celery, beansprouts—which they will mix and toss in a spicy sauce on request.

I haven't seen fresh or frozen spring roll pancakes on sale in any of the Chinese supermarkets I visit: the yellow "egg-roll" wrappers are not the same thing. Making the pancakes at home is extremely difficult at first (and considerably more challenging than any other recipe in this book), but it's really worth it if you fancy an adventure. If you don't, you might try using steamed Peking duck pancakes, which can easily be bought frozen, as a substitute (you would need up to 10 of these). And don't forget that the slivered vegetable filling can be served as a salad in its own right and that you can, if you wish, use other dishes as fillings: Cold Chicken with a Spicy Sichuanese Sauce (see page 48) and Stir-fried Yellow Chives with Venison Slivers (see page 202) are both wonderful.

The following recipe is enough for eight to ten rolls. For the filling, don't feel bound by the quantities I suggest, or even by the particular ingredients: you just want a collection of vegetables of different colors. Serve these on their own as an appetizer, or with other dishes.

For the pancakes
½ tsp salt
2½ cups plus 2 tbsp (200g)
   bread flour, sifted
A little cooking oil

For the filling
4 oz (100g) carrot
4 oz (100g) Asian radish
4 oz (100g) celery
4 oz (100g) red bell pepper

4 oz (100g) beansprouts
3 tbsp finely sliced spring
   onion greens
1 tbsp light soy sauce
2½ tsp Chinkiang vinegar
1½ tsp sugar
½ tsp finely chopped or
   crushed garlic
2 tbsp chilli oil, with sediment
½ tsp sesame oil

To make the pancakes

Place ⅔ cup (175ml) cold water in a bowl with the salt and stir to dissolve. Add the flour, mix well and knead thoroughly to make a thick, shiny, wet dough. Place in a small bowl, gently smooth its surface, cover with a thin layer of cold water (perhaps ½ cup/100ml) and leave to rest for two hours.

Heat a dry, heavy-based frying pan over a gentle flame. Use a thick wad of paper towels to rub it with a little cooking oil and heat over a high flame to seal the surface of the metal. Then transfer to your smallest burner and reduce the heat to a bare minimum. Rub in a little more oil and use the paper to remove all but the merest smear.

Now comes the tricky part. First, check the consistency of the dough. It should be so soft and runny that, when you take a handful out of the bowl, you have to keep your hand moving constantly to prevent it escaping. If it is not sufficiently mobile, mix it with a little of the surface water in your bowl.

Take a handful of dough out of the bowl in your hand and keep your hand moving so it doesn't flow away. Then sweep the handful of dough around the hot surface of the pan so a very thin, circular layer sticks. If there are any little blobs of wet dough on the surface, dab them with your handful of dough to pick them up. Keep moving your hand so the dough doesn't escape and, when the edges of the pancake lift up slightly, use your other hand to peel it gently away. Turn it over for a couple of seconds, then remove it to a plate or clean cloth. The pancake should be just cooked but still completely pale.

Repeat with the remaining dough. Keep the hot surface clean: if any fragments of dough stick, scrape them off, then use a wad of paper towels to apply again the merest smear of oil. If the dough becomes too stiff, simply mix in a few drops of cold water.

Don't be alarmed if your first few wrappers don't work: it takes a while to get a feel for making them. And no one will mind if they are not perfectly round!

Keep the wrappers in a cool, dry place until you need them: they should, however, be eaten within a few hours of making, as they will stick together if left for too long.

To prepare the vegetables

Peel and trim the carrot and radish, then cut as evenly as possible into thin slices, then into fine slivers. De-string the celery and cut into fine slivers. Trim the red pepper and cut into fine slivers. (If your slivers are not extremely fine, mix them all with $^3/_4$ tsp salt and leave for 10-15 minutes before squeezing gently and draining away the water that emerges.)

Bring a little water to a boil and blanch the beansprouts briefly, until softened but still a little crisp. Refresh them under the cold tap and squeeze dry.

Mix all the vegetables together in a bowl. Add all the other ingredients and mix very well. Pile them up on a serving dish.

To serve the spring rolls

Pile up the pancakes on a plate and serve with your vegetable salad (or any other hot or cold dish you fancy, or a selection of dishes).

To make a roll, gently peel away one of the pancakes and lay it on a little plate. Use chopsticks to pile up a little filling along the center of the wrapper. Fold in the right-hand side of the wrapper. Then fold in the side nearest to you and roll away from you to enclose the filling; it will still peep out of one end. Hold the wrapper with the closed side downwards, so the juices don't leak out, and eat immediately.

VARIATION

Slivered vegetables with a mustardy dressing

Prepare the vegetables as in the recipe above but, instead of the seasonings suggested, dress them in chilli oil with salt, a little mustard oil to taste (you will find this in Indian supermarkets) and a little sugar. Vinegar may also be added.

XI'AN POT-STICKER DUMPLINGS
XI'AN GUO TIE 西安鍋貼

If you wander through the tunnel beneath the Drum Tower in the old imperial capital of Xi'an towards the dreamily beautiful Great Mosque, you'll find yourself in the back streets of the Muslim Quarter. Here, especially in the evenings, the air is awaft with aromatic smoke from portable grills and the scents of dumplings and other snacks being steamed or sizzled on outdoor stoves. You'll come across steamed rice dainties scattered with candied fruits and sugar, sticky persimmon cakes, steamed buns stuffed with cumin beef or flower-scented sweet bean paste, lamb kebabs . . . and these delicious pot-sticker dumplings.

Few people can resist their toasty golden bases and slightly glutinous wrappers, their rich flavor sharpened by a vinegar dip. In other parts of China they are pinched into crescent shapes but I love the way they wrap them in Xi'an, with the filling peeping out from both ends. The dumplings can be filled with any kind of meat, mixed with vegetables, or with a vegetarian stuffing, but one of my favorites is this Muslim combination of ground beef and chives.

You'll need a heavy-bottomed frying pan with a close-fitting lid. This recipe serves four as a starter. I like to serve them with a refreshing cold vegetable dish on the side: perhaps Smacked Cucumbers (see page 34) or a Tiger Salad (see page 66).

For the wrappers
½ cup plus 1 tbsp (75g) all-purpose flour, plus more to dust
½ cup plus 1 tbsp (75g) bread flour
½ tsp cooking oil

For the stuffing
4¼ oz (125g) ground beef
½ tsp finely chopped ginger
2 tbsp finely sliced spring onion greens
½ tsp sesame oil
1 tsp light soy sauce
1 tsp Shaoxing wine
4 tbsp chicken stock or water
2 oz (50g) yellow or green Chinese chives, finely chopped
3 tbsp cooking oil

For the dips
Chinkiang vinegar
Finely chopped ginger
Finely chopped garlic

Boil some water in a kettle. Combine the two flours in a mixing bowl with the oil. Pour in about ⅓ cup (80ml) boiling water and mix briskly with a fork. Then add enough cold water to make a dough (about another 2½ tbsp/45ml). When it is cool enough to handle, knead until smooth, then cover with a wet tea towel and set aside to rest for 30 minutes.

Combine all the stuffing ingredients (except the cooking oil) in a bowl and mix well. It's easiest to do this by hand.

Dust a work surface with a little flour. Roll the dough into a long sausage ¾–1 in (2–2½cm) thick. Form the pot-stickers (see page 311).

For each guest, pour about 1 tbsp vinegar in a dipping dish, and add a little ginger and garlic (¼ tsp of each will do).

Boil some water in a kettle. Add the oil to a seasoned cast-iron frying pan or a non-stick pan with a lid over a medium flame, and swirl it around. Then lay the dumplings in neat rows in the pan. Fry them until their bottoms are toasty and golden, moving the pan around for even heating. Then add ½ cup (100ml) water from the kettle, pouring it evenly over. Cover the pan with a tight-fitting lid and allow the dumplings to steam for about four minutes, until cooked through (open one up to check if you are unsure). Remove the lid, allowing the steam to escape and the remaining water to boil away.

Remove from the heat, use a spatula to lift the dumplings from the pan and turn them upside-down on to your serving dish, so you can see their golden, toasty bottoms. Serve with the prepared dip.

TO FORM POT-STICKERS

Use a knife to cut the dough "sausage" into ³⁄₄ in (2cm) pieces, giving it a half roll between cuts (to stop it getting flatter with each cut).

Lay each piece cut end-up on the board, and flatten with the palm of your hand, to make convex discs.

Roll the discs into wrappers 3–3¹⁄₂ (8–9cm) in diameter. The best way to do this (for someone right-handed) is to cradle the far edge of a disc in the fingers of your left hand while you roll from near edge to the center, turning it between rolling movements. You will end up with a slightly curved disc that is thinner at the edges than in the center.

Use a table knife or a bamboo spatula to lay about 1¹⁄₂ tsp of filling along the center of a wrapper.

Firmly pinch together the opposite edges of the wrapper, leaving the ends open.

Lay the dumplings on a lightly floured tray until ready to cook.

MR. LAI'S GLUTINOUS RICE BALLS WITH BLACK SESAME STUFFING
LAI TANG YUAN 賴湯圓

In almost every aspect of the culinary arts, the Chinese reign supreme, except, I must reluctantly concede, in sweet pastries and puddings. There is no dessert course in a classical Chinese meal and no strict division between sweet and savory. A few sweet dishes may crop up in banquets, while cakes and sweet dumplings are part of a rich tradition of snacks and nibbles, especially in certain places such as the picturesque city of Suzhou. Yet, perhaps due to the relative absence of a sweet tooth in most parts of China, or to the lack of the glorious rich cream and butter so important in European traditions, sweet foods are not the greatest strength of Chinese cuisines. However, some sweet snacks are delectable, especially, in my opinion, *tang yuan* or "soup spheres," these soft, voluptuous rice balls with their fragrant black sesame filling. This Sichuanese version—named after a street vendor who worked in Chengdu around the turn of the twentieth century—is a famous street snack, eaten at any time of day.

This recipe makes about 20 spheres, which can be frozen if you don't need them all immediately. Please note that the stuffing is much easier to handle if it is made a few hours in advance, and it will keep in the refrigerator for months.

For the stuffing
1 tbsp (25g) black sesame seeds
1 tbsp (25g) sugar
1½ tbsp all-purpose flour
1 tbsp (20g) lard or coconut oil

For the dough
1½ cups plus 2 tbsp (200g) glutinous rice flour, plus more to dust
1 tsp cooking oil

For the dips
4 tbsp runny sesame paste
4 tsp sugar, to taste

Make the stuffing (this can be done in advance: see the headnote). Toast the sesame seeds in a dry wok or frying pan over a gentle flame, stirring constantly, until they smell and taste delicious. Because they are black, you won't notice a change in color, so do take care not to burn them (they will taste bitter if overdone). Trust your nose and tongue to tell you when they're ready; the roasted taste is unmistakable. (Add a few white sesame seeds as a kind of barometer if you wish: when they are turning golden, all the sesame seeds should be ready.)

When the seeds are done, put them into a mortar and pestle and grind them coarsely (this can be done in a food processor, but take care not to reduce the seeds to a powder, they taste better with a little crunch). Add the sugar and mix well. Place the flour in a dry wok or frying pan and stir over a gentle heat until it smells cooked and toasty. Add it to the sesame seeds and mix well.

Heat the lard or coconut oil over a gentle flame until melted, then stir into the seed mixture. Mix well, then press the stuffing into a small bowl and refrigerate until set. Shortly before you wish to make the *tang yuan*, remove the stuffing from the refrigerator and use a small knife or teaspoon to gouge out small amounts. Roll these into balls the size of small cherries and roll in a scattering of glutinous rice flour.

To make the dough, add the oil and ⅔ cup (150ml) tepid water to the glutinous rice flour and mix to make a soft, squidgy dough with a putty-like consistency. Break off pieces of dough the size of small walnuts, roll them into spheres, then press your thumb into the center of each to make a little cup. Place a ball of filling into a cup.

If you are right-handed, cradle a cup in the fingers of your right hand and gently push your right thumb on to the ball of filling. Turn the dumpling as you use the thumb and index finger of your left hand to draw the edges of the dough up around the ball. Close the dough around the ball. Draw the edges up into a little point to close the rice ball completely, then pinch off the pointy tip (it can be mixed back into the remainder of the dough).

Continued on page 314

Roll the rice ball between your palms into a little sphere and lay on a board lightly dusted with glutinous rice flour.

Combine the sesame paste and sugar and divide between dipping dishes for each of your guests.

Fill a saucepan with water and bring it to a boil. Drop the rice balls into the water, return to a boil, reduce the heat and simmer gently for 5 to 10 minutes until cooked through: the dumplings are ready when they have increased in size and are soft and squeezable when you take them in a pair of chopsticks (break one open to make sure: the black stuffing should be melted and glossy).

As the dumplings are cooking, bring a kettle to a boil. When they are ready, pour a little hot water into a serving bowl for each person and place about four rice balls into each bowl. The water is not to be drunk, but will keep the *tang yuan* hot and silky-soft until they are eaten. Serve with the sweet sesame dip.

VARIATIONS

Tang yuan in sweet glutinous rice soup
Bring enough water to a boil to cook the *tang yuan* and add about 4 tbsp fermented glutinous rice (*lao zao* or *tian jiu*: this is sold in glass jars in Chinese supermarkets and looks like plain long-grain rice in a slightly cloudy liquid), with sugar to taste. Add the prepared *tang yuan* and simmer until cooked. If you wish, reduce the heat at this stage and drizzle a beaten egg or two into the liquid. When the egg has set into golden wisps, divide the *tang yuan* between your serving bowls. This snack is traditionally given to women after childbirth in Sichuan. It is often made with unfilled *tang yuan* (little, cherry-sized spheres of glutinous rice paste).

Tang yuan in roasted peanut flour
Roast some peanuts and grind them with a mortar and pestle. Toss freshly boiled *tang yuan* in this peanut "flour" to cover them completely before serving. *Tang yuan* are often presented like this in Cantonese dim sum restaurants.

LOTUS LEAF BUNS
HE YE BING 荷葉餅

These delicate steamed buns, made to look like folded lotus leaves, are a traditional accompaniment to rich dishes such as bowl-steamed pork in rice meal or roast duck. The bland white dough acts as a counterfoil to the intense flavors and textures of, say, a slice of slow-cooked pork belly, and the buns are fun to stuff and eat too, like Peking duck pancake rolls. They can be made in larger quantities than you need, frozen, then steamed through when you want to eat them.

Try serving lotus leaf buns with Bowl-steamed Pork in Rice Meal (see page 104), Beef with Cumin (see page 106), Twice-cooked Pork (see page 96), or Stir-fried Tofu with Black Bean and Chilli (see page 86).

If you wish to serve these with roast duck, don't forget the traditional trimmings of sweet fermented sauce and slivered spring onion whites, with cucumber strips too, if you wish.

This recipe makes about 30 lotus leaf buns. You will need a clean comb to decorate them. Take a look at the photo on page 105 to see how to decorate the buns.

2 tsp dried yeast
4 cups (500g) bread flour, plus more to dust

2 tbsp cooking oil, plus more to grease
2 tsp sugar

Add the yeast to ½ cup (100ml) tepid water and set aside for five minutes to bloom. Add the flour to a mixing bowl and make a well in the center. Pour the dissolved yeast mixture into the well and mix in enough flour to give a soft paste. Cover with a wet tea towel and leave for about 20 minutes to ferment, by which time the paste should be light and bubbly. Add the oil and sugar, with just enough water to give a soft, kneadable dough (about ¾ cup/225ml). Mix well.

Turn the dough on to a very lightly floured work surface and knead for about 10 minutes until smooth and shiny. Return it to the bowl, cover with a wet tea towel and leave to rise for about 20 minutes.

Knock back the dough by giving it a good punch. Then take a quarter of it and roll it into a sausage about 1¼ in (3cm) thick. Use a knife to cut the sausage into 1¾ in (4cm) sections (weighing about ½ oz/25g each). Lightly dust your hands with flour, turn each section on end and flatten it with the palm of your hand. Then roll it out into a 3 in (8cm) circle. Repeat with the remaining dough.

Take a circle of dough and brush it very lightly with oil. Then use a chopstick laid across its center to help you fold it in half. Lay the folded circle on your work surface and use the teeth of a comb to prick a lotus leaf patten into the dough. Now use the back of the comb to nudge the edges of the bun in at the end of each "leaf vein." Lay on the oiled rack of a steamer and leave to rise for 20 minutes.

Steam the buns over a high heat for 10 minutes, until cooked through. Serve them immediately, or cool then refrigerate or freeze, and simply steam through before serving.

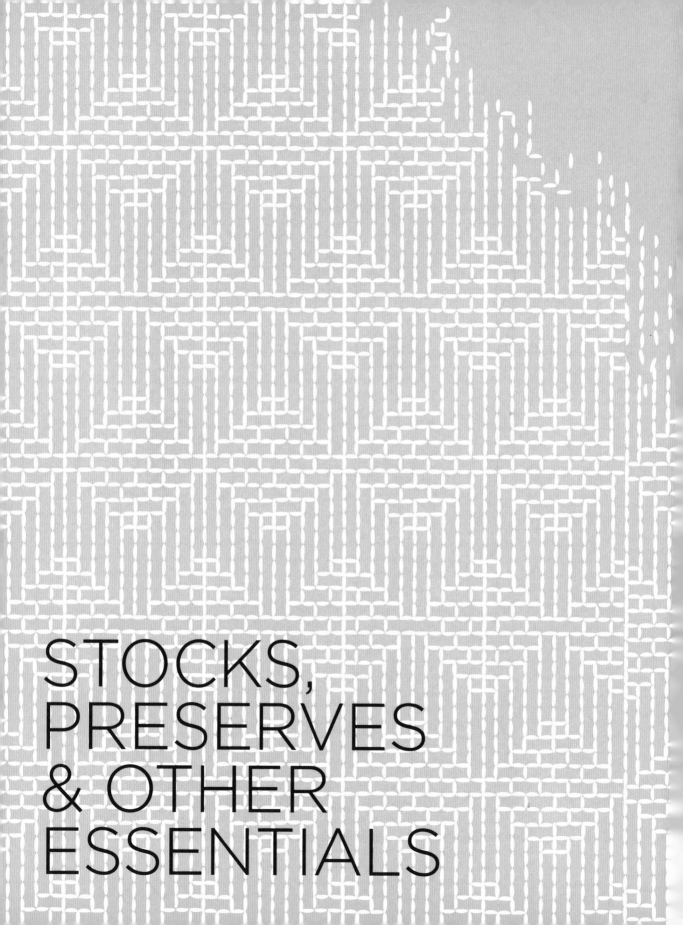

STOCKS,
PRESERVES
& OTHER
ESSENTIALS

A few basic preparations will greatly enhance the flavors of many of the dishes in this book. For the Chinese chef, like the French chef, good stocks are one of the foundation stones of cooking. (A common Chinese saying compares the chef's stocks to the chest of the opera singer, without which he cannot sing a note.) Even for everyday home cooking, a basic homemade stock will be vastly superior to the packaged kinds, unless you buy it fresh from a first-class supplier. While everyone needs to cut corners some of the time, it's really worth making a large batch of stock and keeping it, bagged up in suitable quantities, in the freezer for last-minute meals.

Similarly, learning how to make a few basic seasonings such as chilli oil and spiced aromatic soy sauce is a worthwhile investment of your time: easy to make in large quantities, they keep indefinitely, and will bring light and life to your Sichuanese appetizers, as well as to many dumpling and noodle dishes. This chapter includes recipes for some of these freezer and store-cupboard staples.

EVERYDAY STOCK
XIAN TANG 鮮湯

If you are making soup, a decent stock is essential. It also helps to boost and round out the flavors of other dishes. It's easy to make, but you need to be at home for a few hours to keep an eye on it. I like to make stock on weekends when I'm doing chores around the house. I find something soothing in the way it murmurs away on the back burner, filling the kitchen with wonderful smells. Usually, I buy a big bagful of chicken carcasses and pork ribs, make a huge potful of stock, then freeze it in one-quart (one-liter) containers. If I'm entertaining, I will often start making stock in the afternoon, then let it simmer away at the back of the stove as I cook, scooping it up into my sauces and soup as I need it.

The classic Chinese stock is made from a mixture of chicken and pork, which combine to give an umami-rich yet delicate flavor, but you can make it with chicken alone if you wish. Quantities are not critical, but to intensify the taste it's best to use a pan just large enough to take the meats and only just enough water to cover them.

Raw chicken carcasses
Pork ribs

Piece of ginger, unpeeled
Spring onion whites

Clean the raw meats: the traditional method is to blanch them for a couple of minutes in boiling water but, if you want to save time, just wash them well under the cold and then the hot tap. (Blanching, or rinsing, rids the meats of impurities and gives a cleaner, clearer stock.)

Put the carcasses and ribs in a pan, cover with cold water and bring to a boil. Skim off and discard the froth that rises to the surface of the liquid (you may have to do this a few times). When the surface is fairly clear of froth, add a piece of ginger, crushed slightly, and a couple of spring onion whites (a ½ oz/25g piece of ginger will do for a five- to six-quart pan).

Reduce the heat, half-cover the pan and simmer very gently for two to three hours. If you are not using the stock immediately, let it cool completely, then strain, decant into plastic bags or containers and keep in the refrigerator for a few days, or freeze for later use.

VARIATION

Chicken stock
For a really fine chicken soup or stock, Chinese cooks use an old hen, which may be stringy but will have a magnificent flavor with long, slow cooking. (If you have any friends with free-range birds and can secure a fowl that is at least a year old, make the most of it, as they are hard to buy.) In any case, for the richest flavor use a free-range bird, or parts of it. I tend to buy organic, free-range chicken carcasses from my local market and supplement them with a handful of chicken wings for a richer stock, but I do occasionally use a whole chicken if I'm feeling extravagant. Blanch the bird or its parts in boiling water, or rinse them under the hot tap, and add ginger and spring onions to the pot as in the main recipe.

VEGETARIAN STOCKS
SU XIAN TANG 素鮮湯

Buddhist vegetarian restaurants in China make their own meatless stocks, and rural people may use broths made from pickled vegetables or fermented beans, or the milky liquid left over from cooking rice, for their soups and sauces. Vegetarian stock cubes can be used, but do take care with their saltiness: the recipes in this book are written with unsalted Chinese stocks in mind, so you will need to reduce salt and other salty seasonings if you use them. If you wish to make your own vegetarian stocks, the following are some Chinese possibilities.

Quick vegetarian stock

This is a recipe from the wonderful vegetarian restaurant at the Jade Buddha Temple in Shanghai, where they use it for their noodle and wonton soups. Simply season hot water with light soy sauce and a little sesame oil (for one quart/liter of water, about 2½ tsp light soy sauce and ½ tsp sesame oil will do). Simple, but very savory.

Black bean stock

Bring one quart (liter) of water to a boil with 2 oz (50g) fermented black beans, rinsed and drained, then simmer for about 20 minutes. Strain out and discard the black beans if you wish.

Sprouted soy bean stock

These make a classic vegetarian soup base. The beansprouts, which are longer and thicker than the more common mung beansprouts, are easily available in China but hard to come by in the West, so you may have to sprout your own. To make a "milky" broth, bring a panful of water to a boil, add plenty of soy beansprouts, cover and boil for 10–20 minutes, until the liquid is richly savory. To make a clear broth, boil the water, add the sprouts, return to a boil, then simmer gently, uncovered, for about 30 minutes. Strain the broth, or add the beansprouts to your soups if you wish.

Other variations

Other classic ingredients in vegetarian stocks are fresh bamboo shoots, simmered for a while like the soy beansprouts above, and shiitake mushrooms. For a rich vegetarian stock, use a mixture of soy beansprouts, peeled bamboo shoots and reconstituted dried shiitake mushrooms.

CHILLI OIL
HONG YOU 紅油

One of the essential ingredients in Sichuanese cold dishes, this is also used in dips for dumplings and other snacks. You can buy chilli oil in most Chinese supermarkets, but it's generally much spicier than the Sichuanese version and often has added ingredients such as dried shrimp. For Sichuanese recipes, it's much better to make your own, milder chilli oil, which can be used generously for its color and mouthfeel without any overwhelming heat. It's easy to make, keeps indefinitely, and jars of it can also make rather fine gifts.

Sichuanese ground chillies are hard to find in the West, but the mild, aromatic ground chillies used in Korean kimchi have the same deep terracotta color and make a wonderful substitute. They are increasingly available in Asian stores. If you want to give your chilli oil a bit more of a kick, simply add a dash of hotter ground chillies of your choice to the mix. I almost always buy my chillies ground, because it's more convenient: see the note, right, if you wish to grind your own.

A sugar or oil thermometer is extremely useful, though not essential, for this recipe.

2 cups plus 2 tbsp (500ml) cooking oil
4 oz (100g) Sichuanese or Korean ground chillies

1 tsp sesame seeds
Small piece of ginger, unpeeled, crushed

Heat the oil over a high flame to about 400°F (200°C), then leave for 10 minutes to cool to around 275°F (140°C).

Place the ground chillies, sesame seeds and ginger in a heatproof bowl. Have a little cool oil or a cupful of water on hand. When the oil has cooled to the right temperature, pour a little on to the chillies; it should fizz gently but energetically and release a rich, roasty aroma. Pour over the rest of the oil and stir. If you think the oil is too hot and the chillies are likely to burn, simply add a little cool oil to release the excess heat. Do, though, make sure that the oil is hot enough: without the fizzing, it won't generate the rich, roasty fragrance you need. If you pour all the oil on to the chillies, then discover it's not quite hot enough, you can return the whole lot to a saucepan and heat gently until it smells fabulous and the color is a deep ruby red, but do take care not to burn the chillies. (The chillies will seethe and fizz like a witch's cauldron as you heat them, releasing the most marvellous aromas, but can easily start to burn and blacken.)

When the oil has cooled completely, decant it and the chilli sediment into jars and store in a dark, cool place. Leave it to settle for at least a day before using.

To grind your own chillies
This method comes from the Sichuanese chef Yu Bo. Snip the chillies into halves or sections and discard their seeds as far as possible. Stir them in a dry wok over a very gentle heat until they are fragrant and crisp. (If you wish, you can sift them to get rid of more seeds at this stage.) Then add a very small amount of oil to the wok and continue to stir the chillies over the heat until they are glossy and slightly darker (their color is referred to in the trade as "cockroach color"!). Turn the chillies into a mortar and pestle and pound them into fine flakes; avoid grinding them to a powder.

GROUND ROASTED SICHUAN PEPPER
HUA JIAO MIAN 花椒面

This seasoning is one of the essentials of Sichuanese cooking and is used particularly in dips and cold dishes. Always make it freshly if you can, since it loses its fragrance quickly. A tiny amount goes a long way, so I roast and grind it a tablespoonful or so at a time and try to avoid keeping it for longer than a week.

Stir whole Sichuan pepper in a dry wok over a very gentle heat until it is wonderfully fragrant, taking great care not to burn it. This normally takes three to four minutes. Transfer immediately to a mortar, then grind it to a fine powder with the pestle. For best results, sift the powder through a tea strainer and discard the white husky residue, which has no flavor.

SWEET AROMATIC SOY SAUCE
FU ZHI JIANG YOU 復制醬油

This sweetened, spiced soy sauce is the secret ingredient in the glorious, garlicky dressing used for Sichuanese Wontons (see page 292), as well as salady ingredients such as cucumber and cooked fava beans. It's easy to make and keeps indefinitely.

½ cup (100ml) light or tamari soy sauce
⅓ cinnamon stick or a piece of cassia bark
½ tsp fennel seeds
½ star anise
½ tsp Sichuan pepper
⅓ oz (10g) piece of ginger, crushed slightly
3 tbsp brown sugar

Put the soy sauce into a saucepan with ¾ cup (200ml) water and bring to a boil. Add the spices and ginger, reduce the heat and simmer for 30 minutes.

Add the sugar and stir to dissolve. You should end up with about ½ cup (100ml) of liquid.

LARD
ZHU YOU 豬油

Lard has a poor reputation in the West but, freshly made and used in modest quantities, it's a delicious addition to all kinds of otherwise vegetarian dishes, to which it lends its rich umami flavors. In the Chinese countryside, many households still make their own lard, especially in winter as the Chinese New Year approaches. A small amount of lard will add a subtle luxuriousness to stir-fried mushrooms and other vegetables. It's also often added to the stocks in which noodles or dumplings are served, for a bit of silkiness and extra richness.

Cut pork back fat or belly fat into 1–1¾ in (3–4cm) chunks and put them into a saucepan with a generous covering of water. Bring to a boil, then simmer over a medium heat to allow the water to evaporate. As the water disappears, the liquid will start to spit and crackle. When the noise has subsided, remove from the stove and strain the molten lard into a sterilized container. It will keep for months in the refrigerator. Lard can also be frozen: if you freeze it, I suggest dividing it up into small, useful quantities that are quick and easy to defrost, or letting it set into fairly thin layers from which you can snap off the amount you need.

The same method can be used to render chicken fat, which is often added to banquet dishes just before serving, adding a wonderful umami flavor. A spoonful of chicken fat added to a wokful of mushrooms at the last stage of cooking, or melted over some freshly cooked greens, is a glorious thing.

ROASTED AND FRIED PEANUTS
YOU SU HUA REN 油酥花仁

Roasted or fried peanuts may be used in cold-dressed dishes and also in a few hot dishes, such as Gong Bao Chicken with Peanuts (see page 118). Fried peanuts make a delicious nibble in their own right, perhaps sprinkled with salt and ground roasted Sichuan pepper.

Both fried and roasted peanuts should be stored in an airtight jar if you don't intend to eat them immediately. They are most delicious when freshly fried or roasted.

Roasted peanuts

To roast peanuts, heat an oven to 120°C/250°F/gas mark ½. Place the raw nuts on an oven tray and roast for 15–20 minutes, until fragrant and very slightly golden. Do keep an eye on them, as they are easily burned. If you are not sure if they are ready, remove one peanut, allow to cool slightly, then taste: when done, it will have lost its raw crunchy flavor and have a dry, aromatic crispness. When the nuts are cooked, remove them from the oven and tip on to a plate to cool down. Rub the cooled nuts between your fingertips to loosen the skins. Then stand in the garden or on a balcony and shake the nuts as you blow over them: the skins will blow away.

Fried peanuts

To fry peanuts, heat enough oil to cover the raw nuts in a wok over a gentle flame to 250°F (120°C), adding the peanuts as it starts to warm up. Fry them for about 20 minutes, stirring often and taking care not to burn them. When they are crisp and fragrant, remove them with a slotted spoon or strainer, drain well and spread out to cool completely.

GLOSSARY

Chinese seasonings and dried goods are stocked in increasing numbers and varieties by mainstream supermarkets and health food shops. Those that aren't can be found in Chinese groceries. A few Chinese vegetables—such as bok choy and choy sum—can be found in mainstream supermarkets and I hope more will become available in future. Meanwhile, Chinese supermarkets stock a wonderful and ever-expanding array of Chinese vegetables.

You will need ginger, garlic and spring onions to make many recipes in this book, so keep them in stock. Most other ingredients here are needed only for specific recipes.

TOFU

豆腐
Tofu (*dou fu*)

Tofu is made from dried yellow soy beans that are soaked, ground with water, strained to make soy milk, heated, then curdled with a coagulant (usually gypsum or mineral salts). This basic tofu can be used as it is, or pressed into a more solid form, which in turn can be spiced, smoked or fermented. There are many types; the following are used in this book:

1 | 豆花
Silken tofu (*dou hua*)

Known as flower tofu, or bean flower (*dou hua*) in Chinese, this very light tofu is not pressed and has a consistency reminiscent of pannacotta or crème caramel. It can be eaten hot or cold and with sweet or savory seasonings. You will find it in Chinese and Japanese supermarkets and in health food shops.

2 | 豆腐
Plain white tofu (*dou fu*)

Most tofu is pressed to extract water, so it holds its shape and can be cut with a knife. Its consistency varies depending on how much water has drained away. In this book, plain white tofu refers to the semi-pressed tofu that is the most basic and ubiquitous form. It is generally packaged with water and sold in Chinese groceries, health food shops and mainstream supermarkets. This kind is used mostly in soups and braises. It can also be shallow- or deep-fried until puffy and golden before cooking with other ingredients and seasonings. Most Chinese cooks blanch it in salted water before cooking, to refresh its flavor.

3 | 豆腐乾
Firm tofu (*dou fu gan*)

As more water is pressed out of it, tofu acquires a firmer texture reminiscent of mozzarella, or even Edam. It can be used in cold dishes, or stir-fried. It is stocked by many Chinese supermarkets.

4 | 香乾
Smoked tofu (*xiang gan*)

Made from firm tofu that has been smoked, this is a rich caramel brown on the outside and has a wonderful, aromatic flavor. Like spiced tofu (see below), it can be used in cold dishes or stir-fries and is often sold in health food shops, as well as some Chinese supermarkets. Unopened, it keeps well in the fridge.

5 | 五香豆腐乾
Spiced tofu (*wu xiang dou fu gan*)

This is firm tofu, simmered in aromatic broth. Darker than plain firm tofu, it is sold in Chinese supermarkets and health food shops.

6 | 腐竹
Dried bean milk sticks, or tofu "bamboo" (*fu zhu*)

Made from protein-rich skins that gather on the surface of simmering soy milk, which are crumpled and rolled into sand-colored sticks before drying. Soak in hot water for an hour until supple, cut, then toss into cold dishes, simmer with seasonings, or add to a soup or stew. Bean milk skin is also sold in knots, which may be added to stews, such as Red-braised Beef (see page 108).

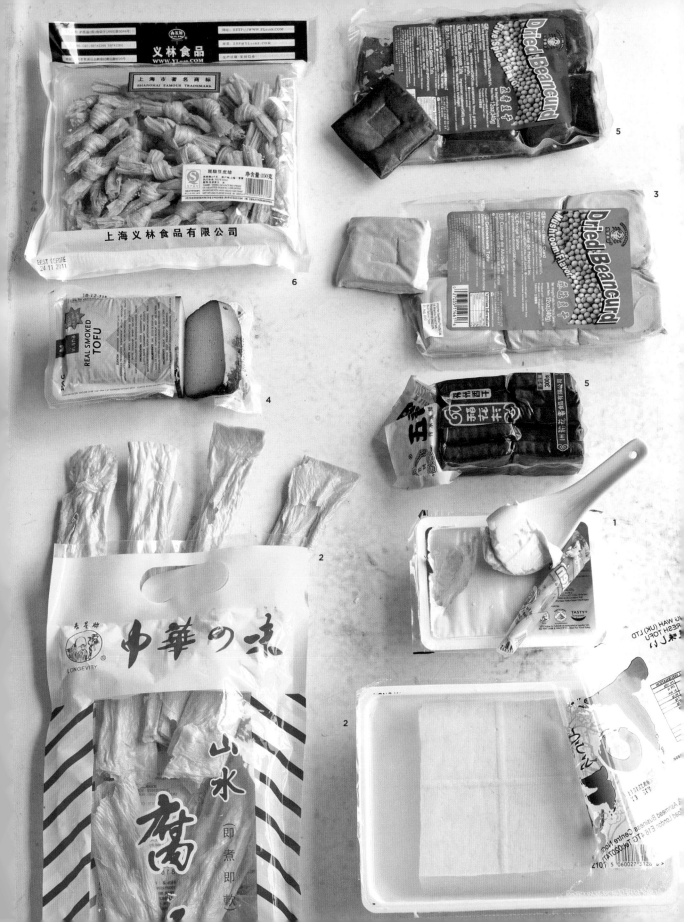

LEAFY GREENS

1 | 芥藍
Chinese broccoli (*jie lan*)

This beautiful, deep green vegetable has a delicious flavor with a hint of bitterness. Dark green leaves grow around its juicy stems and green flower buds. It is commonly eaten in the Cantonese south of China and widely available in Chinese groceries. It is particularly good blanched, then stir-fried with ginger. The Cantonese call it *gai lan*, which is how it is often sold in Chinese supermarkets.

2 | 芹菜
Chinese celery (*qin cai*)

Chinese celery has stems more slender than those of Western celery, and abundant leaves. Its stems can be a little fibrous, but they have a wonderful herby flavor and are often used in stir-fries and cold dishes, or as a garnish. The leaves may be chopped and used as a fragrant garnish for soups and noodle dishes.

3 | 百菜，大白菜
Chinese leaf cabbage (*bai cai, da bai cai*)

Chinese leaf or celery cabbage is sold in most mainstream supermarkets. It has a light, slightly mustardy flavor and a very crisp texture, and is one of the most important vegetables in northern China. With the right treatment, it is juicy and delicious. Most Chinese people pickle it, stir-fry it with a variety of seasonings, or cook it in soups and stews.

4 | 菜心
Choy sum (*cai xin*)

"Vegetable hearts" in Chinese, this is a favorite Cantonese vegetable with deep green leaves, thin, juicy stems and little yellow flowers. It has a delicate, sweet flavor and is beautiful either blanched or stir-fried. In my opinion, the simple Blanched Choy Sum with Sizzling Oil (see page 168) is one of the loveliest recipes in this book. The photograph opposite shows two varieties of choy sum.

5 | 芥菜
Mustard greens (*jie cai*)

This variety of cabbage has broad, mid-green leaves. It is usually pickled, but can also be stir-fried or made into soups (see page 240). The Cantonese call it *gai choy*, which is the name by which it is often sold in the West.

6 | 小白菜
Bok choy (*xiao bai cai*)

Bok choy is now widely available in mainstream supermarkets as well as in Chinese shops. You are likely to come across three main types: regular bok choy (i), which has white midribs blooming out into dark green leaves; baby bok choy (ii), which is the same but smaller and generally tastier; and Shanghai green bok choy (iii), which is grass-green throughout (I find it more interesting in flavor than regular bok choy). They are usually stir-fried, blanched or used in soups.

7 | 豆苗
Pea shoots (*dou miao*)

Pea shoots are a delicate vegetable that was until recently used mainly in banquet cooking. Their slender stalks, leaves and tendrils have a delightful pea flavor. Currently fashionable among Western chefs, they are now available in smarter supermarkets. In Chinese shops, you can recognize them from their small round leaves and snaking tendrils. In Chinese cooking, pea shoots are generally stir-fried, often with garlic, or used as a colorful garnish in clear soups.

8 | 莧菜
Purple amaranth (*xian cai*)

This vegetable (*Amaranth tricolor*), common in southern China and available from time to time in larger Chinese or Vietnamese supermarkets, has thin stems with a profusion of small purple-hearted leaves. It is generally used in soups or in stir-fries, which it delicately colors with pink juices. Try to buy it when young and tender and discard any fibrous stems.

9 | 空心菜，筒菜
Water spinach (*kong xin cai, tong cai*)

Deep green water spinach, known also as "morning glory," has crisp, tubular stems and long, pointed leaves. It is almost always stir-fried, usually with garlic or fermented tofu, but can also be used in soups. The Cantonese sell it as *ong choy*.

GARLIC, CHIVES AND OTHER AROMATICS

1 | 韭菜
Chinese chives (*jiu cai*)
Also known as garlic chives, these have deep green, spear-like leaves and a wonderfully punchy garlicky taste and fragrance. They are used mostly in stir-fries and in dumpling stuffings. They can be bought in many Chinese supermarkets. The photograph shows two varieties: the delicate chives favored in mainland China; and the coarser chives grown in Thailand and exported.

2 | 香菜
Cilantro (*xiang cai*)
One of the few fresh herbs in common use in China. It can be stir-fried or mixed into salads, but is most commonly used as a garnish, especially for ingredients that are considered to have strong "fishy" aspects to their flavors, such as beef, lamb and paddy eels.

3 | 韭菜花
Flowering chives (*jiu cai hua*)
These long, fine stems, topped with little flower buds that should be nipped off and discarded before cooking, have a fantastic garlicky flavor. The stems are normally stir-fried and are particularly delicious with a little pork or bacon.

4 | 大蒜
Garlic (*da suan*)
This needs little explanation, except to say that larger garlic cloves are easier to slice.

5 | 蒜薹，蒜苗，蒜心
Garlic stems (*suan miao, suan tai, suan xin*)
Look out for bundles of these long, pale green stems in Chinese fresh produce shops: they are particularly delicious when stir-fried with a little bacon or with mushrooms.

6 | 姜，生姜
Ginger (*jiang, sheng jiang*)
Try to find plump, smooth-skinned ginger with a strong fragrance that is heavy for its size, indicating that it is full of juice and has not dried out. You may snap off a piece to check that it's not too fibrous: a clean break is a good sign, hair-like fibers sticking out of the break are not. But don't throw away pieces of ginger that are fibrous or drying out: smack them with the side of your cleaver or a rolling pin and use them in stocks and marinades.

7 | 蔥
Spring onions (*cong*)
Chinese green onions, which are normally described in English as spring onions or scallions, resemble long spring onions, without their characteristic swollen bulbs. They are used to refine the flavors of meat and fish ingredients and to give an appetizing fragrance and taste to all kinds of dishes. In southern China there are two common types of spring onion: "small spring onions" (*xiao cong*), which are very slender and almost chive-like; and "large spring onions" (*da cong*), which are longer and thicker. The former are normally finely chopped for a garnish, while the latter are used in marinades and in cooking. The most commonly available spring onions in the West are something between these two Chinese varieties, which is why I generally suggest using the green parts for garnishes and the thicker, more pungent whites in marinades and stews. (In northern China, they use another type of onion, confusingly also known as *da cong*, which is something between a spring onion and a leek: it is leek sized, but has a more delicate texture and can be eaten raw. This kind of *da cong* is one of the traditional garnishes for Peking duck.)

8 | 韭黃
Yellow chives (*jiu huang*)
Yellow or hothouse chives are grown in darkness, like chicory and forced rhubarb, so they have a very pale color and a wonderful aroma. They can be found from time to time in Chinese supermarkets and are usually wrapped in thin paper. They are absolutely delicious but also fragile and they don't keep well, so snap them up when you find them and use them quickly.

蒜苗，大蒜，青蒜
Chinese garlic leaves (*suan miao, da suan* or *qing suan*, not pictured)
Always sold in bunches and resembling, from a distance, long Chinese spring onions, this actually has flat, deep-green leaves rather like those of leeks. It is often used in stir-fries and is delicious in combination with a little smoked bacon. It is a traditional ingredient in classic Sichuanese dishes such as Pock-marked Old Woman's Tofu (*ma po dou fu*, see page 76) and Twice-cooked Pork (see page 96). If you can't find it in a Chinese supermarket, use slender baby leeks, or even spring onions instead. You can also substitute any light green sprouts that emerge from the neglected or forgotten garlic bulbs in your kitchen.

OTHER FRESH VEGETABLES

1 | 蘿蔔
Asian radish (*luo bo*)

The crisp, crystalline flesh of this long white root, known also as daikon and mooli, can have a slightly peppery bite, but it is much less hot than the little red radishes found in the West. It can be eaten raw in salads and garnishes, stir-fried, or simmered in soups and stews; it is particularly good with beef. Chose firm radishes and peel them before use.

2 | 豆芽，芽菜
Beansprouts (*dou ya, ya cai*)

The most common type of these are sprouted from mung beans and are generally used in soups and stir-fries, or blanched and mixed into salady appetizers. Sprouted soy beans, which are less commonly found in the West, are thicker and coarser, but can be simmered in water to make a good vegetarian stock.

3 | 鮮百合
Fresh day lily bulb (*xian bai he*)

Fresh day lily bulbs, which can be found seasonally in some Chinese supermarkets, look rather like garlic bulbs. Peeled, they can be separated into petal-like lobes, which have little flavor of their own but are highly prized for their beautiful crispness in the mouth and their exotic appearance. They are most commonly used in stir-fries, alongside other crisp and crunchy vegetables. Most Chinese stores sell packages of dried lily bulb, which can be reconstituted by soaking in hot water, but I don't recommend this as a substitute for the fresh kind in stir-fries. The fresh bulbs are normally sold vacuum-packed and will keep for several weeks stored in the refrigerator.

4 | 青豆
Fresh green soy beans (*qing dou*)

Unripe soy beans have a bright green color and a lovely flavor. They are wonderful boiled, steamed or stir-fried and can also be used to add a little splash of color to fried rice or noodle dishes. If you can't buy them fresh, look for them frozen in bags in some larger supermarkets and whole food stores. In their pods, these are often known by their Japanese name, "edamame."

5 | 藕
Lotus root (*ou*)

This is actually the segmented underwater stem of the lotus plant. Peeled and sliced, it has a beautiful lace-like appearance and a refreshingly crisp mouthfeel. It can be blanched and then used in cold dishes, stir-fried, or added to soups and stews.

6 | 絲瓜
Silk gourd (*si gua*)

The long silk gourd, otherwise known as loofah gourd, has a coarse reptilian skin and pale flesh that becomes spongy and juicy after cooking. There are two main types, one plump and pale and the other with sharp ridges in its dark green skin (see photo, right). I have found the latter variety on sale in my local Chinatown, but either can be used for the silk gourd recipe in this book, Silk Gourd with Green Soy Beans (see page 220). The skin of the gourd is never eaten, but should be peeled away and discarded before cooking.

7 | 芋頭
Taro (*yu tou*)

This purplish-brown, bristly root vegetable can be found in Chinese and Caribbean or African shops. If you can find them, use tiny young corms, which have a very delicate, milky texture when cooked; otherwise, larger ones, which are more floury, will do. And do make sure you wear rubber gloves when peeling taro: their hairy skins contain a mild toxin, neutralized by cooking, that can otherwise make your wrists and arms itch like crazy for an hour or so.

8 | 馬蹄，荸薺
Water chestnuts (*ma ti, bi qi*)

You can buy these sweet, crisp nuts in cans, ready peeled, but the fresh variety, often sold in larger Chinese groceries, are far superior. If you can buy fresh water chestnuts, wash them well and peel them before use. They can be cooked or eaten raw, like a fruit; the latter is the best way to appreciate their delicate natural sweetness.

9 | 冬瓜
Winter melon (*dong gua*)

These melons, which grow to enormous sizes, have dark, blue-green skins with a thin, frost-like coating and crisp apple-white flesh. They can be a light, refreshing accompaniment to robust ingredients such as meatballs in soups (see page 248), and can also be wok-cooked. Because of their vastness, winter melons are normally sold cut into more manageable slices. Sometimes the smaller melons are carved with spectacular intricate designs, hollowed out and used as soup tureens at banquets.

PRESERVED VEGETABLES

In the past, these preserves were a way of dealing with seasonal gluts of particular crops; these days, they are eaten as much for their delicious tastes as for their nutritional value. Some are pickled in brine: these have a refreshing sour taste. Others are sun-wilted, rubbed with salt and spices and packed into jars to ferment: they are moist and salty and have complex savory flavors that give a real lift to vegetarian dishes, especially those based on peas and beans. Different varieties of these wilted, spiced vegetables have different tastes, but to an extent you can use them interchangeably. The following types are used in this book:

1 | 橄欖菜
"Olive" vegetable (*gan lan cai*)

A speciality of the Cantonese region of Chaozhou, this marvellous relish is made from dark preserved mustard greens, vegetable oil and Chinese olives (unrelated to European olives). Eat it from the jar with rice or noodles, or drain away the oil and use it in stir-fries. You'll find a few Chinese olives in each jar: watch out for their pits. This tends to be sold in larger Chinese supermarkets.

2 | 酸菜，泡菜
Pickled mustard greens (*suan cai, pao cai*)

These are leafy mustard greens pickled in brine. Their stems are a pale ivory and their leaves darker, their color varying from a dull yellow-green to a darker grey-green. They have a juicy texture, a refreshing sour taste and are lovely in soups.

3 | 榨菜
Sichuan preserved vegetable (*zha cai*)

Knobbly dried mustard tubers that have been salted, spiced and packed into jars to ferment. This pickle has a crisp texture and sour-savory taste and makes a wonderful garnish for hot and cold dishes, as well as an ingredient in soups, stir-fries and appetizers. It is sold in cans and should be rinsed before use.

4 | 芽菜
Sichuanese ya cai (*ya cai*)

This dark, sleek, crunchy preserve, the magic ingredient in Sichuanese Dry-fried Green Beans and Classic Dan Dan Noodles (see pages 150 and 280), is usually sold chopped, in sachets. It can be hard to find, but is increasingly available in Chinese supermarkets. If your local Chinese grocery doesn't stock it, use Tianjin preserved vegetable instead.

5 | 雪菜，雪裡蕻
Snow vegetable (*xue cai, xue li hong*)

A juicy preserve made from a variety of salted mustard greens, this has a delicious sour and savory flavor. A favorite in Shanghai and the Southern Yangtze region, it can be found, in sachets, in many Chinese supermarkets. Eat directly, or use in cooking.

6 | 天津冬菜
Tianjin preserved vegetable (*dong cai*)

A salted mustard green reminiscent of Sichuanese *ya cai*, this can be used as a substitute. It is sold in squat, earthenware jars and is very salty, so should be rinsed well and squeezed dry before use.

PRESERVED MEAT AND EGGS

7 | 火腿
Cured ham (*huo tui*)

Chinese cooks, like those in Spain and Italy, use pieces of dark, cured hams to intensify umami flavors. The finest in China come from Yunnan in the south west and Jinhua in eastern Zhejiang Province. They are not available in the West, but Spanish hams make a marvellous substitute: look out for cheaper cuts.

8 | 皮蛋
Preserved duck eggs (*pi dan*)

Known in the West as "1,000-year-old eggs," these are made by treating duck eggs with strong alkalis that "cook" them chemically. It's a technology that dates back at least to the sixteenth century. In the past, the eggs were caked in a paste made from mud, tea, rice husks and salt, with alkaline ingredients such as wood ash, soda, lye and lime; these days they may be simply immersed in an alkaline liquid. The eggs are sold, in boxes, in most Chinese supermarkets. They just need to be peeled before eating.

9 | 鹹蛋
Salted duck eggs (*xian dan*)

These are duck eggs that have been salt-preserved in brine or a salty paste. The salt changes their structure, so the albumen remains runny while the yolks become solid and waxy. The whites can be drizzled into soup and the yolks, which have an amazing umami flavor, chopped and used in soups or stir-fries. They are also hard-boiled and eaten as a relish or appetizer. They are sold in many Chinese food shops.

FERMENTED PRODUCTS, SAUCES AND PASTES

1 | 豆豉
Black fermented soy beans (*dou chi*)

These intensely tasty little beans are the base of black bean sauces and can be used in stir-fries and other wok-cooked dishes. They look withered, but have a rich, savory flavor reminiscent of good soy sauce. Rinse them before use. They keep indefinitely: some in the Hunan Provincial Museum that were found in a tomb dating back to the second century BC still look usable!

2 | 豆腐乳
Fermented tofu (*dou fu ru*)

A delicious Chinese relish that can transform a simple spinach stir-fry into something ambrosial (see Spinach with Chilli and Fermented Tofu, page 170), and add body and umami richness to sauces and marinades. It has a strong, fermented taste somewhat reminiscent of a very ripe Roquefort, and a texture that can be creamily soft or curd-like and crumbly. Serve it straight from the jar: a cube or two in a little dipping dish goes very well with plain rice or noodles for breakfast or a midnight feast (I sometimes also eat it spread sparingly on toast, like anchovy paste). There are many types, but the most useful are the white (i) and red (ii) varieties (*bai dou fu ru* and *hong dou fu ru* or *nan ru*). You will usually find white fermented tofu sold in glass jars filled with brine, either on its own or with a little red chilli. For the recipes in this book, either is fine. Red fermented tofu is eaten in Shanghai and the Southern Yangtze region. It is normally sold in cans or clay jars and has a dramatic, deep crimson color from red yeast rice (*hong qu mi*), and a rich, yeasty, almost biscuity taste. It's delicious with stir-fried spinach and in pork stews (see Tuzi's Slow-cooked Ribs with Red Fermented Tofu, page 102).

3 | 老乾媽
Laoganma black bean sauce (*lao gan ma*)

A zesty relish made from fermented black beans, chillies, vegetable oil and other seasonings. It can be eaten from the jar with noodles or rice and is also used in cooking. Made in Guizhou province, it is now popular all over China and sold in many Chinese supermarkets abroad. Sichuanese chefs in the West are particularly fond of it. Please note that the more common black bean sauce, versions of which are available in most supermarkets, is a completely different product and is not a good substitute.

4 | 醬油
Soy sauce (*jiang you*)

This is made by fermenting cooked soy beans (sometimes with wheat), mixing them with the appropriate mold spores, then immersing them in brine. The fermentation breaks down the proteins and other compounds, which react with one another to create rich and complex flavors (for a detailed description of the process, see Harold McGee's *On Food and Cooking*). Light (i) and dark (ii) soy sauces (*sheng chou* and *lao chou*) are the standard seasonings in Chinese cookbooks in the West, but reflect a recent Cantonese influence; in many parts of China, cooks traditionally rely on one tamari-type soy sauce (see below). I've suggested light and dark soy sauces for most recipes because they are widely available, but a good tamari can be used in place of light soy sauce. Always buy those that are naturally brewed or fermented. Light soy sauce is used primarily as a salt-savory seasoning and is the more widely used; it is also saltier in taste. Dark soy sauce is used, in very small quantities, to lend a rich, dark color to dishes.

5 | 甜麵醬
Sweet fermented sauce (*tian mian jiang*)

Also sold, confusingly, as "sweet bean sauce" and "hoisin sauce," this smooth, dark, glossy paste is made from fermented wheat and salt, sometimes with soy. It is used mainly in dips and stir-fries. Check the Chinese characters on the jar or packet to make sure it's the right thing.

6 | 醬油
Tamari soy sauce (*jiang you*)

Made from fermented soy beans, usually without wheat, this is closer to the traditional soy sauces of Sichuan and the Southern Yangtze region than the light and dark varieties. It has a richer, more balanced flavor than most light soy sauces as well as a slightly darker color. I use the Clearspring version, found in health food shops and some supermarkets. If you are using soy sauce in recipes where it stands out as an ingredient, for example in a sauce or a dip, I strongly recommend using tamari soy sauce.

SESAME

芝麻醬
Sesame paste (*zhi ma jiang*)

Chinese sesame paste is made from roasted sesame seeds, and has a very different taste from that of Middle Eastern tahini. It is sold in glass jars in Chinese supermarkets and usually has a dark, nutty color. As the paste settles in its jar, a layer of oil will form on top. Use a fork or a couple of chopsticks to mix the paste and oil together before using. When a recipe in this book requires "runny sesame paste," this means paste that has been diluted with oil from the top of the jar to the consistency of light cream. If there isn't enough oil on top to dilute it, add a little sesame oil.

芝麻
Sesame seeds (*zhi ma*)

The Chinese use both black and white sesame seeds, although the white are more widely used, while the black are mainly included in sweet dishes. Toasted sesame seeds are often used as a garnish: to toast them, heat them gently for a few minutes in a dry wok or frying pan, stirring constantly, until the white seeds are beginning to turn golden and have a wonderful roasty fragrance. If you are toasting black sesame seeds take great care not to burn them; since they won't change color, you will need to use your nose rather than your eyes to tell when they are ready. A few sesame seeds may be added to ground chillies in the making of chilli oil, to enhance its fragrance. In this book,"sesame seeds" means white sesame seeds unless otherwise stated.

CHILLIES

Chillies are used in many different forms in China, especially in the chilli headquarters of the southern provinces of Sichuan, Hunan, Guizhou and Jiangxi. The following are some of the most common chilli products. If you have sensitive skin, do use rubber gloves when cutting up fresh or dried chillies; if you don't wear gloves, avoid touching your eyes or nose after handling cut chillies.

干辣椒
Chillies, dried (*gan la jiao*)

Choose larger Sichuanese or Indian chillies that have a deep red color but are not too aggressively hot; Mexican de Arbol chillies can also be used. Avoid those tiny, fiery Indian and Thai chillies, which will overwhelm Sichuanese dishes.

辣椒面
Chillies, ground (*la jiao mian*)

Coarsely ground chillies or chilli flakes are used as a dip for cold meats and as a seasoning in many Sichuanese and Hunanese dishes. They are also the key ingredient in Chilli Oil (see page 320). Choose ground chillies with a deep terracotta color, a pleasant fragrance and a heat that is not too aggressive. Korean chilli flakes—the kind that are used for making *kimchi* pickles—are usually the best option to be found in some Chinatowns.

辣椒油，紅油
Chilli oil (*la jiao you, hong you*)

You can find chilli oil in most Chinese groceries, but the most common Cantonese version can be extremely spicy.

For Sichuanese cold dishes a mild chilli oil is best and I recommend making your own, with Sichuanese or Korean ground chillies (see page 320). It takes about 30 minutes to make and keeps indefinitely. It is used mostly in sauces for cold dishes and as a relish for noodles and dumplings. For a milder and more elegant taste, use the oil only; for the hearty taste and mouthfeel of Sichuanese folk cooking, stir in some of the toasted chilli sediment from the bottom of the jar.

豆瓣醬
Sichuan chilli bean paste (*dou ban jiang*)

A rich, fermented paste made from salt-fermented chillies and fava beans, this is one of the essential condiments in Sichuanese cooking. Lee Kum Kee make a bright, light version which is easily available in Chinese supermarkets; for richer, earthier flavors, seek out the more authentic Sichuanese versions from Pixian (郫縣), which are increasingly being sold in the West.

SPICES

The following are a few of the spices commonly used in Chinese cooking. They are all readily available in Chinese groceries. Often, several are used together to flavor aromatic broths (in which meat, poultry, offal or tofu may be simmered), or stews. You can add them directly to your wok or saucepan, or tie them up in pieces of muslin, which makes them easy to remove before serving. The whole spices may also be roasted and ground to make "five-spice" combinations. If you are going to keep only a couple of spices, I recommend cassia bark and star anise, as well as Sichuan pepper.

香葉
Bay leaves (*xiang ye*)
These are often used with other spices in aromatic broths and stews.

桂皮
Cassia bark (*gui pi*)
The dried bark of the Chinese cassia tree, this spice has a cinnamon-like flavor but is considered inferior to true cinnamon. Regular cinnamon sticks can be used instead.

丁香
Cloves (*ding xiang*)
These have a strong flavor and should be used with extreme moderation. Chinese cooks often pinch off and discard their powdery heads.

孜然
Cumin (*zi ran*)
Cumin is the hallmark spice of the great Silk Road region of Xinjiang in the northwest, where Uyghur Muslims sprinkle it on sizzling skewers of lamb;

it is only used occasionally in southern Chinese cooking. It is, however, the most important spice in a fabulous Hunanese beef dish (see Beef with Cumin, page 106), which is why it is included in this list.

小茴香
Fennel seeds (*xiao hui xiang*)
These pale green seeds are often used in spice mixtures.

花椒
Sichuan pepper (*hua jiao*)
The original Chinese pepper, used long before the more familiar black or white pepper (known in Chinese as "barbarian pepper," *hu jiao*) entered China along the old silk routes from the west. This spice is the pimply dried berries of a shrub that grows in dry, mountainous areas. At their best they have an intense, woody, citrussy aroma and induce a tingling sensation on the lips and tongue that can last for several minutes. The flavor is concentrated in the dark pink outer layer of the berries and the black seeds are usually discarded before they are sold. Sichuan pepper can be used whole, or roast and ground (see page 322). Always grind your own in small quantities, as you need them, as the powder quickly loses its fragrance. Store the whole pepper in an airtight jar or, if it's really fresh and zesty, in the fridge or freezer.

八角
Star anise (*ba jiao*)
These beautiful dried fruits are one of the most important spices of the Chinese kitchen. They have a very strong aroma and should be used sparingly. Star anise is often used in conjunction with cassia bark.

草果
Tsao-kuo (*cao guo*)
This spice has no English name, which is why it is often sold by its Chinese name (*cao guo* or *tsao-kuo*), or even its scholarly name (*Amomum tsao-ko*). It consists of dried, brown, ridged seed pods the size of nutmegs and has a cardamom-like flavor. Smack the pods with the flat of a cleaver blade or a rolling pin to open them out before using them (try to avoid smashing them to smithereens).

胡椒
White pepper (*hu jiao*)
The Chinese almost always use white pepper in cooking, largely because it is a common seasoning in so-called *bai wei* or "white-flavored" dishes (pale-colored dishes made without soy sauce or chilli). Black pepper flecks are seen as unsightly in such dishes. If you prefer, you can use black pepper instead.

DRIED GOODS

1 | 臘腸，香腸
Chinese wind-dried sausage (*la chang, xiang chang*)
These pink-and-white, salami-like seasoned sausages can be found in most Chinese supermarkets. Sliced or chopped, they add a rich savory taste, often with a hint of sweetness, to steamed dishes, stir-fries and stuffings; they are never eaten raw. Sometimes, darker pork liver sausages are sold alongside the pinker pork-meat version, but they are harder to find in the West. Wind-dried sausages are made in many parts of China, using different seasonings; those sold in the West tend to be Cantonese. I have sometimes used European salamis and chorizo as a substitute, but I do recommend the Chinese sausages if you can get them. They are easily available in Chinese supermarkets.

2 | 香菇，冬菇，花菇
Dried shiitake mushrooms (*xiang gu, dong gu, hua gu*)
These have an intense flavor, like a Chinese version of Italian porcini. The finest have criss-cross patterns on their caps, which is why they are known as flower mushrooms (*hua gu*). Dried shiitake must be soaked in hot water from the kettle for about 30 minutes until they soften, and they are sometimes also stewed with seasonings before being used in other dishes. Their soaking water may be used to add flavor to vegetarian dishes (if the mushrooms are at all gritty, strain the soaking water before use). The tough mushroom stalks are normally sliced off and discarded and only the caps used in cooking. These mushrooms are sold in Chinese groceries and mainstream supermarkets and keep indefinitely in an airtight box.

3 | 蝦皮，蝦米，開洋
Dried shrimp (*xia pi* or *xia mi*)
These add a dramatic umami edge to other ingredients and can make a simple cabbage stir-fry into something thrilling. There are two main types: tiny, pale, almost paper-thin shrimp known as "shrimp skin" (*xia pi* or *kai yang*) (i) and the more substantial orange or pink dried shrimp (*xia mi*) (ii). The first can be added directly to soups, stuffings and other preparations, while the second should be soaked in hot water for about 30 minutes before use. A bagful of shrimp skin is a very useful thing to have around especially if, like me, you like eating cabbage-type vegetables. Stored in the refrigerator or freezer, they keep for a long time.

4 | 枸杞子
Gouqi or goji berries (*gou qi zi*)
These small, scarlet berries, a traditional Chinese medicine, have become known as a "superfood" in the West in recent years because they are rich in Vitamin C and other nutrients. In Chinese cooking, they are added in small quantities to soups and stews, or used as a vivid garnish for dim sum or other dishes. Gouqi berries can be found in most Chinese supermarkets and medicine shops, as well as in some health food shops.

5 | 紫菜
Laver seaweed (*zi cai*)
Sold dried and pressed into crinkly round sheets that are almost black in color, this seaweed is a delicious addition to Chinese soups. It expands dramatically when soaked in stock or water so a little goes a very long way. It can be found in most Chinese supermarkets. Because of its crinkly, cellophane-like texture, it's not easy to cut with a knife: just tear it into small pieces with your fingers.

6 | 黃花，金針
Lily flowers (*huang hua, jin zhen*)
These dark yellow, long-petalled dried flowers are also known as "golden needles," day lily flowers or tiger lilies. They can be found packaged in most Chinese supermarkets.

7 | 荷葉
Lotus leaves (*he ye*)
These huge dried leaves are a little inconvenient to store, but they have a wonderful fragrance. They are most often used to wrap glutinous rice, meat or poultry for steaming (including that dim sum favorite, chicken with glutinous rice) and are also, in the heat of summer, added to congee, to which they impart their marvellous aroma and medicinally cooling qualities. You can find them in larger Chinese supermarkets.

8 | 黑木耳
Wood ear or Chinese black fungus (*hei muer*)
This dark brown fungus grows in rows of "ears" on damp wood, hence the name. It is sold dried, in a dark, crinkly form, in most Chinese supermarkets, and must be soaked in hot water for about 30 minutes before use.

RICE AND FLOUR

1 | 生粉
Potato flour (*sheng fen*)
Potato flour is a flavorless white powder used to thicken sauces, to clothe small pieces of meat or fish so they have a silky mouthfeel, and to make batters for deep-frying. It can be bought in most Asian food shops and a packet lasts a very long time. Pea starch is used in the same way in some parts of China. Cornstarch can be used as a substitute, but is less gelatinous: I've done some experiments and echo the findings of food writer Yan-kit So, that you need half as much again of cornstarch. Do adjust the quantities in the recipes if you wish to use cornstarch.

2 | 紅曲米，紅曲粉
Red yeast rice (*hong qu mi, hong qu fen*)
This seasoning and natural food coloring is widely used in the Lower Yangtze region. It is made by infecting rice with a kind of yeast (*Monascus purpureus*) that gives it an intense fuchsia color, a technology that dates back about 1,000 years, to the Song Dynasty. Often, it is sold ground, as a deep pink powder (ii), but you may also find the whole pink grains (i) on sale.

3 | 米粉，蒸肉粉
Rice meal (*mi fen, zheng rou fen*)
A coarse meal of rice that has been toasted with spices, then pounded or ground. It is used to steam meats, fish and some vegetables. It can be made at home fairly easily (see page 104), but is also sold in Chinese supermarkets, sometimes translated as "steam powder."

NOODLES

A vast variety of noodles are eaten in China. In the north and central China, they are generally made from wheat flour, while those in the far south often prefer those made from rice. Wheat noodles sometimes have egg added to the dough, perhaps with other seasonings such as shrimp eggs or fish. Noodles can also made from sweet potato starch, mung bean starch and buckwheat.

4 | 粉絲
Bean thread noodles (*fen si*)
Also known as mung bean vermicelli, these fine, transparent noodles should be soaked in hot water for 15 minutes before use. Flavorless in themselves, but with a pleasantly strandy and slippery texture, they can easily be found in most Chinese supermarkets.

5 | 蕎麵
Buckwheat noodles (*qiao mian*)
Eaten in some parts of China, these have a wonderfully nutty, earthy flavor. They are fabulous served with spicy sauces the Sichuanese way. Pure buckwheat noodles are best made to order from buckwheat paste squeezed through holes into a wokful of boiling water; this is because, dried, they have an unfortunate tendency to fall apart while cooking. For this reason I tend to use those noodles made with a mixture of both wheat and buckwheat when I am preparing buckwheat noodle dishes at home. These noodles, in a dried form, can easily be found in Chinese or Korean groceries, or, as *soba*, in Japanese stores.

6 | 米粉，河粉
Rice noodles (*mi fen* or *he fen*)
Rice noodles, known by the Cantonese as *ho fun*, are widely eaten in the far south of China and can be used as a substitute for wheat noodles in most dishes if you don't eat wheat. Fresh rice noodles simply need reheating in boiling water before being used; dried rice noodles should be soaked in hot water for about 30 minutes until supple, then reheated in boiling water when you want to eat them.

7 | 麵調
Wheat noodles, fresh or dried (*mian tiao*)
These are the most commonly used type of noodles in the north, the Southern Yangtze region and Sichuan, as well as other Chinese regions, and can be found in most Chinese groceries. Japanese *udon* can be used as a substitute.

8 | 餛飩皮
Wonton wrappers (*hun dun pi* or *yun tun pi*)
Wonton skins are made from wheat flour and water, usually with added egg, and are thin and supple. They can be found in good Chinese supermarkets.

9 | 糯米粉
Glutinous rice flour (*nuo mi fen*)
This white flour, mixed with water to a putty-like dough, is used to make glutinous rice balls with either sweet or savory stuffings.

COOKING OILS AND FATS

For stir-frying, it is important to use an oil with a high smoke point. I tend to use peanut or rapeseed (canola) oil or occasionally, if I have it, lard. Melted chicken fat is a luxury used in Chinese banquet cooking, so never throw away the fat that solidifies at the top of a cooled chicken stock, or in a roasting pan; instead keep it in the fridge and add it in small quantities to stir-fried mushrooms, steamed or poached vegetables, soups, or soup noodle dishes, just before you serve them, like a gentle, natural MSG. Duck fat can be used in a similar way. Please note that toasted sesame oil is listed separately, because it is used as a seasoning rather than as a cooking oil. The following oils and fats are those most suitable for Chinese cooking:

菜籽油
Rapeseed oil (*cai zi you*)

Yellow rapeseed (canola) oil is the main traditional cooking oil in many parts of southern China, including Sichuan and Zhejiang. It has a high smoke point, which makes it good for wok cooking, and a rich aroma and flavor. I've recently discovered a source of organic rapeseed oil and it's rapidly taking over from peanut oil in my kitchen as my main cooking oil for Chinese dishes.

花生油
Groundnut (peanut) oil (*hua sheng you*)

Peanut oil has a clean, neutral taste and a high smoke point, which makes it suitable for all kinds of wok cooking. It is available in all mainstream supermarkets.

葵花子油
Sunflower oil (*kui hua zi you*)

Another oil with a high smoke point that is used for all kinds of Chinese cooking, including stir-frying and deep-frying.

豬油
Lard (*zhu you*)

Home-made lard lends a wonderful umami richness to stir-fried dishes and transforms stir-fried mushrooms into something sublime. It is one of the important traditional cooking fats of rural China, where many households render it down themselves after they have killed their New Year's pig. To make your own lard at home, see page 324. A small amount of lard can be added to peanut or vegetable oil while stir-frying, as a flavor enhancer.

茶油
Camellia oil (*cha you*)

Also known as tea oil or tea seed oil, this is one of the secret treasures of the southern Chinese kitchen. It is currently little known in the West, although I suspect it won't be long before it is valued as a special delicacy. The golden oil is pressed from the roasted seeds of the *Camellia oleifera* tree, a relative of the plant from which tea is produced. It has a wonderfully nutty flavor, is exceptionally rich in nutrients and low in saturated fats, which is why it is sometimes known as "the oriental olive oil." In the past, it was the main cooking oil in Hunan Province and some other parts of China. Its high smoke point makes it suitable for all kinds of cooking, but these days it is more often used sparingly, for its flavor.

SEASONING OILS

香油，麻油
Sesame oil (*xiang you, ma you*)

Toasted sesame oil, which can be found in mainstream supermarkets as well as in Chinese shops, has a dark caramel color and a strong, nutty aroma. It is never used as a cooking oil, because heat destroys its fragrance, but is added in small quantities to hot dishes in the final stages of cooking, or used in dressings for dumplings, cold dishes and dips. Always choose a pure toasted sesame oil rather than blended versions.

花椒油
Sichuan pepper oil (*hua jiao*)

Sichuan pepper oil, increasingly available in Chinese supermarkets, is made by infusing whole Sichuan pepper in hot oil. Although it rarely has the intense fragrance of the best whole pepper, it has a fruity, zingy flavor and can be used as a substitute for the spice, especially in cold dishes.

RICE WINE AND VINEGAR

鎮江醋，陳醋
Chinkiang vinegar (*zhen jiang cu*) or brown rice vinegar

Dark Chinkiang vinegar, produced in Zhenjiang (Chinkiang) in eastern Jiangsu Province, is one of the most famous Chinese vinegars and is sold in most Chinese supermarkets. It is made from glutinous rice and is naturally colored by charred rice grains. It has a fairly light acidity and a complex flavor that can be a little reminiscent of Italian balsamic vinegars. Many different grades of vinegar are produced in Zhenjiang, but unfortunately only the most basic is currently available in the UK.

白米醋
Clear rice vinegar (*bai mi cu*)

These vinegars tend to be used in pale dishes that might be spoiled by the dark color of a Chinkiang-type vinegar, though they have a sharper, more acidic and less complex taste than the darker vinegars.

紹興酒，黃酒，料酒
Shaoxing wine (*shao xing jiu, huang jiu, liao jiu*)

This amber-colored wine, produced in the ancient city of Shaoxing in eastern China, is used in marinades to refine the flavors of fish and meats and as a flavoring in its own right. Shaoxing cooking wines can be found in all Chinese supermarkets and also in some mainstream supermarkets, but don't try to drink them as wine. Fine Shaoxing wines, which are also suitable for drinking, can be found in some Chinese stores. If you don't have any to hand, medium-dry sherry can be used as a substitute.

Most of the recipes in this book that only use small amounts of Shaoxing wine will work without it, even if the flavors of the final dish will be a little less delicate.

OTHER ESSENTIALS

食鹽
Salt (*shi yan*)

A fine-grained table salt is best for fast wok cooking and for mixing sauces: salt in the form of flakes or larger crystals won't disperse or dissolve quickly enough.

鮮湯
Stock (*xian tang*)

Fresh stock is clearly not a larder ingredient, but it's helpful to have some frozen or canned stock to hand for making soups and stews. Water can generally be used as a substitute for small amounts of stock in sauces, though if you have frozen some homemade stock in ice cube trays, you will have small amounts readily available. I tend to make chicken stock, or chicken and pork bone stock, in large batches when I know I'll be at home for a few hours, then freeze it in one-quart containers. Canned chicken stock can also be used, as can chicken or vegetarian stock granules, although do take care with adding extra salt when using bought stock or granules, which may already be salty. Vegetarians can also make a good stock from sprouted soy beans (see page 319), or fall back on the rustic Chinese tradition of using the silky cooking water left behind after cooking a pot of rice or noodles as a comforting base for soups.

糖
Sugar (*tang*)

White granulated sugar is the main sugar used in the Chinese kitchen. Brown sugar (known as "red sugar," *hong tang*, in Chinese) is used in some dishes, as is rock or crystal sugar (*bing tang*). In this book, sugar means white sugar unless otherwise indicated.

ACKNOWLEDGMENTS

This book, simple as it is, has grown out of many years of cooking and eating in China, and it would be impossible to list here the names of everyone who has played a part in it. I would like, however, to thank a few people in particular.

The team at Barshu restaurant in London have been a fantastic support to me in so many ways. Owner Shao Wei and managers Juanzi, Sherrie Looi and Anne Yim have done everything possible to encourage me in this and many other projects. Head Chef Zhang Xiaozhong has been extraordinarily generous with his expertise, answering innumerable questions and helping me with the testing of recipes on several occasions. I'm also very grateful to Chef Wei Guirong, who assisted me in cooking for the photoshoots, and from whom I have learned so much in terms of dumpling-making. Chefs Fu Bing of Baozi Inn and Li Xue, Zhou Bo and Zheng Qingguo of Bashan have given me advice on certain recipes; and all the other staff have been delightful colleagues.

In China, A Dai (Dai Jianjun), the owner of the Dragon Well Manor restaurant in Hangzhou, has been one of the strongest influences on my research and my cooking in recent years. I find his passion for China's traditional cuisine, culture and agriculture, and his efforts to preserve them for future generations, tremendously inspiring, and I've had the most wonderful times with him and his team, going fishing, gathering wild fruits, sharing meals in rural homes and, of course, eating the incomparable food in his restaurant. So thank you to A Dai and to everyone in the great *cao tang* family for making me feel at home, especially Chefs Dong Jingmu, Guo Ming and Yang Aiping, Qian Lu, Zhou Shifu, He Shifu, Xiatian and Xueyan.

In Chengdu, where my Chinese culinary explorations began and which remains one of my richest sources of recipes,

my old friends Yu Bo and Dai Shuang have patiently answered a stream of questions, accompanied me on market visits and fed me with unbelievable delicacies. Their commitment to their craft is remarkable, and their knowledge of Sichuanese cuisine truly astonishing. A big thank you to them, and to the other staff of their marvellous restaurant, Yu Jia Chu Fang, in particular Xiao Huang and Guo Liang.

For their encouragement and support over many years I would like to thank Wang Xudong, editor of *Sichuan Cuisine* magazine; Professor Jiang Yuxiang of Sichuan University; Professor Du Li of the Sichuan Institute of Higher Cuisine; Liu Yaochun and Liu Jun; Sansan and Liu Wei; Feng Quanxin and Qiu Rongzhen; Li Shurong; Feng Rui; Susan Jung and Nigel Kat; Lai Wu; Lan Guijun; Hugo Martin; Francesca Tarocco; Nunzia Carbone; Gwen Chesnais; and Wu Xiaoming. Special thanks also to the amazing Rose Leng for arranging a couple of emergency shipments from Hong Kong at inconceivably short notice!

Back home, thank you to Lambros Kilaniotis for his ceaseless support and enthusiastic eating—I couldn't have done this without you; Zoë Waldie, my ever-wonderful agent; Carolyn Dunlop, for her help in testing (and tasting!) recipes; Anissa Helou for fun, food adventures and writerly camaraderie; Chef Jerome Henry for trying out some of my recipes; Seema Merchant, for her invaluable advice; Nikki Johnson at the BBC for her patience, forbearance and good humour; the staff of the Shanghai restaurant in Dalston for advice on tofu; and my local guinea pigs Sam Chatterton Dickson, Cathy Roberts and Simon Robey for their comments on my culinary experiments.

I'm also very grateful to my editors, Richard Atkinson and Natalie Hunt at Bloomsbury, and Maria Guarnaschelli

at W. W. Norton, for their enthusiastic commitment to the book and the immense creative effort they have put into its production; to Caroline Clark for her beautiful designs; to the very patient and apparently unflappable Lucy Bannell for her work on the text; to Chris Terry for his mouthwatering photographs; and to Cynthia Inions for her styling of the shoots.

Finally, although I've tried to reproduce recipes faithfully and to write accurately, any errors are entirely my own.

INDEX

For Leonie

Text copyright © 2012 by Fuchsia Dunlop
Photography copyright © 2012 by Chris Terry
Illustrations copyright © 2012 by Caroline Clark
First American Edition 2013

The quotation on page 135 is reproduced by permission of Oxford
University Press and is taken from *The Works of Mencius: A New
Translation Arranged and Annotated for the General Reader*,
translated by W. A. C. H. Dobson (Oxford University Press, 1963),
pages 27–28.

For information about permission to reproduce
selections from this book, write to Permissions,
W. W. Norton & Company, Inc.,
500 Fifth Avenue, New York, NY 10110

For information about special discounts for bulk
purchases, please contact W. W. Norton Special Sales
at specialsales@wwnorton.com or 800-233-4830

Manufacturing by C & C Offset Printing Co. Ltd.
Book design by carolineclark.co.uk

ISBN 978-0-393-08904-2

W. W. Norton & Company, Inc.
500 Fifth Avenue, New York, N.Y. 10110
www.wwnorton.com

W. W. Norton & Company Ltd.
Castle House, 75/76 Wells Street, London W1T 3QT

1 2 3 4 5 6 7 8 9 0

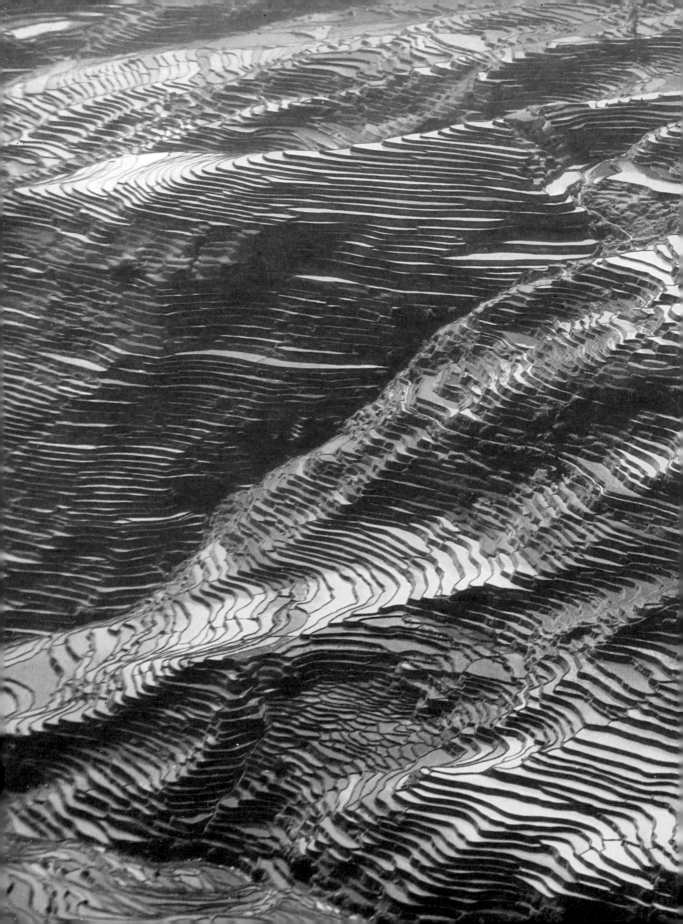